Active Server Pages

Keith Morneau

Jill Batistick

COURSE
TECHNOLOGY

Thomson Learning™

ONE MAIN STREET, CAMBRIDGE, MA 02142

Australia • Canada • Denmark • Japan • Mexico • New Zealand • Philippines
Puerto Rico • Singapore • South Africa • Spain • United Kingdom • United States

Active Server Pages is published by Course Technology.

Managing Editor:	Jennifer Normandin
Senior Product Manager:	Jennifer Muroff
Production Editor:	Megan Cap-Renzi
Associate Product Manager:	Tricia Coia
Editorial Assistant:	Elizabeth Wessen
Composition House:	GEX, Inc.
Text Designer:	GEX, Inc.
Cover Designer:	Sue Yee, Black Fish Design, Inc.
Associate Marketing Manager:	Meagan Walsh
Manufacturing Coordinator:	Denise Widjeskog

Disclaimer

ISBN 0-619-01525-X

Printed in Canada
1 2 3 4 5 WC 05 04 03 02 01

TABLE OF

Contents

PREFACE   **xi**

CHAPTER ONE
The World According to ASP   **1**

    The Way It Was Back Then   2

    The Way It Became   2

    The Way It Is Now   3

        But What Makes an Active Server Page *Work*?   3

    Scripting Languages   4

        Client-side Scripting in VBScript   4

        Client-side Script in JavaScript   5

        Server-side Scripting in VBScript   6

        Server-side Scripting in JavaScript   6

    How a Web Application Works   7

    The Role of the Web Server   9

    Creating a Simple Web Application   10

    Testing a Web Application   13

    Chapter Summary   14

    Review Questions   15

    Hands-on Projects   16

    Case Projects   18

CHAPTER TWO
Using Data   **19**

    Variables and Constants   20

        Application and Session Variables   21

        Data Types   21

        The Scope of a Variable   22

        Declaring Variables   23

        Declaring Constants   24

        Declaring Application and Session Variables   24

        Using Variables and Constants in an Application 25

Creating Modules   29
   Subroutines or Procedures   29
   Functions   33
Creating Objects from Classes   36
   Classes in VBScript   37
   Classes in JavaScript   38
   Declaring an Object from a Class   40
   Using Classes in VBScript   40
   Using Classes in JavaScript   42
Using ASP's Object Model   43
   Application Object   43
   Session Object   44
   Request Object   44
   Response Object   45
Chapter Summary   46
Review Questions   46
Hands-on Projects   49
Case Projects   52

CHAPTER THREE
Arrays, Collections, and Control Structures   53

Arrays and Collections   54
   Arrays   54
   Collections   56
Control Structures   62
   Selection Control Structure   62
   Repetition Control Structure   72
Chapter Summary   78
Review Questions   78
Hands-on Projects   83
Case Projects   86

CHAPTER FOUR
The FileSystemObject Object   87

Review of Drives, Folders, and Files   88
FileSystemObject Object Overview   89
   Drive Object   90
   Folder Object   91

File Object   92

Displaying File and Folder Information   92

Opening New and Existing Files   99

The TextStream Object Steps In   100

Reviewing the Student Contacts Application   101

The QueryString Property of the Request Object   101

Default.htm   102

ClsForm.cls   103

Form.asp   107

register_me.asp   110

Uploading Files to the Server—How It's Really Done   111

SiteGalaxy Upload Component   111

Using the SiteGalaxy Upload Component   112

Chapter Summary   116

Review Questions   117

Hands–on Projects   120

Case Projects   124

CHAPTER FIVE

SQL and Databases for Data-Driven Applications   **125**

Database Overview   126

The DBMSs in the Industry   126

Database Concepts   127

Designing a Database Structure   131

Creating the Web Application to Interact with the Database   134

Querying Databases with SQL   139

SELECT Statement   139

INSERT Statement   146

UPDATE Statement   148

DELETE Statement   148

Chapter Summary   149

Review Questions   149

Hands–on Projects   152

Case Projects   160

CHAPTER SIX
Autogenerating SQL   **161**
    A Program Interface That Intimidates an End User   162
    A Program Interface That Doesn't Intimidate an End User   164
    Understanding ADO   165
        ADO's Role   165
        Connection Object   165
        Recordset Object   166
    Implementing ADO   168
        Changing the Data Source Configuration of the ADO Connection String   169
        How the ADO Recordset Object Queries a Database   170
        How the ADO Recordset Object Inserts Data   172
        How the ADO Fields Collection Allows the Referencing of a Column or Field   172
        Handling Run-Time Errors in ASP   173
    Using ODBC or OLE DB   174
        Setting Up a Microsoft Data Link (OLE DB Data Source)   175
    A Program That Doesn't Intimidate the End User   175
    Tying Together What You've Learned in the First Six Chapters   177
        Default.htm   178
        clsForm.cls   179
        Form.asp   183
        Register_me.asp   187
    Chapter Summary   190
    Review Questions   190
    Hands-on Projects   193
    Case Projects   203

CHAPTER SEVEN
When It's Time to Move Your Database from Access to SQL Server   **205**
    A Typical Scenario with Access   206
    I Know Where I Want to Go, But How Do I Get There?   207
    Converting the Contents of the Access Database to SQL Server 7.0   208
        SQL Server Enterprise Manager   208
        Preparing the SQL Shell   209
        Restoring the Database   210

Stored Procedures	212
What Is a Procedural Language?	212
A Procedural Language and Its Variables	212
The Syntax of Stored Procedures	216
Creating a Stored Procedure in SQL Server	216
Calling a Stored Procedure with the ADO Command Object	218
Updating the SERVER Name	220
Examining the Final Product	221
Key Points in the Code	222
Chapter Summary	230
Review Questions	231
Hands-on Projects	233
Case Projects	241

CHAPTER EIGHT
ASP and E-Commerce **243**

The Role of the Browser Capabilities Component	244
Understanding the Browser Capabilities Component	244
Using the Browser Capabilities Component	246
Maintaining the Browscap.ini File	248
Cookies in Applications	250
How Cookies Come into Existence	250
Response Object	251
Request Object	252
Incorporating Cookies into Applications	252
Key Review Points	258
Login.asp	258
Save_login.asp	259
Chapter Summary	260
Review Questions	261
Hands-on Projects	263
Case Projects	269

CHAPTER NINE
Managing Ads and Tables of Contents in Your Web Application **271**

Using the Ad Rotator Component	272
Creating the Ad Rotator Component	272

Creating the Ad Rotator Component's Schedule File 274

Creating the Ad Rotator's Redirection File 275

The Ad Rotator Component in Action 276

Using the Content Linking Component 277

Create the Content Linking Component Object 278

Creating the Content Linking List File 279

Using Counters 281

Using the PageCounter Object 281

Using the Counters Object 282

Reviewing the Course Tracking Information System Start Page 284

Chapter Summary 287

Review Questions 287

Hands-on Projects 290

Case Projects 293

CHAPTER TEN
Creating User-Defined Components in Visual Basic 6.0   295

Components in Web Applications 296

Components and the Visual Basic 6.0 Environment 298

The Role of Transaction Processing 308

Implementing Transaction Processing 309

High-Level Functions and Organization Strategies for a Software Application 311

Single Tier 311

Two Tiers 311

Three Tiers 312

N-Tier Applications 312

Creating the New Classes ASP Scripts 312

Chapter Summary 316

Review Questions 317

Hands-on Projects 320

Case Projects 330

Preface

Active Server Pages will familiarize you with different approaches for creating server-side scripts using Active Server Pages (ASP). Successfully building, implementing, and executing scripts will allow you to create fully-functional Web applications. The number of Web sites that rely on ASP technology to deliver customer service—in the form of goods, services, and entertainment—is growing. As users come to expect the convenience offered by ASP, implementing Web sites with this feature will be the logical choice for many programmers and ASP developers.

In this book, you will create the scripts that are the basis for active server pages. More importantly, however, you will learn how to develop scripts and pages in real-world environments that take full advantage of the technology. Whether you are creating a simple ASP application or experimenting with the latest shopping cart technology, you will find that *Active Server Pages* provides you with the tools you need to be a successful ASP programmer.

THE INTENDED AUDIENCE

This book is intended for the student who wants to learn to create active server pages that solve everyday business problems. While an introduction to Web applications and Web servers is provided, it is assumed that the student has a basic understanding of these elements. In addition, the student is assumed to have a basic knowledge of variables, constants, arrays, collections, database management systems, HTML, and query languages, even though these items are discussed and addressed in this book. The student should be able to manipulate the Windows operating system, use Internet Explorer to view Web pages, and understand how to create simple Web pages.

THE APPROACH

As you progress through the book, you will practice development techniques by studying code samples, looking at sample active server pages, and creating ASP applications. In addition, where applicable, a student registration ASP application will guide you through your exploration of key terms, techniques, and functions.

Each chapter concludes with a summary and review questions that highlight and reinforce the major concepts of each chapter. Hands-on Projects are included at the end of each chapter to let you practice and reinforce the techniques presented. Additionally, three Case Projects are included with each chapter to let you create ASP applications based on your own hard-won knowledge.

OVERVIEW OF THIS BOOK

The examples, projects, and cases in this book will help you achieve the following objectives:

- Understand the needs that ASP fill
- Learn the roles of variables, constants, and data types
- Understand the use of arrays, keys, collections, and selection control structures
- Learn the use of objects with ASP
- Understand the benefits of SQL and script-generated SQL over Access
- Learn the role of logic flows and migrations in a well-maintained database
- Understand the intricacies and tools behind the shopping cart
- Learn the use of components in maintaining banner ad schedules
- Understand the role of the Visual Basic environment in creating active server pages

In **Chapter 1**, you will learn how browsers and servers interacted on the Internet when the Internet first became popular and how Active Server Pages were created. **Chapter 2** reviews variables and constants and the use of data types and variable declarations. In addition, it explains the use of modules and classes. In **Chapter 3**, you will learn about the benefits and limitations of arrays. You will also come to understand structures, operators, and loops and their roles in ASP. **Chapter 4** provides a review of the drive, the folder, and the file, and covers key objects and components that are used to gather, use, and share information. In **Chapter 5**, you will learn about DBMSs and how a Web application interacts with one. In the process, you will learn the intricacies of a few key statements. **Chapter 6** provides a guideline for the benefits of HTML forms and script-generated SQL. It also explains the different applications of ODBC and OLE DB. In **Chapter 7**, you will learn about the importance of logic flows, conversions, and stored procedures. **Chapter 8** describes how the variety of browsers in the marketplace will affect your ASP programming. It also gives instruction on how to create a shopping cart. In **Chapter 9**, you will learn the role ASP plays in managing the insertion and timing of Web advertisements. In the process, you will become familiar with the Ad Rotator Component and the Schedule and Redirection Files. Finally, **Chapter 10** explains the role that the Visual Basic environment has in ASP programming.

FEATURES

- **Chapter Objectives:** Each chapter in this book begins with a list of the important concepts to be mastered within the chapter. This list provides you with a quick reference to the contents of the chapter as well as a useful study aid.

- **Data Disks:** Data disks provide files for use in each chapter and for other files needed to complete the projects. Please refer to the Read This Before You Begin section for more information.

- **Figures and Tables:** Figures help you visualize Web architecture components and relationships, and also provide code samples. Tables list examples of code components and their variations in a visual and readable format.

- **Tips:** Chapters contain Tips designed to provide you with practical advice and proven strategies related to the concept being discussed. Tips also provide suggestions for resolving problems you might encounter while proceeding through the chapter tutorials.

- **Chapter Summaries:** Each chapter's text is followed by a summary of chapter concepts. These summaries provide a helpful way to recap and revisit the ideas covered in each chapter.

- **Review Questions:** End-of-chapter assessment begins with a set of approximately 20 review questions that reinforce the main ideas introduced in each chapter. These questions ensure that you have mastered the concepts and understand the information you have learned.

- **Hands-on Projects:** Along with conceptual explanations and step-by-step tutorials, each chapter provides Hands-on Projects related to each major topic. These projects are aimed at providing you with practical experience. Some involve enhancing or extending the exercises in the chapter tutorials, and some involve creating new applications. Some of the Hands-on Projects provide detailed instructions, while others provide less detailed instructions that require you to apply the materials presented in the current chapter and previous chapters with less guidance. As a result, the Hands-on Projects provide you with practice implementing database-driven Web site development skills in real-world situations.

- **Case Projects:** Three Case Projects that run throughout the book are presented at the end of each chapter. These cases are designed to help you apply what you have learned in each chapter to real-world situations. They give you the opportunity to independently synthesize and evaluate information, examine potential solutions, and make recommendations, much as you would in an actual business situation. The content of each chapter is cumulatively applied to the Cases, allowing you to create programs that build upon the knowledge you gain throughout the book.

TEACHING TOOLS

The following supplemental materials are available when this book is used in a classroom setting. All the teaching tools available with this book are provided to the instructor on a single CD.

Electronic Instructor's Manual. The Instructor's Manual that accompanies this textbook includes:

- Additional instructional material to assist in class preparation, including suggestions for lecture topics.
- Solutions to all end-of-chapter materials, including the Review Questions, and when applicable, Hands-on Projects and Case Projects.

Course Test Manager 1.2. Accompanying this book is a powerful assessment tool known as the Course Test Manager. Designed by Course Technology, this cutting-edge Windows-based testing software helps instructors design and administer tests and pre-tests. In addition to generating tests that can be printed and administered, this full-featured program also has an online testing component that allows students to take tests at the computer and have their exams graded automatically.

PowerPoint presentations. This book comes with Microsoft PowerPoint slides for each chapter. These are included as a teaching aid for classroom presentation, to make available to students on the network for chapter review, or to be printed for classroom distribution. Instructors can add their own slides for additional topics they introduce to the class.

ACKNOWLEDGMENTS

We thank Jennifer Muroff for her vision; she carried the team to the finish line. We would also like to thank the reviewers for their feedback: Bob Nelson, Spokane Community College; Katie Kalata, Oakton Community College; John Gaulden, Southern Nazarene University; Brad Hunt, South Plains College; Doug Stoddard, Clovis Community College; Bret Dickey, Spokane Community College; as well as Ann Shaffer.

Keith Morneau

Jill Batistick

Read This Before You Begin

TO THE USER

Data Disks

To complete the chapters and exercises in this book, you will need a Data Disk. The term "Data Disk" does not refer to a floppy disk; instead, it refers to a collection of files that reside on your hard drive. The Data Disk contains all of the source files you will need. You will also save the files that you create while completing the chapters onto your Data Disk. Because of the size and quantity of the files you will be working with, you will need to store your Data Disk on your local workstation or on a network file server to which you can connect.

Hard Disk Installation

If you are going to copy the Data Disk source files from a file server, your instructor will tell you the drive letter and folder that contains the source files that you need. To create your Data Disk, start Windows Explorer, navigate to the Data Disk folder provided by your instructor, select all the subfolders, and copy them to the folder on your hard drive in which you want to store your Data Disk files. There are folders for Chapters 1 through 10 in the book. All the folders contain files you will need to complete the tutorials and end-of-chapter Hands-on Projects, and some of the folders contain subfolders.

Many of the code examples in this book require you to enter a folder path to your Data Disk. Figures that accompany these instructions will show the path as it is typed via a virtual directory in PWS. This use of the virtual path will allow you to store your Data Disk in a location that is convenient to you and that can hold the large volume of files that accompany most of the chapters.

Throughout this book, you will be instructed to open files from or save files to your Data Disk (for example, "Open the default.htm file from the Chapter_4 folder on your Data Disk.") Therefore, it is important to make sure that you are using the correct Data Disk when you begin working on each chapter.

Using Your Own Computer

You can use your own computer to complete the tutorials, Hands-on Projects, and Cases in this book. To use your own computer, you will need the following:

- **Microsoft Windows 98 with the latest Windows 98 Service Pack installed.**
- **An evaluation copy of SQL Server 7.0.**

- **Microsoft Visual Basic Version 6.0 Professional or Enterprise Edition.**
- **Microsoft Personal Web Server (PWS).** PWS is distributed with some versions of Windows 98 and Office 2000, and with Windows 2000 Professional. To determine if PWS is already installed on your computer, start Windows Explorer, and look to see if the PWS files are installed in a folder named Windows\System\Inetsrv.

  Windows 98 users can download the software from Microsoft's Web site at no cost. To download the software, connect to **http://www.microsoft.com**, search for "Personal Web Server," and then follow the links to the download pages.
- **Microsoft Internet Explorer 5.** You can download a copy of Internet Explorer 5 and the available service packs from the Internet Explorer home page at no cost. Connect to **http://www.microsoft.com/windows/ie/**, and then click the Download link from the menu near the top of the Web page.
- **Data Disk.** You can get the Data Disk files from your instructor. You will not be able to complete the tutorials and projects in this book using your own computer unless you have the Data Disk files. See the Data Disk section for information on setting up your Data Disk files. The Data Disk files can also be obtained electronically from the Course Technology Web site by connecting to **http://www.course.com**, and then searching for this book title.

Visit Our World Wide Web Site

Additional materials designed especially for you might be available for your course on the World Wide Web. Go to **http://www.course.com**. Search for this book title periodically on the Course Technology Web site for more details.

TO THE INSTRUCTOR

To complete the chapters in this book, your users must have a set of user files, which are referred to throughout the book as Data Disk files. These files are included in the Instructor's Resource Kit. They may also be obtained electronically through the Course Technology Web site at **http://www.course.com**. Follow the instructions in the Help file to copy the user files to your server or standalone computer. You can view the Help file using a text editor such as WordPad or Notepad. Because of the volume of Data Disk files, we recommend that you assist your students in installing and accessing these files on their own hard drives.

Course Technology Data Disk Files

You are granted a license to copy the Data Disk files to any computer or computer network used by individuals who have purchased this book.

1

THE WORLD ACCORDING TO ASP

In this chapter, you will:

♦ Learn how browsers and servers interacted on the Internet when the Internet first became popular

♦ Learn what first-generation Internet/intranet applications brought to the browser/server relationship

♦ Learn why Active Server Pages were created

♦ Learn the role of scripting languages

♦ Learn how a Web application works

♦ Learn the role of the Web server

♦ Learn how to create and test a simple Active Server Page application

Have you seen any good Web sites lately? Have you cruised a few of the large financial, news, or sports sites? If you have, did you notice how they fed you custom information that reflects whom you are and what you have decided to share with the site? Those sites are able to provide that custom information because they run on Active Server Page technology. In this chapter, you will learn how Active Server Pages fit into the timeline of Web development. Then, you will take a look at a live Active Server Page application. Finally, to wrap it all up, you'll get a brief overview of what you can expect in the coming chapters. So, that being said, hold on to your keyboards, because we're about to take a jump back in Internet time to take a look at the way it was.

THE WAY IT WAS BACK THEN

Not too long ago in Internet time, the relationship between your browser and a distant server was pretty simple. You requested a Web page via your browser, the server received your request, and the server sent back the page that you wanted.

It was in this simple environment that most of us picked up our basic Web literacy. For instance, we learned that the user requests Web resources by typing a Uniform Resource Locator (URL) in the address box of the browser screen. We also learned that the first part of the URL (http://) indicates the application-level protocol used for the request, and that the second part of the URL is the name of the Web server where the Web resource resides. Through additional experience, we learned that the third part of the URL is the folder path and that it indicates the precise folder on the Web server in which the Web resource is stored. The last part of the URL, of course, specifies the Web resource we requested.

As we cruised around, we became very familiar with the following types of resources:

- **Hypertext Markup Language (HTML) documents**: Specialized pages that provide content (such as a newspaper article) in an easy-to-read format
- **Graphics**: Images stored in either GIF or JPEG format

The first Web sites consisted of static HTML pages that could not change in response to input from the user. Although the Internet was enjoyable in spite of this fact, Web sites needed to become dynamic and responsive to user input. And they did.

THE WAY IT BECAME

Internet time marched on to new and better things. One of those better things was the first-generation Internet/intranet application. It was an extension to Web servers and was called **Common Gateway Interface (CGI)**.

CGI allowed Web sites to dynamically create Web pages from a program typically written in C or a scripting language such as Perl. A CGI program could access information from HTML forms and store this information in databases. CGI programs were designed to run in a UNIX environment as a separate running application program or process. Each time a CGI request was made, a new process was created to handle the request.

CGI added functionality to the Web. Unfortunately, however, running multiple processes in Windows environments used up a lot of network resources and slowed network performance significantly when a large number of users were involved. As a result, CGI programs often exhausted memory space on Windows computers. These shortcomings eventually led to Active Server Pages, or ASP.

THE WAY IT IS NOW

Active Server Pages (ASP) generate HTML and pass the dynamically created HTML to the browser to be displayed to the user. Microsoft created Active Server Pages to make it easier for developers to create dynamic Web sites in a Windows environment.

ASP applications run in a **thread**, which is the smallest unit of execution of a process. Windows handles multiple threads very efficiently, regardless of the number of users; therefore, ASP provides a better solution for Web applications in Windows environments than does CGI. In fact, ASP applications run three to five times faster than their CGI counterparts and can incorporate HTML pages and forms, scripts written in VBScript or JavaScript, and ActiveX components.

You can create Active Server Pages manually with Notepad or by using Visual InterDev as a development platform. (In this book, you will use a text editor such as Notepad to create ASP pages.) No matter how you create them, ASP application files use the ".asp" file extension that tells the Web server that the Web page contains scripts that must be executed before the page can be sent to the browser.

As Web users became more experienced with this environment, they began running into elements such as the following:

- **Java Applets**: Programs that are created in the Java programming language and that are downloaded to and run on a Web browser. The technology behind the Java programming language was created by Sun Microsystems.

- **ActiveX controls**: A self-contained application that a programmer can reuse in different applications, and that usually supplies an interface such as a label, textbox, and listbox. Microsoft created the technology behind ActiveX.

- **Extensible Markup Language (XML) documents**: Special Web pages that provide a structured way of representing and manipulating data from different applications

But What Makes an Active Server Page *Work*?

Active Server Pages create their value through the scripts that they contain. **Scripts**, or **scripting**, are lines of code that accomplish a specific task, such as retrieving data from a file. You can mix HTML tags and scripts in an ASP by using a special <SCRIPT>...</SCRIPT> tag. The beauty of scripting is that it gives you the ability to create executable code within the Web page. It's the executable code that allows you to create customized content for your Web visitors.

There are two kinds of scripting: client-side and server-side. Client-side scripts download to and execute on the client. When developing client-side scripting, you have to worry about the features supported by browsers, to make sure your scripts are compatible with all kinds of browsers. In most cases, you cannot assume that everyone will use the same browser, and in the case of older browsers, you can't even be certain that the browser will support scripting at all. Although this chapter will provide sample client-side scripts for your general background knowledge, they will not be the focus of this book.

While client-side scripts must be downloaded to the client so that they can run in the browser, server-side scripts run directly on the server and generate data to be viewed by the browser in HTML format. As you can imagine, running scripts on the server side can be extremely useful if you are trying to create a Web application that will be accessed by many types and kinds of browsers. Because server-side scripts run on the server, you don't have to concern yourself with the capabilities of the various browsers accessing them. Instead, the scripts that programmers create can generate HTML tags that almost all browsers support.

Most Web users have encountered server-side scripts, even if they weren't aware of it. A common place to encounter these scripts is at the Web site of a search engine, such as Yahoo!. At such a site, the user accesses a search engine to find Web sites related to specific topics.

To use the search engine, the user enters keywords into a text box and then clicks the Search button. When the user clicks the Search button, the data entered into the search text box is sent to a script on an ASP on the Web server. The script takes the data from the form, creates a query from the data, and creates HTML to display the results returned from the query. That HTML is sent from the Web server back to the browser for display.

Search engines can get thousands of requests a day. Individual static pages showing the results of anticipated search queries cannot realistically exist on a Web server. The potential combinations of information would quickly exhaust even the largest and most powerful server. That is why ASP is so valuable—with it, each user can have pages that are dynamically custom-generated.

SCRIPTING LANGUAGES

You can create client- or server-side scripts in one of two scripting languages: VBScript or JavaScript (also known in Microsoft environments as JScript). VBScript is a scripting language created by Microsoft that works very similarly to the programming language Visual Basic. JavaScript is a scripting language created by Netscape. Internet Explorer supports both scripting languages. Netscape Communicator supports only JavaScript. Throughout this book, you will be exposed to examples in both languages.

Before you can jump into the rest of this book and start manipulating scripts like a serious script master, you have to understand how to read scripts. We begin with client-side scripting in VBScript and then move on to JavaScript. (Although client-side scripting is not the focus of this book, you should be familiar with the basic elements.) Then, we'll give server-side scripting the same treatment.

Client-side Scripting in VBScript

The following is an example of a document that contains HTML and a simple VBScript script. The script displays the message "Hello, world!" in a message box.

```
<HTML>
<HEAD>
</HEAD>
<BODY>
```

```
<SCRIPT LANGUAGE=VBScript>
<!--
msgbox("Hello, world!")
//-->
</SCRIPT>
</BODY>
</HTML>
```

Code Dissection

- The tag

  ```
  <SCRIPT LANGUAGE=VBScript>...</SCRIPT>
  ```

  tells the browser that what follows is a VBScript script. The data between the tags is the actual script.

- `<!-- ... //-->` is a comment in HTML and prevents browsers that cannot read scripts from displaying the script on the page.

- Note that in this scripting language, you use a msgbox statement to display messages to the user.

Client-side Script in JavaScript

The following is an example of a file that contains HTML and a simple script written in JavaScript. The script displays the message "Hello, world!" in a message box.

```
<HTML>
<HEAD>
</HEAD>
<BODY>
<SCRIPT LANGUAGE=JavaScript>
<!--
alert("Hello, world!")
//-->
</SCRIPT>
</BODY>
</HTML>
```

Code Dissection

- The tag

  ```
  <SCRIPT LANGUAGE=JavaScript>...</SCRIPT>
  ```

  tells the browser that the following code is in JavaScript. The data between the tags is the script.

- `<!-- ... //-->` is a comment in HTML and prevents browsers that cannot read scripts from displaying the script on the page.

- Note that in contrast to VBScript, you use the alert statement in JavaScript to display messages to the user.

Server-side Scripting in VBScript

The following HTML page includes a simple server-side script written in VBScript.

```
<HTML>
<HEAD>
<SCRIPT LANGUAGE="VBScript" RUNAT="Server">
 Server-side script that runs on the server
</SCRIPT>
<SCRIPT LANGUAGE="VBScript">
 Client-side script that runs on the client
</SCRIPT>
</HEAD>
<BODY>
<% Server-side VBScript that runs on the server %>
</BODY>
</HTML>
```

Code Dissection

- A Web page can contain HTML tags along with scripts. The scripting sections that run on the server must execute before the entire page is sent to the browser. The scripting sections usually result in additional HTML tags and data that become part of the generated Web page.

- The line

  ```
  <SCRIPT LANGUAGE="VBScript" RUNAT="Server">...</SCRIPT>
  ```

  tells the Web server that this script runs on the server first, before the HTML page can be transmitted to the client.

- The line

  ```
  <SCRIPT LANGUAGE="VBScript">...</SCRIPT>
  ```

  tells the Web server that this script should be transmitted to the client and tells the browser to run this script on the client, rather than on the server.

- The <% ... %> tag combination tells the Web server to run the script on the server and pass the results to the client.

Server-side Scripting in JavaScript

The following HTML page includes a simple server-side script written in JavaScript.

```
<HTML>
<HEAD>
<SCRIPT LANGUAGE="JavaScript" RUNAT="Server">
 Server-side script that runs on the server
</SCRIPT>
<SCRIPT LANGUAGE="JavaScript">
 Client-side script that runs on the client
</SCRIPT>
</HEAD>
```

```
<BODY>
<% Server-side JavaScript that runs on the server %>
</BODY>
</HTML>
```

Code Dissection

- A Web page can contain HTML tags along with scripts. The scripting sections that run on the server must execute before the entire page is sent to the browser. The scripting sections usually result in additional HTML tags and data that become part of the generated Web page.

- The line

  ```
  <SCRIPT LANGUAGE="JavaScript" RUNAT="Server">...</SCRIPT>
  ```

  tells the Web server that this script runs on the server first, before the HTML page can be transmitted to the client.

- The line

  ```
  <SCRIPT LANGUAGE="JavaScript">...</SCRIPT>
  ```

  tells the Web server that this script should be transmitted to the client and tells the browser to run this script on the client, rather than on the server.

- The <% ... %> tag combination tells the Web server to run the script on the server and pass the results to the client.

HOW A WEB APPLICATION WORKS

One ASP is good. Two are better. When you get a whole herd of them together on one server, that's best of all. When that happens, you have the makings of a great Web application.

A **Web application** is a special type of Web site that contains pages of static HTML and server-side scripts that interact with a user. The Web applications that you will encounter in this book share some common attributes. We'll explore these attributes now to give you an overview. You'll encounter them in more detail in later chapters.

We begin the discussion with one of the main components of a Web application: the object. Programmers routinely use objects to create reusable code that can be used in many applications. An object in the real world is, conveniently enough, very similar to an object in programming. For instance, a photograph that you can hold in your hand has properties, such as size, color, and paper weight. An image on a Web page also has properties, such as alignment, color, and resolution.

No doubt, you are very adept at manipulating the properties of real-world objects. For instance, you could take a pair of scissors and trim your photograph to a different size. Likewise, in programming, you can "trim" the size of an online image, by changing the appropriate property.

Objects also have methods. Think of the method as something the object can do. So, let's take a look at another real-world example of an object: the clipboard. A clipboard can hold a printout of your document. Likewise, your Clipboard in Windows "holds" your document for you.

Properties and methods are useful, but the fun starts when an event, the other main component, enters the scenario. An event occurs when a stimulus affects an object. For example, when a user clicks a Submit button on a form on a Web page, a script on a server runs. The event in this example is the clicking of the Submit button.

Events don't exist in a vacuum; they can also create or modify an object. For instance, consider the event that occurs when the first end user accesses a Web application. As a result of such an event, Personal Web Server (PWS) or Internet Information Server (IIS; hereafter, we'll only mention PWS) creates an Application object. This object stores data on the server that contains values that you can use in your Web application. PWS will be discussed in the next section.

Once the Application object is created, an event called Application_OnStart fires, or starts, in the Global.asa file in the Web application directory. **Global.asa** is a file that contains events that are activated when Application and Session objects are created and when they are destroyed. So, one event can create an object, and the creation of that object can trigger another event.

So, now you have an Application object. What does it actually do? Well, its main job is to store any settings that are the same between sessions. (**Sessions** are special environments that the Web server creates for each user of an application.) These settings travel with the individual user, from session to session.

The sessions themselves are also objects—Session objects. One is created at the same time that the Application object is being created. As a result of the creation of the Session Object, the Session_OnStart event fires in the Global.asa file. This allows the Web application to store data that is active during the entire session and that is available to all Web pages and scripts in the Web application. The Session object contains the environment in which the user interacts with the application. Each session of an individual user is contained in its own Session object and contains the settings that are particular to the user.

Let's drape all this theory over a hypothetical situation. In the situation, we'll say that a Web user is looking at a Web page. When this user causes the Application and Session objects to be created, we'll say that a form Web page is displayed on the browser. When the user fills in the form and clicks the Submit button, this event (i.e., the Submit button being clicked) results in the creation of a Request object. This object (remember, an object has properties and methods) grabs all the data from the form and packages it in a way that the receiving server can easily interpret and that a developer can manipulate in his or her scripts.

Once the server receives the Request object, it begins to respond to the request, resulting in the creation of a Response object. The Response object creates a response—a Web page that contains lots of HTML and other information. Some of that HTML was hard-coded into the page by the developer; some of that code was created by the script that interpreted the Request object.

When the session is completed, either by the user or by the Web server, the Session_OnEnd event fires, signaling the end of the session in the Global.asa file. When the session ends, the Session, Request, and Response objects are destroyed, at the behest of the Application object. The Application object itself is not destroyed until PWS shuts down.

1

The Application, Session, Request, and Response objects are the most important objects in ASP. You will use them over and over again in this book and learn more details about their existence. As you explore them in the next several chapters, remember the basic discussion here and refer to it as necessary.

THE ROLE OF THE WEB SERVER

PWS is a Web server that allows you to create and test applications in Windows 98. In other words, you use PWS to develop and test Web applications. Once you complete your Web application and want to use it over the Internet, you use IIS. You would not use PWS for Web sites accessed over the Internet, because PWS is designed only as a development environment to be used to create and test Web applications. PWS cannot handle the thousands or millions of users that real Web sites need to be able to handle.

In the environment of this book, you will use PWS, which runs on Windows 98. To actually create your application, you will use Notepad or your own text editor. You will view your work using Internet Explorer or Netscape Navigator.

Typically, you must adapt to and use a Web server's existing folder structure. For instance, in Windows environments, all Web sites and applications that reside on the server actually reside at c:\inetpub\wwwroot. If you want to use other folders besides the default wwwroot folder, you need to create a virtual directory. We will now create a virtual directory so that we can store our Web applications in a location that is convenient to the project.

To create a PWS virtual directory in Windows 98:

1. Click **Start**, point to **Programs**, point to **Microsoft Personal Web Server**, and then click **Personal Web Manager**. The Personal Web Manager window opens.

You can also access the Personal Web Server through the task area at the bottom of the desktop, if you have elected to show the tray icon.

If you install PWS off the Windows 98 CD, it will be placed in Start/Internet Explorer/Personal Web Server.

2. If the Tip of the Day dialog box appears, click **Close**.

3. Verify that Web publishing is on, and then click the **Advanced** icon on the left side of the window. The Advanced Options window opens.

4. Click the **Add** button. The Add Directory dialog box opens.

5. In the Alias text box, type **Chapter_1** folder. The alias is the name of the folder you are using.

6. In the Directory text box, type the full pathname to the Chapter_1 folder.

7. Click the **OK** button, and then click **Yes** in the resulting dialog box. You return to the Advanced Options window.

8. Verify that your new virtual directory appears in the list.

9. Close the Personal Web Manager window.

CREATING A SIMPLE WEB APPLICATION

Theory is great, but seeing is believing. For our first adventure, we are going to create the Web pages for a student contact information application. The application will consist of two parts. The first is the user registration form, Register.htm. The second is the class registration script, Register_me.asp.

To create the Register.htm page:

1. Start a text editor such as Notepad. (This will be our default choice from this point forward.)

2. Type the following HTML in a blank document:

```
<HTML>

<HEAD>
<TITLE>User Registration Form</TITLE>
</HEAD>

<BODY>

<H1 align="center">User Registration Form</H1>

<FORM id="frmRegister" name="frmRegister"
action="register_me.asp" method="post">

<CENTER><P>First name: <input id="txtFirstName"
name="txtFirstName" style="LEFT: 119px; TOP: 69px"
size="35">*<BR>
 Last name: 

<INPUT id="txtLastName" name="txtLastName"
size="35"><STRONG>*</STRONG> </P>

E-mail: <INPUT type="text" name="txtemail"
size="30"><STRONG>*</STRONG></p>
</CENTER>

<CENTER><P><INPUT id="cmdSubmit" name="cmdSubmit"
type="submit" value="Submit">
<INPUT id="cmdReset" name="cmdReset" type="reset"
value="Reset"> </P>
```

```
</CENTER>
</FORM>

</BODY>
</HTML>
```

3. Create a folder named **Myregister** in the Chapter_1 folder on your Data Disk.

4. Save the Web page as **Register.htm** in the Chapter_1\myregister folder on your Data Disk.

5. Close the text editor.

6. Open **Register.htm** in your browser. It appears as a Web page, as shown in Figure 1-1.

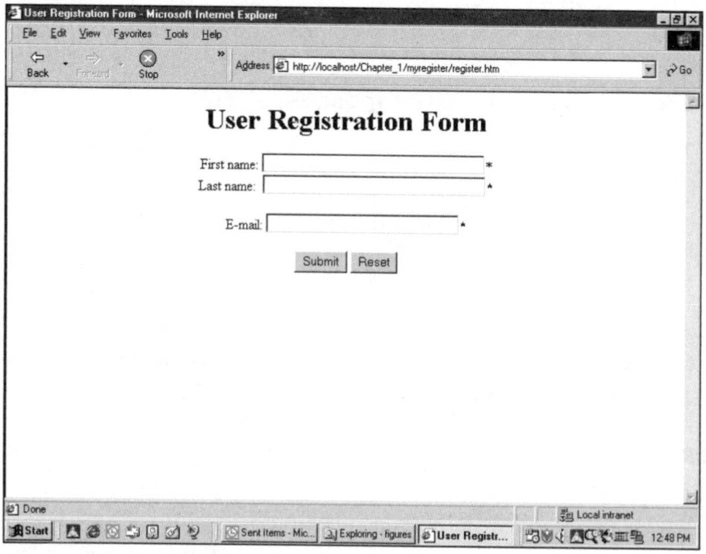

Figure 1-1   User Registration Form

7. Close the file.

Many text editors such as Notepad attach their own filename extension (.txt in Notepad) to a saved file. Verify that your file does not include a double extension. If it does, rename the file. You can use quotes around the filename to make sure that the text editor does not add a second extension to your filename. As an alternate, you can select "All Files [*.*]" in the Save as type list box in the Save dialog box.

In the seventh line of the code that you just typed, you'll find "action." This "action" is the action attribute of the form tag. It specifies the ASP to which the Web browser will pass the form data. The script on that page will receive the form data and create a response. In the code you just typed, the form data will be sent to Register_me.asp. You will create that ASP next, using the VBScript scripting language introduced earlier in this chapter.

When you create an ASP, you need to add an extension, .asp, to the filename. You will also use the <%...%> tag to specify the part of the file that constitutes the script. Inside the <%...%> tags, you will include script that will cause the Web server to generate the results of the script and replace the script (and the <%. . .%>tag) with HTML. For example, if you place <% = 1+2+3 %> in your ASP, the Web server will generate and send to the browser a 6 in place of the <%...%> tags.

To create the Register_me.asp script in the VBScript language:

1. Open your text editor.

2. Type the following:

```
<%@ Language=VBScript %>
<% Response.Buffer = True %>
<HTML>

<HEAD>

<TITLE>User Registration Response</TITLE>

<BODY>

<CENTER><H1>User Registration Response</H1></CENTER>
<center>
<P>The information you entered: <BR>
<UL>
<LI>First name: <%=Request.Form("txtFirstName")%></LI>
<LI>Last name: <%=Request.Form("txtLastName")%></LI>
<LI>E-Mail: <%=Request.Form("txtemail")%></LI>
</UL>
</CENTER>
</BODY>
</HTML>
```

3. Save the script as **Register_me.asp** in the Chapter_1\myregister folder of your Data Disk.

4. Close the text editor.

Let's investigate this ASP in a little more detail:

Code Dissection

- The line

```
<%@ Language=VBScript %>
```

specifies the scripting language being used. The <%. . .%> tells the Web server that the enclosed script code must run before the Web page is transmitted to the browser.

- The line

```
<% Response.Buffer = True %>
```

tells the Web server to create the entire Web page in memory before sending it to the client. By default, a Web page is sent to the browser line by line as it is generated. By telling the server to create the entire page before sending it to the client, you have the power to clear the buffer and start over if necessary. If you do not store the entire page in memory first, the page will be sent to the browser as it is created; this makes it impossible to clear the buffer and start over if an error should occur.

- The line

```
<%=Request.Form("txtFirstName")%>
```

tells the Web server to insert the contents of the form element txtFirstName. txtFirstName is the name of a form element specified in the Register.htm page. This line is one example of a Request object. (See how much you know already!) This Request object has a property called Form, where the Web server stores the form's data.

TESTING A WEB APPLICATION

The next step in developing a Web application is testing what you have created.

To test the new application:

1. Start your Web browser.

2. In the address field, type
   http://localhost/Chapter_1/myregister/register.htm. The "localhost" part of the URL refers to your computer, which is acting as the Web server.

3. Press **Enter**.

 If you have trouble opening this file, consult the setup instructions contained in the front of this book, or ask your instructor or technical support person for assistance.

4. Type your personal information in the appropriate text boxes.

5. Click the **Reset** button. The information you typed is cleared from the form.

6. Reenter your personal information.

7. Click the **Submit** button. Your screen should resemble Figure 1-2.

8. Close the browser.

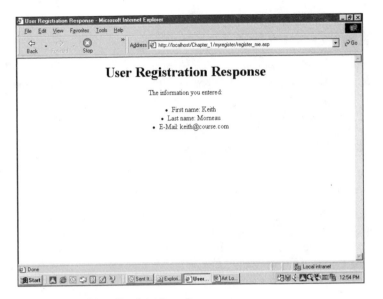

Figure 1-2   User Registration Response

When you click Submit, the Web server creates an Application and Session object, the Web server creates the Request object, and the Web server gathers the information from the form and stuffs that information into the Form property of the Request object.

The User Registration Response Web page now appears with your personal information. The script in Register_me.asp uses the data in the Form property of the Request object to generate HTML code. The result first goes to memory and then on to your browser.

This sample application is actually an information system; it receives input, processes the input, and provides output. The user registration form contains the data input into the system. The ASP, Register_me.asp, processes the data entered into the form and creates the HTML that produces the response.

You have just created a working version of an application, and so have come to the end of Chapter 1. Congratulations on completing your first ASP application. In the course of this book, you will apply these same techniques and processes to create other more complicated applications. To assist you in these creations, you'll learn in Chapter 2 the intricacies of variables and constants and the joys of using modules and functions. Once you master these, you'll be off and running into Chapter 3 and its discussion of arrays, collections, and control structures.

CHAPTER SUMMARY

- ❑ Web pages used to be simple items. You requested a page, the server processed your request, and you then received the page for viewing. It was in this environment that most people became familiar with the basic concepts related to the World Wide Web.

- ❑ After simple static Web pages, the industry moved on to utilize CGI scripts, even with their shortcomings. Later came the Active Server Pages technology. This technique for creating Web applications has become the de facto standard in Web application development.

❑ The term *script*, or *scripting*, refers to lines of code that accomplish a specific task, such as retrieving data from a file. Scripting gives you the ability to create executable code. Client-side scripts download to and execute on the client. By contrast, server-side scripts execute on the Web server and can generate additional data to be viewed by the browser in HTML format. You can create client- or server-side scripts in VBScript or JavaScript.

❑ In programming, objects are discrete entities with two main characteristics: properties and methods. Properties are the data that describes an object. A method is a task that the object can perform. An operation is triggered by an external stimulus, or event. Programmers routinely use objects to create reusable code that can be used in many applications. The Application, Session, Request, and Response objects are the most important objects in ASP.

❑ In this book, you will use Personal Web Server (PWS), which runs on Windows 98. To actually create the application, you will use Notepad or your own text editor. If you want to use other folders besides the default wwwroot folder, you need to create a virtual directory.

REVIEW QUESTIONS

1. A user can request a Web resource by typing a URL into the _____ of the browser screen.

   a. address box

   b. protocol

   c. Web resource

   d. folder

2. Images that you find on the Web can be in GIF or JPEG format. True or False?

3. The first-generation Internet/intranet application was called _____.

   a. HTML

   b. CGI

   c. URL

   d. PERL

4. A CGI program can access information from HTML forms. True or False?

5. Who created the technology behind the Java programming language?

   a. Microsoft

   b. Sun Microsystems

   c. IBM

   d. Big Blue

6. The technology behind ActiveX was created by _____.

7. CGI programs often exhausted the _____ on computers.

8. A _____ is the smallest unit of execution of a process.

   a. CGI

   b. Windows environment

   c. thread

   d. ActiveX dump

9. CGI applications run faster than their ASP counterparts. True or False?

10. Lines of code that accomplish a specific task are called _____.

11. VBScript and JavaScript are the same programming language. True or False?

12. In JavaScript, you use the _____ statement to display messages to the user.

13. The _____ tag combination tells a Web server to run a script on the server and then pass the results to the client.

    a. <#...#>

    b. <OPEN%...%>/<%...%END>

    c. <SCRIPT%...SCRIPT%>

    d. <%...%>

14. PWS is a Web _____.

15. In Windows environments, all Web sites and applications that reside on the server actually reside at _____.

    a. c:\inetpub\wwwroot

    b. a:\inetpub\wwwroot

    c. http://localhost.com

    d. a:\Chapter_1

16. Notepad is a(n) _____ editor.

17. The _____ attribute of the form tag specifies the ASP to which a browser will pass form data.

18. The ASP technology generates HTML. True or False?

19. Windows cannot handle threads efficiently. True or False?

20. If necessary, you can mix HTML and scripts on one ASP. True or False?

HANDS-ON PROJECTS

Hands-on
Project

Project 1-1

Amazon.com is the pioneer in online book ordering. You have just been hired by a competitor, CollegeBooks.com, to evaluate current online bookstores and to recommend the minimum functionality needed to compete with Amazon.com. You notice that there is a search form on their start page. You decide to investigate how the search form works.

1. Start your Web browser and connect to the Internet.

2. Type *http://www.amazon.com* in the Address field of the browser, and press the [Enter] key to load the page.

3. Click the View menu, and then click Source to view the HTML for the Amazon.com start page. (If you are using Netscape, click View, and then click Page Source.)

4. Search for the HTML form on this page and look at the Search form and its contents. Make sure to note the different form elements and their functions.

5. Describe to yourself the purpose of the method and action attributes of the form tag.

6. Click the File menu and then the Close button to exit the browser.

Project 1-2

Wish Auction House is losing business to e-Bay, the extremely successful Internet auction house. As a result, Wish wants to create a Web application that will compete with e-Bay, and has asked you to help. You notice two forms on e-Bay's start page, and you decide to learn how they use HTML forms on their site.

1. Start your Web browser and connect to the Internet.

2. Type *http://www.ebay.com* and press the [Enter] key to load the start page.

3. Click the View menu, and then click Source to view the HTML for the start page. (If you are using Netscape, click View, then click Page Source.)

4. Search for the HTML forms on this page and document the forms and their contents.

5. Click the File menu and then the Close button to exit the browser.

Project 1-3

The IS Manager at NOVA University recently hired you to help create a Web application that requests information for their contact database. This application should store the following information for each University employee: first name, last name, address, city, state, zip, work number, fax number, e-mail address, division, and department. You also need to create an ASP script that displays the results of the form entry. You need to execute the following steps to create this Web application:

1. Create a directory in the Chapter_1 folder on your Data Disk called contacts.

2. Create a virtual directory called contacts in your Web server that points to the contacts folder.

3. Copy the Register.htm page from this chapter into an HTML form called Personal.htm. Change the form elements to first name, last name, address, city, state, zip, work number, fax number, e-mail address, division, and department.

4. Create an ASP called response.asp with the appropriate HTML tags and similar to Register_me.asp in this chapter.

5. Test your Web application to make sure it works.

Project 1-4

The marketing director of Online Books has hired you to help regain market share that Online has lost to Amazon.com. Your job is to create a Web application that requests users to enter information regarding the book they want to purchase. This information includes title, author, and ISBN number. After the user clicks Submit, the application should display the information entered in the form. You need to do the following:

1. Create a directory called books in the Chapter_1 folder on the Data Disk.

2. Create a virtual directory called books in your Web server that points to the books folder.

3. Copy the Register.htm form from the chapter into an HTML form called Books.htm. Change the HTML tags to Title, Author, and ISBN number. Make sure to delete any extra form elements if necessary, and change the name of the form elements to appropriate names.

4. Create an ASP called Response.asp with the appropriate HTML tags and similar to Register_me.asp in this chapter.

5. Test your Web application to make sure it works.

Project 1-5

The customer relations manager at First Bank of Madison has hired you to create an e-commerce site that helps customers balance their checkbooks on a monthly basis. For starters, you need to create a simple Web application that requests users to enter information similar to the information that appears on the back of a checking account statement. You also need to create a response page that displays what the user has entered in the form. You need to do the following:

1. Create a directory called checkbook in the Chapter_1 folder on the Data Disk.

2. Create a virtual directory called checkbook in your Web server that points to the checkbook folder.

3. Copy the Register.htm page into an HTML form called Personal.htm. Change the form elements to match the back of a checking account statement. Add or delete HTML form elements as necessary.

4. Create an ASP called Response.asp with the appropriate HTML tags, and another ASP similar to Register_me.asp in this chapter.

5. Test your Web application to make sure it works.

CASE PROJECTS

1. Use the Internet to investigate two or three Web applications. Explain what each application does, who the target user is, and the functions of the application.

2. On the Internet, investigate Personal Web Server on Microsoft's Web site, *www.microsoft.com*. Write a one-page summary on this Web server.

3. On the Internet, investigate the concept of objects. Define objects in your own terms. Give two to three different examples of objects not presented in this chapter. Give the properties and methods of your objects.

2

USING DATA

In this chapter, you will:

- ◆ Learn about variables and constants
- ◆ Explore application and session variables
- ◆ Learn the use of data types and variable declarations
- ◆ Learn the role that variables and constants have in an application
- ◆ Learn the benefits and types of modules
- ◆ Learn how to create objects from classes
- ◆ Learn about ASP's object model

Programming is a highly skilled trade. As with any trade, you must learn the tools before you learn about the techniques and situations in which you will apply them. In the spirit of that maxim, this chapter will begin with a thorough discussion of variables and constants and their use in ASP programming. Once you have that down, we would like to think of you as an experienced apprentice who is ready to move on to modules and classes, both of which are the stock in trade for the master programmer.

VARIABLES AND CONSTANTS

At the heart of every program is data. Data exists in a program as a variable or as a constant. A **constant** is a memory location that cannot change throughout the life of a program, which means that the value stored at this location will always be the same value. A **variable** is a memory location that stores values that can change throughout the life of a program. The value of a variable can be updated with a new value whenever necessary.

Constants are useful for storing data that does not change. Constants allow you to declare a value once, and then refer to this value throughout your program. If the constant (such as a standard sales commission) were to change, you would only need to change the constant in one location—where you originally declared it. This makes your program easier to maintain.

Conversely, your program is harder to maintain if you choose not to use a constant, and instead decide to use the actual value of the constant directly in different lines of code. When you do this, you are forced to update every instance of the value each time it is changed. This opens your program to more potential problems, because you might miss one or more instances of the value.

To use a variable in your code, you must give it a name. Variable names in VBScript are not case sensitive—that is, they can be lowercase, uppercase, or a mixture of uppercase and lowercase. For example, VARname, varname, and VARNAME are considered identical in VBScript. By contrast, variables in JavaScript *are* case sensitive, which means VARname, varname, and VARNAME are each considered to be different variable names.

In VBScript, variables names must follow these rules:

- Must begin with an alphabetic character
- Cannot contain an embedded period
- Cannot exceed 255 characters
- Must be unique in the scope in which they are declared. For example, you cannot have two different variables with the same name in a script.
- Cannot be a reserved word (see *msdn.microsoft.com/scripting* for a complete listing of reserved words)

Variable names in JavaScript must also follow some standard rules:

- Must begin with a letter (either uppercase or lowercase), an underscore (_), or a dollar sign ($). All subsequent characters can be letters, numbers, underscores, or dollar signs.
- Cannot be a reserved word.

Application and Session Variables

Active server pages are dynamic. In fact, when an ASP is processed, its variables are active only while the response page is being generated by the ASP script. After the page is generated, the variables are no longer available to the active server pages, Application objects, and Session objects within your Web page.

Fortunately, though, you can make data available after the response pages generate. You do this by using special variables. One type, the Application variable, can be used by everyone who accesses the application. Session variables, on the other hand, can only be used by the user who is logged on to the application during that session. The following examples show how to use Application and Session variables in ASP.

Code Example

```
Application("myVar")
```

Code Dissection

- This example defines an Application variable named myVar. It is stored on the server in the Application object.

Code Example

```
Session("myVar")
```

Code Dissection

- This example defines a Session variable called myVar. It is stored on the server in the Session object.

Data Types

Variables contain data; data comes in **data types**. The data type indicates characteristics of the contained data. For example, an integer data type stores only numbers, and a Boolean data type stores only the values True or False. Table 2-1 lists the character prefixes that programmers use to designate data types. These data types are for your benefit and for the benefit of programmers down the road. VBScript does not need them; to VBScript, all data types are variant.

Different programming languages allow for different data types. For instance, VBScript allows for only one data type, called a **variant**. A variant can store different types of data at different times. For example, a variable named Sales could store the number 10 at one time and the text string "Joe" at another.

 Like VBScript, JavaScript allows storage of any type of data in a variable.

Table 2-1   Data types and their three-character prefixes

Prefix	Type
int	Integer
bln	Boolean
dbl	double
sng	single
cur	currency
dtm	date (time)
byt	byte
ing	long
obj	object
str	string
vnt (use this when you do not know the type of the variable)	variant

The Scope of a Variable

A variable's **scope** specifies when the application does and does not have access to the variable. You indicate the scope that you want a variable to have by declaring the variable in a specific place, such as:

- **Application object**: A variable declared here is a **global** variable, which means that it can be seen and used by anyone who uses the application. You can use this scope to pass variables between pages in ASP. In Chapter 1, you were introduced to global.asa. This file will, among other things, store application-level variables and objects for use by your application.

- **Session object**: A variable declared here can be accessed only by the session that creates it and by any scripts that are run in the user's session. You can use this scope to pass variables between pages in ASP.

- **Script**: A variable declared here can be accessed by all subroutines and functions in the script and by all statements run as part of the script.

- **Procedure**: A variable declared here can only be accessed by the procedure that creates it. Once you declare a variable in a procedure, you can use it only during that procedure. When the procedure ends, the script destroys the variable.

Declaring Variables

Once you decide to use a variable or constant and then pick its data type, the next step is to declare the variable. A **variable declaration** is a line of code that tells the program what variables you will use. In VBScript, a typical variable declaration includes the following:

Code Example

```
Dim myVar
```

Code Dissection

- Dim states that a variable declaration is taking place.

- myVar is a valid variable name in VBScript.

- You can declare two variables on one line; you need only separate their names with a comma.

- The variable declarations are generally found at the beginning of an ASP script, usually in the first couple of lines.

A typical variable declaration in JavaScript is as follows:

Code Example

```
var myVar;
```

Code Dissection

- var is a keyword in JavaScript that states that a variable declaration is taking place.

- myVar is a valid variable name in JavaScript.

- You can declare two variables on one line; you need only separate their names with a comma.

- The variable declarations are found at the beginning of an ASP script, usually in the first couple of lines.

- Unlike in VBScript, each line in JavaScript ends in a semicolon.

While VBScript and JavaScript do not require it, you should declare all variables at the beginning of the script. This provides a convenient place to keep track of the variables included in a script. Second, it prevents invalid results that might arise if you accidentally misspell a variable later on in the script.

In VBScript, typing "Option Explicit" prior to Dim statements forces variables to be defined:

```
<%@ Language=VBScript%>
<% Option Explicit %>
```

JavaScript does not have anything equivalent to the VBScript Option Explicit statement.

Declaring Constants

The next example shows how to declare constants in VBScript. JavaScript does not support constants; therefore, in JavaScript, you need to use a regular variable set to a specific value in place of a constant.

Code Example

```
Const myConst = 2
```

Code Dissection

- Const is a keyword that tells VBScript a constant follows.

- myConst is assigned the value 2. myConst cannot change throughout the life of a script, after it has been declared.

Declaring Application and Session Variables

You declare an Application or Session variable with an **assignment statement**, which allows you to give a variable a value. (When you give the variable a value of zero, you have initialized the variable. Initialization is used when you need to do a calculation using that variable.) VBScript and JavaScript declare variables in this manner:

Code Example

```
Application("myVar") = 0
```
Or
```
Application("myVar") = "This is a string"
```
```
Application("myVar") = 0;
```
Or
```
Application("myVar") = "This is a string";
```

Code Dissection

- In both scripting languages, the first declaration uses an assignment statement to set the variable myVar to 0 in the Application object. The myVar variable is an integer data type.

- The second declaration sets the variable myVar to "This is a string" in the Application object. The myVar variable is a string data type.

Using Variables and Constants in an Application

Now that you have a good grounding in variables and constants, it's time to take a look at them within an application. Before you take a look at the application, however, we will create a virtual directory for it.

1. Click **Start**, point to **Programs**, point to **Microsoft Personal Web Server**, and then click **Personal Web Manager**. The Personal Web Manager window opens.

2. If the Tip of the Day dialog box appears, click **Close**. Verify that Web publishing is turned on.

3. Click the **Advanced** icon on the left side of the window. The Advanced Options window opens.

4. Click the **Add** button. The Add Directory dialog box opens.

5. In the Alias text box, type **Chapter_2**. The alias is the name of the folder you are using.

6. In the Directory text box, browse to the **Chapter_2** folder.

7. Repeat Steps 5 and 6 for Chapter_2/feet_conv.

8. Click the **OK** button, and then click **Yes** in the resulting dialog box. You return to the Advanced Options window. Make sure the Enable Default Document check box is checked. Close the Personal Web Manager window.

9. Open the program by typing **http://localhost/Chapter_2/feet_conv** into your browser. Your screen should resemble Figure 2-1.

10. Enter **12** into the text box, and then press the **Submit** button. Your screen should now resemble Figure 2-2.

11. Close your browser.

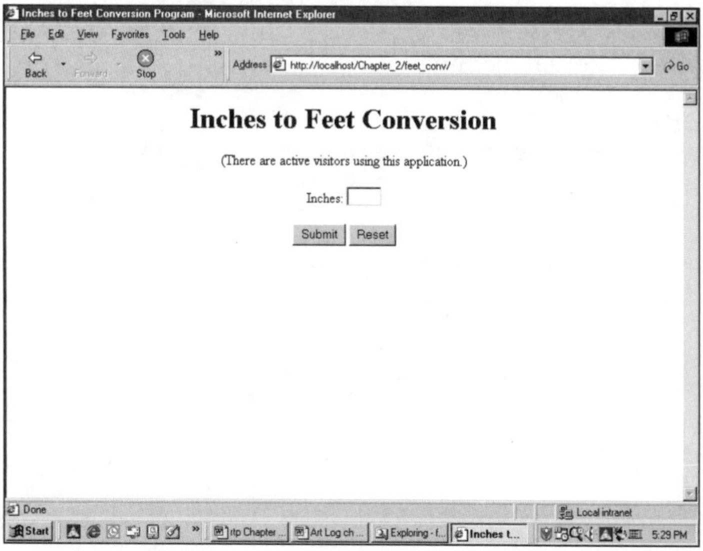

Figure 2-1   The Inches to Feet program

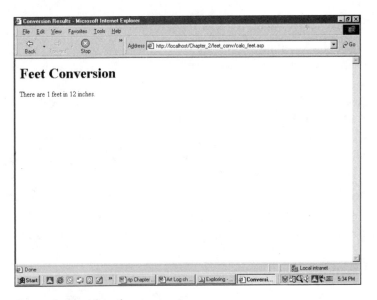

Figure 2-2   After the conversion

Let's take a look at the code behind the program:

Code Example

```
1 <%@ Language=VBScript%>
2 <%Option Explicit%>
3 <%Response.buffer=true%>
4 <HTML>
5 <!--
6  ************************************************
7  *** Script Name: conv_feet               ***
8  *** Author:      Keith Morneau            ***
9  *** Date:        7/22/01                  ***
10 *** Description:                          ***
11 ***  This script generates the number     ***
12 ***  of feet in a number of inches.        ***
13 ***                                       ***
14 *** Revisions:                            ***
15 ************************************************
16 -->
17
18 <HEAD>
19 <TITLE>Conversion Results</TITLE>
20 </HEAD>
21 <BODY>
22<H1>Feet Conversion</H1>
23 <%
24 Dim intInches, sngFeet
```

```
25 Const conConvFactor = 12
26
27 'Change the entry on the form to an integer
28 intInches = CInt(Request.Form("txtInches"))
29
30 'Convert feet to inches
31 sngFeet = round((intInches / conConvFactor),1)
32
33 'Write out the result
34 Response.Write("There are " & sngFeet & " feet in " &
   intInches & " inches.")
35
36 'End the session
37 Session.Abandon
38 %>
39 </BODY>
40 </HTML>
```

Code Dissection

- Line 2 is the Option Explicit statement, which forces all variables to be declared in the script.

- Lines 6–15 shows how to document your HTML pages.

- Line 27 shows how to document a line in VBScript using the ' character as the first character in a line.

- Line 24 shows an example of a variable declaration.

- Line 25 shows an example of a constant declaration.

- Line 28 shows how to convert a value (which the user has typed into the form) to the integer type, using the Cint function.

- Line 31 shows another built-in function called round. Round(expression, number of decimal places) rounds a value to a given number of decimal places. See *www.msdn.microsoft.com/scripting* if you are not familiar with the round function.

- Line 34 shows a way of writing a line of text to the HTML page. You can directly use text in your ASP scripts by inserting the text with HTML tags, or you can use a function called Response.Write. The Response.Write function allows the application to insert a line of text into a Web page as the Web page is generated. In the function, you use an **&**, the concatenation operator, to connect one or more strings. See *msdn.microsoft.com/scripting* if you are not familiar with the **&** concatenation function.

- Line 37 shows how to end a Session in ASP, using Session.Abandon.

Here is JavaScript that produces the same result:

Code Example

```
1 <%@ Language=JavaScript%>
2 <%Response.buffer=true%>
3 <HTML>
4 <!--
5   **********************************************
6   *** Script Name: conv_feet              ***
7   *** Author:      Keith Morneau          ***
8   *** Date:        7/22/01                ***
9   *** Description:                        ***
10  ***   This script generates the number ***
11  ***   of feet in a number of inches.    ***
12  ***                                     ***
13  *** Revisions:                          ***
14  **********************************************
15 -->
16
17 <HEAD>
18 <TITLE>Conversion Results</TITLE>
19 </HEAD>
20 <BODY>
21 <H1>Feet Conversion</H1>
22 <%
23 var intInches, sngFeet;
24 var conConvFactor = 12;
25
26 //Change the entry on the form to an integer
27 intInches = Request.Form("txtInches");
28
29 //Convert feet to inches
30 sngFeet = Math.round((intInches / conConvFactor));
31
32 //Write out the result
33 Response.Write("There are " + sngFeet + " feet in " +
intInches + " inches.");
34
35 //End the session
36 Session.Abandon();
37 %>
38 </BODY>
39 </HTML>
```

Code Dissection

- Lines 23 and 24 show how to declare variables in JavaScript. In line 24 the constant becomes a variable that is assigned a particular value.

- Each line in JavaScript ends with a ;.

- Lines 26, 29, 32, and 35 are comments, which are indicated by two forward slashes (//).

- Line 30 uses the built-in function round, from the Math object in JavaScript. Refer to *www.msdn.microsoft.com/scripting* for details about the Math object.

- Line 36 shows how to call a function in JavaScript. You will investigate calling functions later in this chapter.

CREATING MODULES

As with any of the skilled trades, once you learn the basic tools and their uses, you begin to look for ways to economize on your effort. In programming, you can economize by using modules. A **module** is a series of steps designed to perform a single task. Using module names within code allows you to build your application more efficiently; rather than retyping many lines of code, you can simply refer to the relevant module name.

Modularization is the dividing of an application into two parts. In the first part, you place your input code. In the second part, you place your processing and output code. Modularization allows you to create discrete units of code devoted to solving a particular problem. Code organized in this manner allows you to write very complex programs that are easy to read and understand.

There are two different kinds of modules: subroutines (also known as procedures) and functions. We will discuss them in the following sections. Both allow you to reuse a segment of code over and over again in your programs. You will use a subroutine when you want to repeat a series of statements but do not need to return a value to the user. You will use a function when you want to repeat a series of statements and return a value.

Subroutines or Procedures

A **subroutine** is a series of steps that accomplishes a task but does not usually return a value. There are two steps involved in creating a subroutine: defining and calling. The following shows how to define a subroutine in VBScript:

```
SUB subroutine_name
    . . . [Code goes here]
END SUB
```

A module in VBScript is defined with the keyword SUB followed by the name of the subroutine. The line "[Code goes here]" would be replaced by the actual steps of the subroutine in a real subroutine. The keyword END SUB ends the subroutine.

A module in JavaScript looks a little different from VBScript:

```
function function_name()
{
[CODE GOES HERE]
}
[END CODE]
```

In JavaScript, a subroutine begins with the keyword FUNCTION followed by the name of the function. A { curly brace begins the function and a } curly brace ends the function.

Once you go through the effort of defining a subroutine or procedure, your next step is to call the subroutine or module, as shown in the following code:

```
call subroutine_name
```

The preceding example calls and runs a subroutine named subroutine_name. The Call keyword is optional, but should be used for the sake of clarity.

To make the same call in JavaScript, you would use the following:

```
function_name();
```

A subroutine call in JavaScript consists of the name of the subroutine followed by parentheses and a semicolon. When JavaScript processes this line of code, it will run the contents of the specified subroutine.

Creating a VBScript Subroutine

At this point, we are going to use a VBScript subroutine in the conversion application in this chapter. Then, we will investigate the JavaScript version of the same code.

To modify the calc_feet.asp file in VBScript:

1. Start Notepad.

2. Open the **calc_feet.asp** file, located in the feet_conv subfolder within the Chapter_2 folder.

3. Modify the file so that it resembles the following (new code shown in bold):

```
<%@ Language=VBScript%>
<%Option Explicit%>
<%Response.buffer=true%>
<HTML>
<!--
   ***********************************************
   *** Script Name: conv_feet                 ***
   *** Author:      Keith Morneau             ***
   *** Date:        7/22/01                   ***
   *** Description:                           ***
   ***   This script generates the number     ***
   ***   of feet in a number of inches.       ***
   ***                                        ***
   *** Revisions:                             ***
   ***   7/25/01     Add a subroutine to script ***
   ***********************************************
-->
```

```
<HEAD>
<TITLE>Conversion Results</TITLE>
<%
 SUB inches_to_feet()
    Dim intInches, sngFeet
    Const conConvFactor = 12

'Change the entry on the form to an integer
    intInches = CInt(Request.Form("txtInches"))

'Convert feet from inches
    sngFeet = round((intInches / conConvFactor),1)

'Write out the result
    Response.Write("There are " & sngFeet & " feet in " &
    intInches & " inches.")

  END SUB
%>
</HEAD>
<BODY>
<H1>Feet Conversion</H1>
<%
Call inches_to_feet
'End the session
Session.Abandon
%>
</BODY>
</HTML>
```

4. Save the file.

5. Close Notepad.

6. Test your changes in Internet Explorer by requesting the Web application using **http://localhost/chapter_2/feet_conv/default.asp**.

7. Type **12** into the text box, and then click the **Submit** button. Your screen should resemble Figure 2-3.

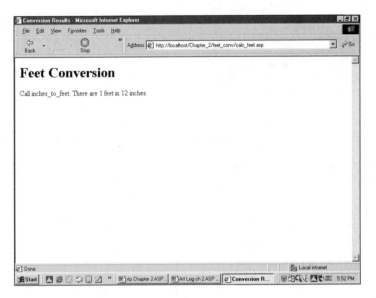

Figure 2-3   Calling inches_to_feet

In the code that you just typed, the 13 lines of code after the <TITLE>...</TITLE> tag pair defined the subroutine. The next line of bold code called the subroutine.

Reviewing a JavaScript Subroutine

If you wanted to accomplish the same task with JavaScript, you would use the following code. (Note that the bolded sections reflect the differences between the JavaScript and VBScript versions and that "..." was used to indicate code that was unchanged and thus deleted for brevity.)

Code Example

```
<%@ Language=JavaScript%>
...
 <% function inches_to_feet()
    {
    var intInches, sngFeet;
    var conConvFactor = 12;

 //Change the entry on the form to an integer
    intInches = Request.Form("txtInches");

 //Convert feet from inches
    sngFeet = Math.round((intInches / conConvFactor));

 //Write out the result
    Response.Write("There are " + sngFeet + " feet in " +
    intInches + " inches.");
```

2

```
   }
%>
...
 inches_to_feet();
 //End the session
 Session.Abandon();
...
```

Code Dissection

- In the first line of code, the language tag specified JavaScript instead of VBScript.

- The second block of code shows how to create a subroutine in JavaScript. You will notice that VBScript uses SUB…END SUB, and JavaScript uses function…{…}.

- The third block of code shows you how to call the subroutine in JavaScript. Notice that you do not use the call keyword, and you need to include the ( ) in a JavaScript subroutine call.

Functions

While subroutines accomplish a series of steps, a function accomplishes a series of steps *and* returns a single value. The following code shows a VBScript function that adds two numbers. The two numbers passed into the function are called arguments. An **argument** is a variable used to do calculations in the function itself. A function can have zero or more arguments, separated by commas.

Code Example

VBScript

```
FUNCTION Add(number1,number2)
Add = number1 + number2
END FUNCTION
```

Code Dissection

- The function name is Add, as shown in the first line of code. The function involves two arguments: number1 and number2, separated by commas.

- The second line of code returns the result of the operation.

Now, let's take a look at the same example in JavaScript:

Code Example

JavaScript

```
function Add(number1,number2)
{
return (number1+number2);
}
```

Code Dissection

- The first line is similar to the corresponding line in VBScript.
- The third line differs from the return line VBScript, but it still returns the result of the Add function.

Calling a Function

Once again, creating a function is only half the battle. You have to call the function to put it to work. The following, written in VBScript, calls a function:

Code Example

```
Dim result
result = Add(1,2)
```

Code Dissection

- To call a function in VBScript, you must allow the function to return a value into a variable.
- The variable result in this example will store the contents of 1 + 2, which is 3.

To do the same in JavaScript, you would write the following code:

Code Example

```
var result;
result = Add(1,2);
```

Code Dissection

- Note that in the JavaScript example, the code looks identical to VBScript except for the var and the semicolon at the end of the lines.

Adding a VBScript Function to calc_feet.asp

In the following steps, you will add a function to the calc_feet.asp page in VBScript. This function will be responsible for converting inches into feet.

To add a function to the calc_feet.asp page in VBScript:

1. Start NotePad.

2. Open the **calc_feet.asp** file.

3. Modify the file by replacing the text between the <TITLE> and the </HEAD> tags with the block of text shown below in bold, and then change the single line

of bold text as shown (the "..." notation indicates lines of code that do not change and that were removed for brevity):

VBScript

```
...
<TITLE>Conversion Results</TITLE>
<%
    FUNCTION convert_to_feet(intInches)
    convert_to_feet = round(intInches / 12,1)
    END FUNCTION
%>
</HEAD>
...
'Convert feet from inches
sngFeet = convert_to_feet(intInches)
'Write out the result
...
```

4. Save the file, close NotePad, and test your changes in Internet Explorer.

Now, let's take a closer look at the code you just changed:

Code Dissection

- The first bold line of code is the function definition: FUNCTION convert_to_feet(intinches). Note that the definition contains a function name and an argument. In this case, the argument is the value assigned to the variable intInches, which is used to calculate the feet measurement.

- The first block of bold code includes the FUNCTION … END FUNCTION keywords, which declare a function in VBScript. This block also constitutes the function's code.

- In the first block of bold code, the line that begins with convert_to_feet = round(intinches/12,1) is the actual function. Following the order of operations, this function divides the intinches argument by 12, and then rounds the value to the nearest whole number (which is what 1 stands for). Finally, the built-in round function rounds the resulting value to sngFeet in the main script. Note that in VBScript, the name of the function must be positioned to the right of the equal sign.

- The last bold line calls the function. You will notice that a variable is set equal to the function call. Since functions return values, you need a variable to accept the value from the function.

Reviewing a Function in JavaScript

In JavaScript, a function uses the keyword "return" to return a value from the function. The following code shows the JavaScript version of the previous function example. Again, the differences between VBScript and JavaScript are bolded, and some lines have been deleted for brevity.

Code Example

```
<%@ Language=JavaScript%>
...
<TITLE>Conversion Results</TITLE>
<% function convert_to_feet(intInches)
   {
   var conConvFactor = 12;

//Convert feet from inches
     return (Math.round(intInches / conConvFactor));

   }
 %>
...
 <%
 var sngFeet;
 sngFeet = convert_to_feet(Request.Form("txtInches"));
 //Write out the result
 Response.Write("There are " + sngFeet + " feet in " +
Request.Form("txtInches") + " inches.");

 //End the session
 Session.Abandon();
 %>
...
```

Code Dissection

■ The first block of bold code shows how to create a function in JavaScript. The line that begins with "return" is what makes this a JavaScript function. This line is also different from VBScript regarding the use of round. Round in JavaScript belongs to an object called Math. There is no object needed in VBScript.

■ The second block of code shows how to call a function in JavaScript.

CREATING OBJECTS FROM CLASSES

You can create objects efficiently by using a class. A **class** defines the properties and methods of the objects that reside in it. Once you create a class, you can use it to create multiple objects. Essentially, a class functions like a cookie cutter—you can use it to create a series of similar objects.

You can create classes in VBScript or in JavaScript. We'll start with the former.

Classes in VBScript

Within VBScript, you declare properties and methods associated with a class inside the CLASS...END CLASS keywords. You name a class by using the three letter prefix "cls" and the name of your choice.

In the following steps, you will create your own class in VBScript.

To create a class in VBScript:

1. Open NotePad and create a new file.
2. Type the following:

```
<%

CLASS clsConversion

Private intInches
Private sngFeet

Public Sub Convert_to_Feet

sngFeet = round(intInches/12,1)

End Sub

'Create a property called Inches
Public Property Get Inches

Inches = intInches

End Property

Public Property Let Inches(newInches)

intInches = newInches

End Property

'Create a property called Feet
Public Property Get Feet

Feet = sngFeet

End Property

Public Property Let Feet(newFeet)

sngFeet = newFeet

End Property
```

```
      END CLASS

      %>
```

3. Save the class with filename **clsConversion.cls** in the **feet_conv** subfolder within the **chapter_2** folder on your Data Disk.

4. Close NotePad.

Code Dissection

- The second line of code to the third to last line of code show how to declare properties and methods inside the CLASS…END CLASS keywords.

- The class is actually declared in the second line of code. Notice that the class name begins with "cls" (as explained earlier) and then includes a descriptive word, in this case, conversion.

- The object's properties are declared in the third and fourth lines of code. Notice the keyword PRIVATE before the property names. A property can be either public or private. Declaring a property as private allows an object to change internally without affecting the overall operation of the object. Declaring a property as public makes it possible for a developer to access that property directly. (In other words, it creates an interface to the class.)

- In the next three lines of code, you'll find the convert_to_feet subroutine, which converts inches to feet, using the intInches variable in your properties. Private variables have global scope in relation to each of the subroutines and functions declared in the class. You can use these variables in the class itself. Notice that the subroutine is declared public, which means that it can be accessed by users of the object and is therefore part of its interface.

- The remaining code declares two public properties, Inches and Feet, using special property procedures called Get and Let. The Get property function allows you to return the internal representation of intInches and sngFeet. The Let property subroutine allows you to set the internal representation of intInches and sngFeet. When you modify the calc_feet.asp page, you will see an example of how to use Get and Let property procedures. You will notice that they are declared as public, which means that you, as the developer, can use these properties in your code.

Classes in JavaScript

To create a class in JavaScript, you need to create a function that creates the class (which is an object in and of itself) and that declares the properties and methods that will be given to any subsequent objects from that class. The function name should be the name of the class, which in the example below is clsConversion:

Code Example

```
1 <%
2
3 function clsConversion()
```

```
 4 {
 5
 6 // Property declarations
 7
 8 this.intInches = 0;
 9 this.sngFeet = 0;
10
11 // Method declarations
12
13 this.Convert_to_Feet = Convert_to_Feet;
14 this.getFeet = getFeet;
15 this.setFeet = setFeet;
16 this.getInches = getInches;
17 this.setInches = setInches;
18 }
19
20 function Convert_to_Feet()
21 {
22 this.sngFeet = Math.round(this.intInches/12,1);
23 }
24
25
26 //Create an accessor method called getInches
27 function getInches()
28 {
29 return (this.intInches);
30 }
31
32 function setInches(newInches)
33 {
34 this.intInches = newInches;
35 }
36
37 // Create an accessor method for Feet
38 function getFeet()
39 {
40 return (this.sngFeet);
41 }
42
43 function setFeet(newFeet)
44 {
45 this.sngFeet = newFeet;
46 }
47
48 %>
```

Code Dissection

- Lines 3 through 18 provide the clsConversion function that creates the class. To declare a property you need to use this.intInches = 0;. This is a special keyword that indicates that you are creating this object. Inches is the name of the property. To declare a method, you need to use this.Convert_to_Feet = Convert_to_Feet. This line indicates that you want to make the Convert_to_Feet function a method of the object.

- Lines 20–46 define each of the methods of clsConversion. Toward the end of the code, notice the functions that contain get and set. These functions operate similarly to the Get and Let modules in VBScript and are called **accessor methods** in JavaScript.

Declaring an Object from a Class

The next step after you create a class in VBScript or JavaScript is to declare an object that will be based on the class. Declaring an object from a class is called creating an **instance** of the class.

Code Example

The following shows how to declare an object from a VBScript class:

```
Dim objConversion
Set objConversion = new clsConversion
```

The following shows how to declare an object from a JavaScript class:

```
var objConversion;
objConversion = new clsConversion();
```

Code Dissection

- The first line of the VBScript and JavaScript examples declares the variable to use.

- The second line of the VBScript and JavaScript examples creates an object from the class, using the new keyword. The new keyword creates the object from the class.

- In the VBScript example, when you use object variables, you must use the set keyword in the beginning of the line that creates an object.

Using Classes in VBScript

The running example in this chapter converts inches to feet. The use of classes allows the developer of the class to hide from the programmer the details of how the conversion is done. Thus, the use of a class makes it possible for the programmer to create an application object without actually having to learn how to do the conversion itself. For instance, to include the clsConversion.cls class in his or her script, the programmer would use the following line:

```
<!-- #include file="clsConversion.cls" -->
```

In the above example, the code did not specify where clsConversion.cls is located. Thus, the class file you just created is called a **Server-Side Include (SSI)** file. SSI files are handy if you have scripts that you need to reuse in different ASP pages. ASP scripts assume that the SSI file is in the same directory or folder as the page you requested in your Web application.

Sometimes, however, for management reasons, you will want your shared script files to reside in their own directories. To do this, you will need to use a **virtual path**, which is a directory path that assumes that the Web application's root folder is the virtual directory created for this application.

To illustrate this concept, let's say that the includes folder is located up one directory from the feet_conv. You would specify the include line as follows:

```
<!-- #include file="../includes/clsConversion.cls" -->
```

You can also specify the include file by using the physical path—that is, the actual path of the directory as seen by Windows. You would specify the include line as follows:

```
<!--
 #include file="a:\chapter_2\includes\clsConversion.cls" -->
```

Notice the difference in the slashes between the virtual folder and the physical folder. The forward slash (/) assumes that the start of the directory path begins at the virtual directory. The back slash (\) assumes that the start of the directory path begins with a drive letter in Windows.

In the next set of steps, you will modify the calc_feet.asp page to use the clsConversion class you just created in VBScript.

To modify the calc_feet.asp to use the clsConversion class:

1. Open **calc_feet.asp** in NotePad.

2. Modify the file by making its code match the bold lines shown below. Note that some lines of nonchanging code have been eliminated for brevity:

VBScript

```
...
<%Response.buffer=true%>
<!-- #include file="clsConversion.cls" -->
<HTML>
...
<H1>Feet Conversion</H1>
<%
Dim objConversion
Set objConversion = New clsConversion

objConversion.Inches = CInt(Request.Form("txtInches"))
objConversion.Convert_to_Feet

'Write out the result
Response.Write("There are " & objConversion.Feet & " feet
in " & objConversion.Inches & " inches.")

'End the session
Session.Abandon
%>
</BODY>
</HTML>
```

3. Save the file, close Notepad, and then test your changes in your browser, as you have done before.

Code Dissection

- The first bold line of code shows how to incorporate an existing class file into a script.

- The second and third lines of bold code show how to declare an object that is based on an existing class. Notice that you declare an object by using the key word "Dim," just as when you declare a variable. The keyword Dim is followed by the object's name, which begins with the three-letter prefix "obj" (short for "object").

- The third line of bold code creates the instance of the class—that is, it creates an object called objConversion from the class clsConversion. You only use the keyword **Set** and **New** when you are declaring an object. Set is used when assigning an object variable, and New is used only when creating an instance of a class.

- Look at the additional lines of bold code and notice the lines that employ decimal dotted notation to access the object's properties and methods, which are specified by the class. object_name.property and object_name.method access the object's public properties and methods. For example, the objConversion object contains a property called Inches. To access the inches property, you need to use the object_name.property, objConversion.Inches. The same rule applies to methods. Notice that these lines refer to the Inches and Feet properties, which are the special property procedures you created when you defined the class.

Using Classes in JavaScript

The following shows the modifications to calc_feet.asp necessary to support JavaScript objects. Again, some nonchanging code has been eliminated for brevity.

Code Example

```
<%@ Language=JavaScript%>
<%Response.buffer=true%>
...
<H1>Feet Conversion</H1>
 <%

 var objConversion;
 objConversion = new clsConversion();

 objConversion.setInches(Request.Form("txtInches"));
 objConversion.Convert_to_Feet();

 Response.write("There are " + objConversion.getFeet() + " feet
in " + Request.Form("txtInches") + " inches!");
```

2

```
//End the session
Session.Abandon();
%>
</BODY>
</HTML>
```

Code Dissection

- The third and fourth lines of bold code show you how to declare an object called objConversion from a class called clsConversion. You will notice that JavaScript does not need a set keyword in front of an object variable assignment.

- Look farther down the lines of code. The line that begins "objConversion" shows how to set a property in JavaScript. The next line shows how to call a method in JavaScript.

- The line that begins with "Response.write" shows how to retrieve the feet measurement from the object, using the getFeet method.

In this section, you learned how to use a class in your scripts. This knowledge gives you the ability to create your own user-defined objects in your scripts. You can use these objects to hide the functionality of your scripts from the user.

USING ASP'S OBJECT MODEL

Throughout the first two chapters of this book, you have encountered brief mentions of the Application, Session, Request, and Response objects. It is now time, however, to review them in detail so that you understand properties, methods, and events and that are available to you for use in future chapters.

Application Object

The Application object, which initializes server variables that are used throughout the life of a Web application, supplies the necessary interface you need to create Web applications. Table 2-2 describes the properties, methods, and events of the Application object.

Table 2-2   Useful properties, methods, and events of the Application object

Property/Method/Event	Name	Description
Property	Contents	A collection of all the items (such as variables and objects) created during the processing of ASP scripts
Property	StaticObjects	A collection of all the items added through the <OBJECT> tag
Method	lock	A method that prevents any other client from modifying Web application properties
Method	unlock	A method that allows other clients to modify Web application properties
Event	onstart	An event that fires when an application first starts
Event	onend	An event that fires when an application exits

Session Object

The Session object, which initializes a user's session inside a Web application, provides a mechanism for creating server variables and firing common events related to a user's session. Table 2-3 describes the properties, methods, and events of the session object.

Table 2-3   Useful properties, methods, and events of the Session object

Property/Method/Event	Name	Description
Property	Contents	A collection of all the items created during the processing of ASP scripts
Property	staticObjects	A collection of all the items added through the <OBJECT> tag
Property	timeout	This property sets the timeout property for the session state in the application, in minutes.
Method	Abandon	This method ends a session.
Event	onstart	This event fires when a new client accesses a Web application.
Event	onend	This event fires when a client ends the session.

Request Object

The Request object supplies information regarding the request the user sends to the Web application. Table 2-4 lists the properties and methods of the Request object.

Table 2-4   Useful properties and methods of the Request object

Property/Method	Name	Description
Property	TotalBytes	The size of the request in bytes
Property	ClientCertificate	A special security object that contains the user's electronic signature; used in implementing security in ASP
Property	Cookies	A collection of cookies
Property	Form	Values from the form elements sent by the browser
Property	QueryString	Values of the variables in an HTTP query string, which is data sent to the server from the Web address
Property	ServerVariables	Values of the Web server's environment
Method	BinaryRead	A method that is used to retrieve data sent to the server as part of the user's POST request

Response Object

The Response object provides a way of sending a response message to the client in HTML. The Response object allows the application to create a unique response to a particular request. Table 2-5 describes the Response object's properties and methods.

Table 2-5   Useful properties and methods of the Response object

Property/Method	Name	Description
Property	Cookies	Contents of the cookie collection to be sent to the browser
Property	buffer	Indicates whether to buffer the contents of the response until complete
Property	status	The status of the HTTP request, as returned by the server
Method	Appendtolog	Adds text to a Web server log
Method	Binarywrite	Sends text to the browser without any text conversions, which means that the object will not add HTML tags to the data before sending it
Method	clear	Removes any buffered output
Method	end	Stops processing the page and returns results to the browser
Method	flush	Sends buffered output immediately
Method	Redirect	Redirects a browser to a different URL
Method	write	Writes text or variables to the current page as a string

CHAPTER SUMMARY

- Data exists in a program as a variable or as a constant. A constant is a memory location that cannot change throughout the life of a program. A variable is a memory location that stores values that can change throughout the life of a program. A special type of variable, the Application variable, can be used by everyone who accesses the application. Session variables, on the other hand, can only be used by the user who is logged in to the application during that session.

- Variables contain data; data comes in data types. The data type indicates characteristics of the contained data. Different programming languages allow for different data types. A variable's scope specifies when the application does or does not have access to the variable.

- A variable declaration is a line of code that tells the program what variables you will use. While VBScript and JavaScript do not require it, you should declare all variables at the beginning of the script. While you can declare constants in VBScript, you cannot do so in JavaScript. To declare an Application or Session variable, you use an assignment statement.

- A module is a series of steps designed to perform a single task. Using module names within code allows you to build your application more efficiently; rather than retyping many lines of code, you can simply refer to the relevant module name. There are two different kinds of modules: subroutines (also known as procedures) and functions. A subroutine is a series of steps that accomplishes a task but does not usually return a value. While a subroutine accomplishes a series of steps, a function accomplishes a series of steps and returns a single value.

- You can create objects efficiently by using a class. A class defines the properties and methods of the objects that reside in it. Once you create a class, you can use it to create multiple objects. Declaring an object from a class is called creating an instance of the class.

- The Application, Session, Request, and Response objects are common in ASP. Each has its own unique combination of available properties, methods, and events.

REVIEW QUESTIONS

1. A(n) ――――――― is a memory location that varies or changes.
   a. module
   b. constant
   c. variable
   d. none of the above

2. A(n) ――――――― is a memory location that cannot change throughout the life of a program.
   a. module
   b. constant
   c. variable
   d. none of the above

3. You can declare variables by using the Application and Session objects. True or False?

4. Which of the following is a concatenation operator in VBScript?

   a. +

   b. #

   c. $

   d. &

5. Which of the following is a concatenation operator in JavaScript?

   a. +

   b. #

   c. $

   d. &

6. The only data type in VBScript is _____.

   a. Integer

   b. String

   c. Variant

   d. Single

7. Assume that the strCity variable contains "Boston" and that the strState variable contains "MA". Which of the following will concatenate the strCity variable with the strState variable in VBScript?

   a. strCity + strState

   b. strCity & ", " & strState

   c. strCity ! ", " ! strState

   d. strCity ^ strState

8. Assume that the strCity variable contains "Boston" and that the strState variable contains "MA". Which of the following will concatenate the strCity variable with the strState variable in JavaScript?

   a. strCity + strState

   b. strCity & ", " & strState

   c. strCity ! ", " ! strState

   d. strCity ^ strState

9. A(n) _____ is a module consisting of a series of steps that usually does not return a result.

   a. subroutine

   b. function

   c. procedure

   d. none of the above

10. The _____ is a module consisting of a series of steps that returns a single value.

    a. subroutine

    b. function

    c. procedure

    d. none of the above

11. The cookie cutter is an analogy for a(n) _____ in software development.

    a. class

    b. object

    c. property

    d. method

12. A(n) _____ is an instance of a class.

    a. attribute

    b. object

    c. property

    d. method

13. The color of a ball is an example of a(n) _____.

    a. class

    b. object

    c. property

    d. method

14. Bouncing a ball is an example of a(n) _____.

    a. class

    b. object

    c. property

    d. method

15. A class contains both properties and methods. True or False?

16. A class and an object are synonymous. True or False?

17. Classes use _____ as the three-letter prefix in their names.

    a. cls

    b. obj

    c. met

    d. pro

18. Objects use _____ as the three-letter prefix in their names.

    a. cls

    b. obj

    c. met

    d. pro

HANDS-ON PROJECTS

 For the projects below that do not specify a scripting language, ask your instructor to specify one. Remember to create a virtual directory for your Hands-on Projects.

Project 2-1

Write a Web application that computes the area and circumference of a circle. The application should accept the radius of the circle as input. (Remember that the area of a circle is $\pi * r^2$, and the circumference is $C = 2 * \pi * r$. Make sure to use a constant for π.)

Complete these steps:

1. Create a folder called circle on your Data Disk.
2. Create a virtual directory on your Web server for the circle folder.
3. Create a file called default.htm that requests the radius of a circle using an HTML form and save it in the circle folder.
4. Create a file called calculate.asp that calculates the circumference and area of a circle, using the formulas above. Make sure to display the results of the calculations. Save this file in the circle folder.
5. Test your Web application in Internet Explorer by requesting the Web application, using *http://localhost/circle/default.htm*.
6. Change the calculate.asp script to incorporate a function or a subroutine similar to what you learned in this chapter.
7. Test your Web application in Internet Explorer by requesting the Web application, using *http://localhost/circle/default.htm*.
8. Change the calculate.asp script to incorporate objects. (*Hint:* You will need to create a class file called circle.cls in the circle folder before you alter the calculate.asp script.)
9. Test your Web application in Internet Explorer by requesting the Web application using *http://localhost/circle/default.htm*.

Project 2-2

Write a Web application that computes and displays the total pay for an employee. The application should accept regular hours, overtime hours, and the hourly wage rate for one employee, using an employee time sheet as input.

Complete these steps:

1. Create a folder called pay on your Data Disk.

2. Create a virtual directory on your Web server for the pay folder.

3. Create a file called default.htm that requests regular hours, overtime hours, and the hourly wage rate for one employee, using an HTML form, and save it in the pay folder.

4. Create a file called calculate.asp that calculates the total pay of an employee, using the regular hours*hourly wage rate+overtime*hourly wage rate*1.5 formula. Make sure to display the results of the calculations. Save this file in the pay folder.

5. Test your Web application in Internet Explorer by requesting the Web application, using *http://localhost/pay/default.htm*.

6. Change the calculate.asp script to incorporate a function or a subroutine similar to what you learned in this chapter.

7. Test your Web application in Internet Explorer by requesting the Web application, using *http://localhost/pay/default.htm*.

8. Change the calculate.asp script to incorporate objects. (*Hint:* You will need to create a class file called pay.cls in the pay folder before you alter the calculate.asp script.)

9. Test your Web application in Internet Explorer by requesting the Web application, using *http://localhost/pay/default.htm*.

Project 2-3

Write a Web application that computes the average of five grades. Create a form that accepts the five grades and displays the average and the five grades.

Complete these steps:

1. Create a folder called grades on your Data Disk.

2. Create a virtual directory on your Web server for the grades folder.

3. Create a file called default.htm that requests five grades, using an HTML form, and save it in the grades folder.

4. Create a file called calculate.asp that calculates the average of the five grades, using the (grade1+grade2+grade3+grade4+grade5)/5 formula. Make sure to display the results of the calculations. Save this file in the grades folder.

5. Test your Web application in Internet Explorer by requesting the Web application using *http://localhost/grades/default.htm*.

6. Change the calculate.asp script to incorporate a function or a subroutine similar to what you learned in this chapter.

7. Test your Web application in Internet Explorer by requesting the Web application using *http://localhost/grades/default.htm.*

8. Change the calculate.asp script to incorporate objects. (*Hint:* You will need to create a class file called grades.cls in the grades folder before you alter the calculate.asp script.)

9. Test your Web application in Internet Explorer by requesting the Web application, using *http://localhost/grades/default.htm.*

Project 2-4

Write a Web application that computes the area and perimeter of a rectangle. The application should accept the length and width of the rectangle as input. The output should include the length, width, area, and perimeter of the rectangle.

Complete these steps:

1. Create a folder called rectangle on your Data Disk.

2. Create a virtual directory on your Web server for the rectangle folder.

3. Create a file called default.htm that requests length and width of a rectangle, using an HTML form, and save it in the rectangle folder.

4. Create a file called calculate.asp that calculates the perimeter (2*length+2*width) and area (length*width). Make sure to display the results of the calculations. Save this file in the rectangle folder.

5. Test your Web application in Internet Explorer by requesting the Web application, using *http://localhost/rectangle/default.htm.*

6. Change the calculate.asp script to incorporate a function or a subroutine similar to what you learned in this chapter.

7. Test your Web application in Internet Explorer by requesting the Web application, using *http://localhost/rectangle/default.htm.*

8. Change the calculate.asp script to incorporate objects.

9. Test your Web application in Internet Explorer by requesting the Web application, using *http://localhost/rectangle/default.htm.*

Project 2-5

Write a Web application that converts the Fahrenheit temperature to the Celsius temperature.

Complete these steps:

1. Create a folder called temp on your Data Disk.

2. Create a virtual directory on your Web server for the temp folder.

3. Create a file called default.htm that requests Fahrenheit temperature, using an HTML form, and save it in the temp folder.

4. Create a file called calculate.asp that calculates the Celsius temperature. Make sure to display the results of the calculations. Save this file in the temp folder.

5. Test your Web application in Internet Explorer by requesting the Web application, using *http://localhost/temp/default.htm*.

6. Change the calculate.asp script to incorporate a function or a subroutine similar to what you learned in this chapter.

7. Test your Web application in Internet Explorer by requesting the Web application, using *http://localhost/temp/default.htm*.

8. Change the calculate.asp script to incorporate objects.

9. Test your Web application in Internet Explorer by requesting the Web application, via PWS.

CASE PROJECTS

1. While you are taking a class in ASP, you decide to work as a shoe salesman for a major department store. You will get paid a 6% commission for all sales you accumulate over a two-week period, on top of your regular salary. Create a Web application to calculate your commission, with your total sales as input.

2. Your manager just found out that you are learning how to create Web applications using ASP. Your manager wants you to create a Web application that will calculate the sales price of any item in the store. He wants the application to request the item name, the regular price of the item, and the discount percentage. The application should then display the item name, the regular price, the discount percent, and the sales price.

3. After completing the assignment in Case 2, you decide to change your Web application so that it calculates the commission and total gross pay for the two-week period. Employees are paid an hourly rate and time and a half for overtime.

3

ARRAYS, COLLECTIONS, AND CONTROL STRUCTURES

In this chapter, you will:

♦ Understand the arrays and their limitations
♦ Create collections using correct key and objects
♦ Modify a Dictionary object
♦ Understand selection control structures and the role of operators in control structures
♦ Understand repetition control structures and the use of loops

When you finished the last chapter, we could think of you as a pretty skilled apprentice in the art of ASP. Now, we're going to introduce you to two new tools—arrays and collections—that will allow you to handle multiple variables. You will discover that the former has a limitation that the latter will overcome. Later in the chapter, you'll learn how to write code that will allow your application to make decisions based on the content of variables. In the process of this exploration, you'll learn how the server can prevent end users from introducing errors into an application.

ARRAYS AND COLLECTIONS

So far in this book, you have been exposed to programming situations in which a single variable was sufficient for a programmer's needs. In many situations, however, employing a single variable is too restrictive. For example, consider the situation in which a user needs to enter four exam grades into a program. Your job as the programmer is pretty simple: you decide to define grade1, grade2, grade3, and grade4 as variables. Simple enough, but what happens if the instructor later wants to add two more exams to her course? You would have to add two more variables to support the new grades.

The above scenario may sound like no big deal, but if you multiply the situation by 350 instructors each teaching four classes, you can see yourself being pulled into a vortex of endless updating of code. Fortunately, to avoid having to add variables to complement data increases (or remove variables to accommodate data decreases), you can employ arrays or collections, which are specifically designed to handle lists of variables as a single group. The next two sections show you how to use arrays and collections in ASP.

Arrays

An **array** stores multiple pieces of data, and programmers typically use the array to store a finite number of related pieces of data. For example, a programmer would use the array to store four grades, such as 90, 90, 80, and 70. Each grade is a piece of data, and an array assigns each piece of data its own memory location.

VBScript or JavaScript assigns each memory location a unique number called a **subscript**. Thus, the code can refer to a particular piece of data (or memory location) within an array, using a combination of the array name (such as "A") followed by the appropriate subscript. In VBScript the subscript is in parentheses; in JavaScript the subscript is in brackets. So, an array named A at location 0 is A(0) in VBScript and A[0] in JavaScript.

Arrays in VBScript and JavaScript

To use an array, you would declare the array, determine the number of items in the array, and then assign each memory location a data item. The following code declares an array in VBScript:

Code Example

VBScript

```
Dim Grade()
Redim Grade(4)
Grade(0) = 95
Grade(1) = 90
Grade(2) = 91
Grade(3) = 92
```

Code Dissection

- The first line declares an array named Grade.

- The second line indicates that the array will store up to four values.

- The remaining lines assign subscripts (the numbers in parentheses) to the elements of the array. In VBScript, arrays start at subscript zero and end at the number that is one less than the number of elements in the array. In this case, you are storing 4 grades in the array, which are assigned the subscripts 0–3.

Now examine the JavaScript version of the same example:

Code Example

JavaScript

```
var Grade = new Array();
Grade[0] = 95;
Grade[1] = 90;
Grade[2] = 91;
Grade[3] = 92;
```

Code Dissection

- The first line declares an array named Grade.

- The second through fifth lines assign subscripts (the numbers in brackets) to the elements of the array. In JavaScript, arrays start at subscript zero and end at the number that is one less than the number of elements in the array.

Two-dimensional Arrays

So far, we have discussed one-dimensional arrays, which contain one set of data for one entity. For example, the exam grade array contained grades (data) for one entity (student). To store information for multiple entities, however, you need to use two-dimensional arrays, which store data in rows and columns.

A two-dimensional array is like a teacher's grade book that has one row for each student and one column for each exam grade. Each piece of data in a two-dimensional array is identified by two subscripts; one subscript is for the row, and one is for the column. Consider the following code:

Code Example

VBScript

```
Dim Grades()
Redim Grades(2,4) '2 is the number of rows, and 4 is the number
of columns
Grades(0,0) = "Joe"
Grades(0,1) = 95
Grades(0,2) = 80
Grades(0,3) = 60
```

```
Grades(1,0) = "Sally"
Grades(1,1) = 85
Grades(1,2) = 75
Grades(1,3) = 80
```

Code Dissection

- The Grades array places a student name in the first column and that student's grades in the subsequent four columns. The name and the grades will occupy one row of the array.

- The Grades array will contain at most two students, with four grades each.

- The code in the second line (minus the comment) shows the format for declaring the number of rows and columns in an array. The subscript starts at zero for both the row and the column.

Here is the JavaScript version of the same example:

Code Example

JavaScript

```
Grades = new Array();
Grades[0,0] = "Joe";
Grades[0,1] = 95;
Grades[0,2] = 80;
Grades[0,3] = 60;

Grades[1,0] = "Sally";
Grades[1,1] = 85;
Grades[1,2] = 75;
Grades[1,3] = 80;
```

Two-dimensional arrays store tables of information. Arrays of more than two dimensions are used in mathematical applications and are beyond the scope of this book.

Collections

Arrays are only useful if you know the maximum number of items in a list. When you cannot predict the number of items, you use a collection instead. A **collection** stores multiple pieces of data and accommodates fluctuations in the total number of data items. Thus, a collection offers more flexibility than does an array.

The following sections discuss specific ways for implementing collections.

Using Keys

A collection is more than a group of memory locations. It is an object, and you can only retrieve or add a value to a collection by using the appropriate method. A method interacts with a value by referencing that value's **key**, which is a special identifier assigned to each data item in the collection.

A key is similar to a subscript in that it uniquely refers to a particular item in a list. However, a key does not have to be a number and can instead be a letter or a word. A key is unique within a collection and uses the following convention:

```
(key,value)
```

For example, suppose the grades application used a collection to store the grade values. The values 90, 90, 80, and 70 would each be assigned a unique key. The grades would be then represented as ("grade1",90), ("grade2",90), ("grade3",80), and ("grade4",70), where grade1, grade2, grade3, and grade4 are the unique keys. To retrieve the fourth grade, for instance, your method would request grade4 from the collection. You will see how this is done later in this chapter.

Creating Collections

In ASP, you create a collection by using the Dictionary object. Table 3-1 lists the properties and methods of this object.

Table 3-1 Useful Properties and Methods of the Dictionary Object in VBScript

Property/Method	Name	Description
Property	CompareMode	Sets or returns the string comparison mode used. "String comparison" is the process of comparing two strings to each other. The comparison returns a value of true or false. A string comparison is case sensitive; a text comparison is not case sensitive.
Property	Count	Returns the number of (key,value) pairs in the collection
Property	Item(key)	Sets or returns a value (item) associated with a particular key
Property	Key(key)	Sets or returns the value of the key. That is, it allows the programmer to change the key itself.
Method	Add key, item	Adds the (key,value) pair to the Dictionary object
Method	Exists(key)	Returns true if the key exists; otherwise, returns false
Method	Items	Returns an array of all items in the collection
Method	Keys	Returns an array of all keys in the collection
Method	Remove(key)	Removes a single (key,value) pair that matches the specified key
Method	RemoveAll	Removes all (key,value) pairs in the collection

To use the Dictionary object, you must first declare it. The following example shows how to declare a Dictionary object in VBScript:

Code Example

```
Dim objCollection
set objCollection = CreateObject("Scripting.Dictionary")
```

Code Dissection

- The first line declares the variable that will point to the collection.
- The second line creates the object from the Dictionary class using the CreateObject function.

Here's the same functionality in JavaScript:

Code Example

```
var objCollection;
objCollection = Server.CreateObject("Scripting.Dictionary");
```

Code Dissection

- The first line declares the variable.
- The second line creates the object from the Dictionary class using the CreateObject function.

Modifying a Dictionary Object

After you have created a collection (in the form of a Dictionary object), you need to be able to modify the collection. You can modify it by adding a value with the Add method. Adding a value to the collection, creates a memory location for the new value and assigns the new value to the new location. When your program no longer needs a value in a collection, your program can remove that value from the collection, using the Remove method.

Other useful methods include the Item method (retrieves or looks up a value from the collection), the Exists method (determines if a key already exists), and the RemoveAll method (removes all items from a collection).

The following code adds, removes, and retrieves values from a collection in VBScript:

```
objCollection.Add "A Key", "A Value" 'Adds a value to a
dictionary
objCollection.Remove("A Key") 'Removes the item with key "A
Key" from the dictionary
blnExists = objCollection.Exists("A Key") ' Checks to see if
the key named "A Key" already exists
strItem = objCollection.Item("A Key") 'Retrieves the value of
the key in the collection
objCollection.RemoveAll 'Removes all values from the
collection
```

The following code shows how to do the same in JavaScript:

```
objCollection.Add("A Key", "A Value"); //Adds a value to a
dictionary
objCollection.Remove("A Key"); //Removes the value with key
"A Key" from the dictionary
```

```
blnExists = objCollection.Exists("A Key"); //Checks to see if
the key named "A Key" already exists
strItem = objCollection.Item("A Key"); //Retrieves the value
of the key in the collection
objCollection.RemoveAll(); //Removes all values from the
collection
```

3

Reviewing a Sample Dictionary Object

Now that you're familiar with the various properties and methods of the Dictionary object, you're ready to apply what you know to the application for this chapter. As always, we begin by making a virtual directory.

To make a virtual directory:

1. Open the **Personal Web Manager,** and click the **Advanced** icon on the left side of the window. The Advanced Options window opens.

2. Click the **Add** button. The Add Directory dialog box opens.

3. In the Alias text box, type **Chapter_3**. The alias is the name of the folder you are using.

4. In the Directory text box, type the pathname to the Chapter_3 folder.

5. Click the **OK** button and then close the Personal Web Manager window.

6. Open your browser, and navigate to **http://localhost/Chapter_3/grades/ default.asp**. Your screen should resemble Figure 3-1.

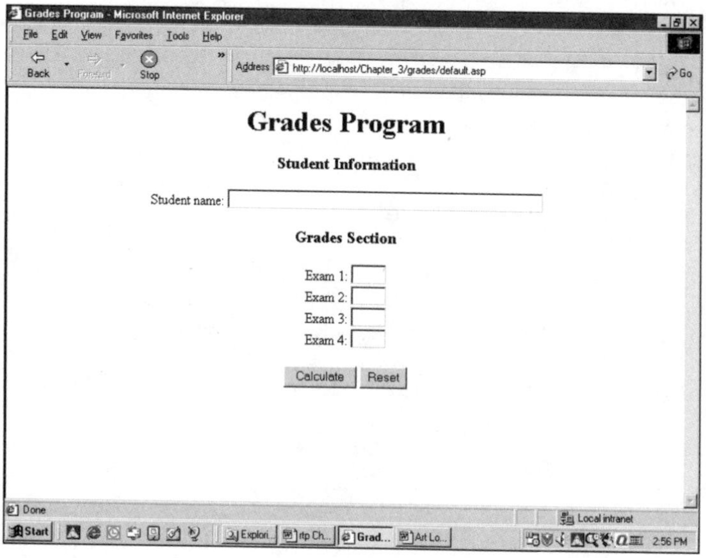

Figure 3-1 Grades application

7. Enter a student name and four grades (make sure that the grades are between 1 and 100), and then click the **Calculate** button. Your screen should resemble Figure 3-2.

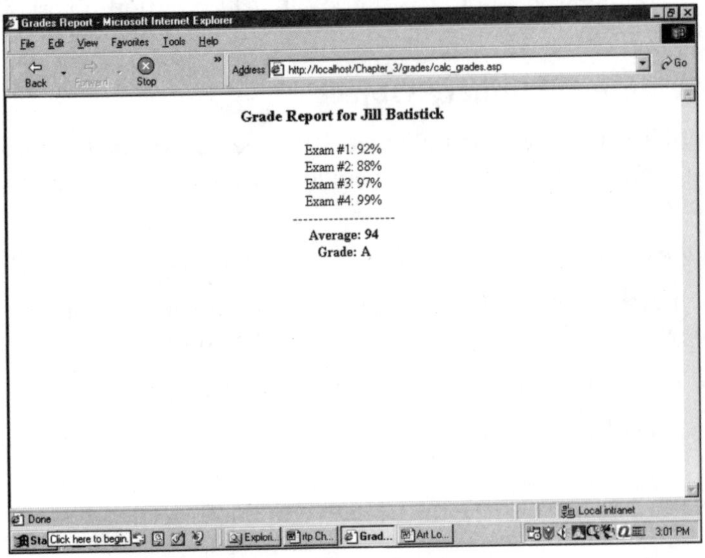

Figure 3-2   Calculated average

8. Close your browser, open **clsGrades.cls** in Notepad, and modify the code so that it resembles the following:

```
<%
CLASS clsGrades

Private strStudentName
Private sngAverage
Private objCollection
Public Sub Class_Initialize

   Set objCollection = CreateObject("Scripting.Dictionary")
   objCollection.Add "grade0", Request.Form("txtGrade0")
   objCollection.Add "grade1", Request.Form("txtGrade1")
   objCollection.Add "grade2", Request.Form("txtGrade2")
   objCollection.Add "grade3", Request.Form("txtGrade3")


End Sub

Public Function Calc_Average

   Dim sum, i, intGrade
   i = 0
```

```
      strStudentName = cstr(Request.Form("txtStudentname"))
      for i = 0 to objCollection.Count - 1
        sum = sum + CInt(objCollection.Item("grade" & i))
      next

      Calc_Average = round(sum/objCollection.Count,0)

End Function

Public Sub PrintReport

  Dim i,grade
  Response.Write("<CENTER><H3>Grade Report for " & _
strStudentName & "</H3>")

  for i = 0 to objCollection.Count - 1
    Response.Write("Exam #" & i + 1 & ": " & _
objCollection.Item("grade" & i) & "%<br>")
  next
  Response.Write "--------------------<br>"
  Response.Write("<b>Average: " & sngAverage & "<br>")

  if sngAverage > 89 then
    grade = "A"
  else
    if sngAverage > 79 then
      grade = "B"
    else
      if sngAverage > 69 then
        grade = "C"
      else
        if sngAverage > 59 then
          grade = "D"
        else
          grade = "F"
        end if
      end if
    end if
  end if

  Response.Write("<b>Grade: " & Grade & "</p>")


End Sub

'Create a property called Average
Public Property Get Average

Average = sngAverage

End Property
```

```
Public Property Let Average(newAverage)

sngAverage = newAverage

End Property


END CLASS

%>
```

9. Save your code, and close Notepad. Your code now declares the variable that points to a collection object, adds grades to the collection, and accesses an item in a collection.

10. Repeat Steps 6 and 7. You as the end user will see the same result in your browser. However, you as the programmer now have additional information at your disposal. This will come in handy later.

The following code shows the salient points in the JavaScript version of the changes in subclass_Initialize:

```
var objCollection;
objCollection = CreateObject("Scripting.Dictionary");
objCollection.Add("grade0", Request.Form("txtGrade0"));
objCollection.Add("grade1", Request.Form("txtGrade1"));
objCollection.Add("grade2", Request.Form("txtGrade2"));
objCollection.Add("grade3", Request.Form("txtGrade3"));
```

CONTROL STRUCTURES

Now that you know how to use arrays and collections, you need to learn how to use control structures to manipulate the data that they contain. A **control structure** is special code that allows a program to vary the sequence of steps depending upon certain conditions. For example, in the grade application with a control structure, if the user enters a grade that is not between 0 and 100, the application will display an error message; however, if the user enters valid data, the application will process the data. These two outcomes are made possible by the use of a control structure. The following sections discuss two types of control structures: selection and repetition.

Selection Control Structure

Control structures can be fairly complicated. Suppose that an application needs to determine what letter grade to assign a student, and that each letter grade is associated with a range of scores. For example, if a student receives a score between 90 and 100, the application assigns an A. To perform this task, you need to incorporate a selection control structure into the application. You can use two kinds of selection control structures, the IFTHENELSE statement or the CASE statement.

IFTHENELSE Statement

You use the IFTHENELSE statement when the application must make a decision based on whether a specific condition is met. The heart of an IFTHENELSE statement is a condition that evaluates to true or false. When the condition evaluates to true, the application executes one set of steps. When the condition evaluates to false, the application executes another set of steps.

3

As an example of this scenario, consider the following story that may run inside your head as you get ready to leave the house in the morning to go to work or school: *If it is raining, I will take the bus; otherwise I will walk.*

In this statement, the condition is "it is raining." The phrase "then I will take the bus" indicates the action that occurs when the condition evaluates to true (that is, when it rains). The phrase "otherwise I will walk" indicates the action that occurs when the condition evaluates to false (that is, when it does not rain).

The following code shows how to structure an IFTHENELSE statement in VBScript:

Code Example

```
IF        [condition] THEN
[instructions run if condition is true]
ELSE
[instructions run if condition is false]
END IF
```

Code Dissection

- In the first line, you would replace the condition with an actual conditional statement such as A<5 or ABC=5.

- In the second line, if the condition is true, the code after THEN runs.

- In the fourth line, if the condition is false, the code after ELSE runs.

The following code shows how to structure an IFTHENELSE statement in JavaScript.

Code Example

```
if        ([condition]) {
[instructions run if condition is true]
}
else
{
[instructions run if condition is false]
}
```

Relational Operators in IFTHENELSE Statements

The condition in an IFTHENELSE statement usually contains, in its simplest form, a variable or constant, a relational operator such as =, <, or >, and another variable or constant. Grouped together, they might appear like this: strName = "Joe". Table 3-2 lists the relational operators used with IFTHENELSE statements.

Table 3-2   Relational Operators

Relational Operator	Description	Example
= (VBScript) == (JavaScript)	Equal to	10=10 evaluates to true for VBScript. 10==10 evaluates to true for JavaScript.
>	Greater than	10>5, evaluates to true
<	Less than	5<1 evaluates to false
>=	Greater than or equal to	4>=3 evaluates to true
<=	Less than or equal to	4<=3 evaluates to false
<> != (also used in JavaScript)	Not equal to	4<>4 evaluates to false

As you may remember from your math class, arithmetic expressions (such as 5 + 2) are evaluated before a relational expression. For example, in 10 > 7 + 2, you evaluate 7+2 first. Once you have determined that 7 + 2 = 9, you then evaluate 10 > 9. In this case, the expression evaluates to true.

The following code incorporates a relational operator (the IFTHENELSE statement will be explained later in the chapter):

Code Example

VBScript

```
IF grade > 89 THEN
   Response.Write("Excellent!")
ELSE
   IF grade > 79 THEN
     Response.Write("Above Average!")
     ELSE
        IF grade > 69 THEN
           Response.Write("Average!")
           END IF
              END IF
END IF
```

Code Dissection

- If the student receives a grade of 85, then the application displays the message "Above Average!" Why? The condition, 85 > 89, is false, which means that the code after ELSE runs.

- If the student receives a grade of 90, then the application displays the message "Excellent!" Why? The condition, 90 > 89, is true, which means that the code after THEN runs.

The following code shows an IFTHENELSE statement (in JavaScript) that incorporates a relational operator:

Code Example

```
if (grade > 89) {
 Response.Write("Excellent!");
}
ELSE
{
  if (grade > 79) {
    Response.Write("Above Average!");
}
 else
{
 if (grade > 69) {
   Response.Write("Average!");
 }
 }
}
```

Logical Operators in IFTHENELSE Statements

Sometimes, you need to create compound conditions within IFTHENELSE statements. A **compound condition** is two or more conditions separated by a logical operator. Table 3-3 lists the logical operators you can use in your code.

Table 3-3   Logical Operators

Logical Operator	Description	Example
Not (VBScript) ! (JavaScript)	Negates the value of the condition. If the condition is true, "not true" is false. If the condition is false, "not false" is true. Note that "Not" has the highest precedence of all logical operators.	Not grade>5 (VBScript) !(grade>5) (JavaScript) If grade is 6, then the condition evaluates to false.

Table 3-3   Logical Operators (continued)

Logical Operator	Description	Example
And (VBScript) && (JavaScript)	All conditions connected to an And logical operator must be true for the entire compound condition to be true; otherwise it evaluates to false. The And logical operator has second precedence after Not.	grade>=90 and grade<=100 for VBScript ((grade>=90) && (grade<=100)) for JavaScript If grade is 89, then this condition evaluates to false. In this situation only one condition needs to be false for the entire compound condition to be false. If grade is 90, then the condition evaluates to true (because both conditions are true).
Or (VBScript) || (Java Script)	Only one condition using an Or logical operator must be true for the entire compound condition to be true. If all are false, then the compound condition evaluates to false. The Or logical operator has the lowest precedence of all operators.	grade<50 or grade>= 80 for VBScript (grade<50) || (grade>=80) for JavaScript If grade is 48, then the entire condition is true. If grade is 60, then the entire condition is false. If grade is 85, then the entire condition is true.

The following code shows an IFTHENELSE statement (in VBScript) that incorporates a logical operator:

```
IF grade>89 and grade<=100 THEN
grade_letter = "A"
END IF
```

The following code shows an IFTHENELSE statement (in JavaScript) that incorporates a logical operator:

```
if ((grade>89 && grade<=100))
{
    grade_letter = "A";
}
```

Nested IFTHENELSE Statements

In a nested IFTHENELSE structure, another IFTHENELSE statement can replace the set of steps that would normally follow one outcome of the condition. For instance, a condition evaluating to false might lead to another IFTHENELSE statement, rather than to a simple set of steps. In the following VBScript example, a false value leads to a nested IFTHENELSE statement.

Code Example

VBScript

```
1      IF          grade > 89 THEN
2         grade_letter = "A"
3      ELSE
4        IF        grade > 79 THEN
5         grade_letter = "B"
6        ELSE
7         ...
8        END IF
9      END IF
```

Code Dissection

- In line 1, if the condition evaluates to true (that is, if the grade is greater than 89), then the letter grade "A" is assigned.

- In line 1, if the condition evaluates to false (that is, if the grade is not greater than 89), then a second IFTHENELSE statement in line 4 (nested inside the first one) executes. This statement has its own condition, which assigns the letter grade "B" if the grade is greater than 79.

- In line 4, if the condition evaluates to false (that is, if the grade is not greater than 79), then a third IFTHENELSE statement (nested inside the second one) in line 7 could execute (this third statement is not included, for brevity). You can nest IFTHENELSE structures to as many levels as you wish.

- In lines 8 and 9, note that each IFTHENELSE statement must end with the line END IF. When nesting multiple IFTHENELSE statements, be sure to end each of the nested statements properly.

The JavaScript version of the same example is as follows:

Code Example

JavaScript

```
1 if          (grade > 89) {
2  grade_letter = "A";
3 }
4 else
5 {
6   if         (grade > 79) {
7      grade_letter = "B";
8  }
9  else
10  {
11     ...
12  }
13 }
```

Case Sensitivity in IFTHENELSE Statements

When using an IFTHENELSE statement to compare strings of data, you need to be aware that string comparisons are case sensitive. This means that "Joe" and "JOE" are not identical strings of data. Thus the statement Joe=JOE will evaluate to false.

If you do not want the string comparisons to be case sensitive, then you need to use a function called UCASE. The **UCASE** function accepts a string, converts the string to all caps, and then returns the string to the script for further processing.

Consider this example in VBScript:

Code Example

```
If UCASE(strStudent1) = UCASE(strStudent2) Then
   [do something]
END IF
```

Code Dissection

- The string in strStudent1 and strStudent2 returns from the UCASE function in all caps. After strStudent1 and strStudent2 are compared to see if they are the same, the code inside the IF statement runs.

The JavaScript version follows:

Code Example

```
if (ucase(strStudent1) == ucase(strStudent2)) {
   [do something]
}
```

CASE Statement

In contrast to the IFTHENELSE statement, the CASE statement compares an expression to a list of values; when it finds a match, it executes the steps associated with the matching value.

As an example of this type of comparison, suppose you want the grade application to display a message that varies with the grade the student receives. For an A, the student should see the message "Excellent." For a B, the student should see the message "Above Average." For a C, the student should see the message "Average." A CASE statement would compare the letter grade to a list consisting of the values A, B, and C. When it found a match (the letter grade A, for instance), it would display the corresponding message (for the letter grade A, the message would be "Excellent").

While a series of nested IFTHENELSE statements could perform the same function as a CASE statement, nested IFTHENELSE statements can be difficult to decipher, which can, in turn, make an application difficult to update and maintain. Whenever possible, you should use a single CASE statement rather than multiple nested IFTHENELSE statements.

The following code illustrates the generic structure of a CASE statement in VBScript:

Code Example

```
SELECT CASE testexpression
[Case expressionlist1
  [instructions for this case]
[Case expressionlist2]
  [instructions for this case]
[Case Else]
   [instructions for when no testexpression matches any of the
   expressionlists.]
END SELECT
```

Code Dissection

- A CASE statement in VBScript begins with the keyword SELECT CASE and ends with the keyword END SELECT.

- When processing a SELECT CASE statement, VBScript compares the values in the test-expression with the values in the expressionlist. The values are compared in the order in which the Case lines appear in the code. When the testexpression matches a value, then the code immediately after that line runs, after which the SELECT CASE ends. If nothing matches, the code in the CASE ELSE option runs.

- A testexpression is a statement that contains variables, constants, functions, or operators. For example, total_sales is an example of a testexpression.

- An expressionlist is one or more numeric or string expressions. For example, <=200 is an example of a expressionlist.

Here's a CASE statement in JavaScript:

Code Example

```
switch (testexpression) {
[case expressionlist1:]
  [instructions for this case]
break;
[case expressionlist2:]
  [instructions for this case]
break;
[default:]
   [instructions for when no testexpression matches any of the
expressionlists.]
}
```

Code Dissection

- When processing a CASE statement, JavaScript compares the values in the testexpression with the values in the expressionlists in the order in which they appear in the code. If a value matches the test expression, then the code in line immediately after that value runs, after which the CASE ends. If nothing matches, the code in the default option runs. When the code reaches a break statement, the CASE statement is exited.

- The CASE statement begins with switch and ends with }.

- A testexpression is a statement that contains variables, constants, functions, or operators. For example, total_sales is an example of a testexpression.

- An expressionlist is one or more numeric or string expressions. For example, <=200 is an example of an expressionlist.

Server-side Validation

Server-side validation is a technique that verifies that the data entered in a form is valid or in the correct format. If an application cannot validate input data, the application could produce erroneous results. For instance, if the user failed to enter data into a field that required a number, the form would send a "" character to the server, which would then erroneously attempt to use this character in a number calculation.

Server-side validation requires a script, a subroutine, or a function (running on the server) that consists of nested IF statements. In some cases, you may want to combine all nested IFTHENELSE statements into a subroutine that you call in a script. You can accomplish the same thing if you use the IFTHENELSE statements directly or combine them into a subroutine, such as a FormValidation subroutine. These statements verify that data was entered on a form. An example of such a check would be:

```
If txtStudentName = "" Then
[display an error message]
END IF
```

The preceding code checks to see if nothing was entered into a particular part of the form. If that part of the form is indeed empty, then an error message is displayed.

Reviewing Server-side Validation

With the application in this chapter, you can easily observe the validation of user input by server-side validation. We'll do that next.

To view errors when entering data:

1. Open **calc_grades.asp** in Notepad, delete the Sub FormValidation script, and comment out **Call FormValidation**.

2. Save the code, close Notepad, open your browser, and then navigate to **http://localhost/Chapter_3/grades/default.asp**.

3. Enter a student name and three grades (make sure that the grades are between 1 and 100, and leave the last grade blank), and then click the **Calculate** button. Your screen should resemble Figure 3-3.

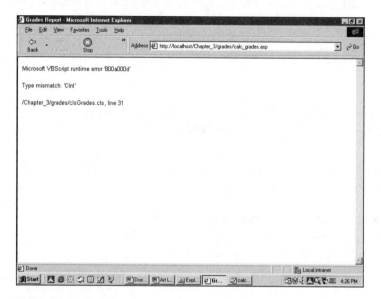

Figure 3-3   Runtime error

When you do not use server-side validation, you can end up with runtime errors like the one shown in Figure 3-3. We'll now put the server-side validation code into the calc_grades.asp page and view the difference.

4. Close your browser, open **calc_grades.asp** in Notepad, add the following code between <TITLE>...</TITLE> and the </HEAD> tags, and uncomment **Call FormValidation**.

```
<%
Sub FormValidation

Dim blnOK
If  Request.Form("txtStudentName") = "" Then
    Response.Write("<CENTER><H1>Error Information</H1>")
    Response.Write("<H3>You enter a student " & _
"name!</H3><BR>")
    Response.Write("You click the back button " & _
"on your browser to fix your errors!</CENTER>")
    Response.End
 Else
    blnOK = (Trim(Request.Form("txtGrade0")) = "") & _
OR (Trim(Request.Form("txtGrade1")) = "") OR & _
(Trim(Request.Form("txtGrade2")) = "") & _
OR (Trim(Request.Form("txtGrade3")) = "")
    If blnOK Then
       Response.Write("<CENTER><H1>Error Information</H1>")
```

```
                Response.Write("<H3>You must enter all the " &_
                "grades!</H3><BR>")
                Response.Write("You click the back button " &_
                "on your browser to fix your errors!</CENTER>")
                Response.End
            End If
        End If

    End Sub
    %>
```

5. Save the changes, close Notepad, open your browser, and navigate to **http://localhost/Chapter_3/grades/default.asp**.

6. Enter a student name and three grades (make sure that the grades are between 1 and 100, and leave the last grade blank), and then click the **Calculate** button. Your screen should resemble Figure 3-4. Now that's some information you can use.

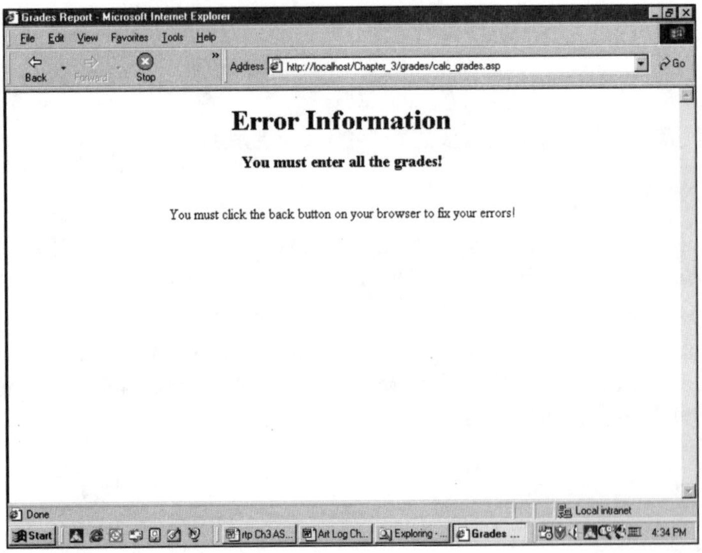

Figure 3-4   Server-side validation

When you use server-side validation, you create an error page like the one in Figure 3-4 to keep runtime errors from appearing in your programs. Good programming practice dictates that you validate user input on HTML forms.

Repetition Control Structure

Another kind of control structure, known as a **loop** or **repetition control structure,** repeats a sequence of steps until a special condition becomes true. For example, you might create a loop that reads, processes, and outputs grades for different students. Instead of repeating the code for each student, you would use a loop that repeats the same steps over and over again until the user exits the program.

To understand the concept of a loop, consider the process involved in washing your hair. You need to rinse your hair, put a small amount of shampoo in your hair, rub the shampoo in your hair, rinse your hair with water, and repeat the steps if necessary. Your judgment of what is necessary forms the basis of this "shampoo" repetition control structure.

In the following sections, you will investigate two types of loops.

FOR Loop

Programmers use a **FOR** loop, also known as a counter-controlled loop, to repeat a block of code a specified number of times. The following example shows the syntax of a FOR loop in VBScript:

Code Example

```
FOR counter = startvalue TO endvalue [STEP stepvalue]
    [INSTRUCTIONS]
NEXT
```

Code Dissection

- A **counter** is a numeric variable used to count something, such as the number of people present during a meeting. The counter variable is a counter that increments itself by a stepvalue (usually by 1) each time the loop repeats itself.

- The startvalue is the initial value of the counter.

- The endvalue is the stop value of the counter. When the counter is greater than the endvalue, the loop ends when the stepvalue is a positive number. When the step value is a negative number, the opposite is true.

- The stepvalue increments the counter by a certain value. By default, the counter increments by 1 if no stepvalue is used.

The following code shows the generic structure of a FOR loop in JavaScript:

Code Example

```
for (initial_expression; conditional_expression;
update_expression) {
[loop code goes here]
}
```

Code Dissection

- `Initial_expression` is the expression that assigns the initial value to the counter, such as counter=1.

- `Conditional_expression` is the expression that provides the condition to test whether to continue the loop. This also provides the stop value of the counter. When the counter is greater than the stop value, the loop ends when the stepvalue is a positive number. When the stepvalue is a negative number, the opposite is true.

- `Update_expression` is the expression that increments the counter by a certain value. By default, you always use an expression that increments the counter by 1.

Now that you are familiar with the syntax of a FOR loop, consider this specific example in VBScript:

Code Example

```
FOR counter = 1 to 10
[instructions]
NEXT
```

Code Dissection

- The counter variable initializes to 1.

- When the program reaches the Next statement, the counter increments by the step-value (in this case, 1).

- The loop continues until counter > 10.

- When the loop finishes, the counter is 11.

Here is the JavaScript version of the same example:

Code Example

```
for   (counter = 1; counter<=10; counter++)
{
[instructions]
}
```

An array has a fixed number of items; therefore, looping that involves calculating values in an array is usually handled by FOR loops.

Let's apply our knowledge to a discussion of the application in this chapter. This application calculates an average grade based on four exam grades. To calculate the grade, the application must sum the grades from the four exams, and then divide the sum by the number of exam grades. This situation requires a counter because the application must know the number of grades in the list before it can perform the division. If you used such a counter, the application would contain code similar to the following (VBScript):

Code Example

VBScript

```
1 Dim Grade(), Sum, Average
2 ReDim Grade(4)
3 Grade(0) = 90
4 Grade(1) = 80
5 Grade(2) = 75
6 Grade(3) = 75
7 For count = 0 to 3
8   Sum = Sum + Grade(count)
9 Next
10 Average = Sum / count
```

Code Dissection

- Lines 1 and 2: The first step is to declare the grade array and indicate that it will contain 4 items.

- Lines 3–6: These lines assign each item in the grade array to the grade earned in the class.

- Line 7: Because the array subscripts start at 0 and end at 3, a For loop is used to count from 0 to 3. This For loop calculates the sum of all the grades. The loop will process all the grades and exit when the counter is 4.

- Line 8: `Sum = Sum + Grade(count)` uses the variable, **Sum,** to add the grades.

- Line 10: This line calculates the average grade by dividing the sum by the counter.

Let's look at the JavaScript version of the same example.

Code Example

JavaScript

```
1 var Sum, Average;
2 Grade= new Array();
3 Grade[0] = 90;
4 Grade[1] = 80;
5 Grade[2] = 75;
6 Grade[3] = 75;
7 for (count = 0; count < 4; count++)
8 {
9   Sum = Sum + Grade[count];
10 }
11 Average = Sum / count;
```

Code Dissection

- Line 2: The first step is to declare the grade array.

- Lines 3–6: These lines assign each item in the grade array to a specific grade.

- Line 7: Because the array subscripts start at 0 and end at 3, a For loop is used to count from 0 to 3. This For loop calculates the sum of all the grades. The loop will process all the grades and exit when the counter is 4.

- Line 9: `Sum = Sum + Grade[count]`, uses the variable named `Sum` to add the grades.

- Line 11: This line calculates the average grade by dividing the sum by the counter.

WHILE Loop

A FOR loop continues to run until the counter reaches a specified value. In contrast, a **WHILE** loop repeats while a certain condition is true. It stops running when the condition becomes false. Note that you can use WHILE loops to accomplish the same task that a FOR loop performs, as you will see below.

The syntax for a WHILE loop in VBScript is as follows:

Code Example

```
DO WHILE condition
[instructions]

LOOP
```

Code Dissection

- As you can see, a WHILE loop begins with a DO WHILE clause and ends with a LOOP clause.

- The condition in a WHILE loop follows the same rules as conditions in IFTHENELSE statements.

- The instructions in a WHILE loop process while the condition is true and exit when the condition is false.

Let's look at a JavaScript example of a WHILE loop.

Code Example

```
while (condition) {
[instructions]

}
```

Code Dissection

- As you can see, a WHILE loop begins with a WHILE clause and ends with a }.

- The condition in a WHILE loop follows the same rules as conditions in IFTHENELSE statements.

- The instructions in a WHILE loop process while the condition is true and exit when the condition is false.

In the preceding section you saw how to use a FOR loop to average four exam grades. The following example shows how to use a WHILE loop in VBScript to perform the same calculation.

Code Example

```
DIM Grade(),count,sum,average
REDIM Grade(4)
count = 0
DO WHILE count < 4
   sum = sum + Grade(count)
   count = count + 1
LOOP
average = sum / count
```

Code Dissection

- Unlike in the FOR loop, the counter variable, **count**, must be initialized to 0.

- The code must contain a counter statement (such as count = count + 1) to increment the counter by 1.

- The condition, count < 4, would be understood in a FOR loop.

- The WHILE loop processes until the count is 4.

The following code shows the same example in JavaScript.

Code Example

```
var Grade = new Array(),count,sum,average
count = 0;
while (count < 4) {
   sum = sum + Grade[count];
   count = count + 1;
}
average = sum / count;
```

Code Dissection

- The WHILE loop processes until the count is 4.

As you can see, you can use FOR loops and WHILE loops in your ASP scripts to repeat a block of code.

You have come to the end of this chapter and have learned a great deal about the intricacies of arrays and collections, and the ways in which you can apply control structures to your programming logic. In the next chapter, you will explore the File System object and the functionality it brings to your programming.

CHAPTER SUMMARY

❑ In many programming situations, employing a single variable is too restrictive. To handle the need for multiple variables, you can employ arrays or collections, which are specifically designed to handle lists of variables as a single group.

❑ An array stores multiple pieces of data, and programmers typically use the array to store a finite number of related pieces of data. To use an array, you would declare the array, determine the number of items in the array, and then assign each memory location a data item. To store information for multiple entities, however, you need to use two-dimensional arrays, which store data in rows and columns.

❑ A collection stores multiple pieces of data and accommodates fluctuations in the total number of data items. Thus, a collection offers more flexibility than does an array. A collection is more than a group of memory locations. It is an object, and you can only retrieve or add a value to a collection by using the appropriate method. A method interacts with a value by referencing that value's key, which is a special identifier assigned to each data item in the collection. In ASP, you create a collection by using the Dictionary object. After you have created a Dictionary object, you can modify it.

❑ A control structure is special code that allows a program to vary the sequence of steps depending upon certain conditions. You can use two kinds of selection control structures, the IFTHENELSE statement or the CASE statement. You use the IFTHENELSE statement when the application must make a decision based on whether a specific condition is met. In contrast to the IFTHENELSE statement, the CASE statement compares an expression to a list of values; when it finds a match, it executes the steps associated with the matching value.

❑ Server-side validation is a technique that verifies that the data entered in a form is valid or in the correct format. If an application cannot validate input data, the application could produce erroneous results.

❑ Another kind of control structure, known as a loop or repetition control structure repeats a sequence of steps until a special condition becomes true. Programmers use a FOR loop, also known as a counter-controlled loop, to repeat a block of code a specified number of times. In contrast, a WHILE loop repeats while a certain condition is true. It stops running when the condition becomes false.

REVIEW QUESTIONS

1. A(n) _____ is a fixed-size list of items.

   a. collection

   b. array

   c. variable

   d. none of the above

2. A(n) _____ is a dynamically sized list of items.

   a. collection

   b. array

   c. variable

   d. none of the above

3

3. Which statement will size an array with seven items in VBScript?

   a. ReDim(4)

   b. ReDim(5)

   c. ReDim(6)

   d. ReDim(7)

4. Which is a valid assignment statement for an array at subscript two in VBScript?

   a. A(0)

   b. A(2)

   c. A(1)

   d. A(3)

5. Arrays can be multidimensional. True or False?

6. A collection contains a unique _____ that cannot be duplicated.

   a. value

   b. key

   c. Key/Value

   d. none of the above

7. ASP uses a _____ object to provide the functionality of a collection.

   a. collection

   b. dictionary

   c. item

   d. none of the above

8. Which property in the Dictionary object allows you to determine the number of items in the collection?

   a. Item

   b. Key

   c. Count

   d. CompareMode

9. A(n) _____ is a sequence of steps that repeats a number of times.

   a. loop

   b. block

   c. selection

   d. none of the above

10. A(n) _____ statement evaluates to true or false in an IF clause.

   a. condition

   b. loop

   c. WHILE

   d. FOR

11. Which of the following is not a relational operator?

   a. or

   b. <

   c. >

   d. =

12. Which of the following is not a logical operator?

   a. and

   b. or

   c. not

   d. =

13. A(n) _____ is more than one statement separated by a logical operator.

   a. condition

   b. compound condition

   c. loop

   d. none of the above

14. An IFTHENELSE statement can contain more than one constant. True or False?

15. Which function do you use if you want to change input to all uppercase?

   a. UCASE

   b. TRIM

   c. CDBL

   d. none of the above

16. A CASE statement can be used in place of the IFTHENELSE statement. True or False?

3

17. Which looping syntax should you use if you know the number of times a loop must execute?

   a. FOR...NEXT

   b. DO WHILE...LOOP

   c. IFTHENELSE

   d. none of the above

18. Which looping syntax should you use if you do not know the number of times a loop must execute?

   a. FOR...NEXT

   b. DO WHILE...LOOP

   c. IFTHENELSE

   d. none of the above

19. A(n) _____ is a numeric variable used to count something, such as the number of people in a class.

   a. counter

   b. accumulator

   c. array

   d. none of the above

20. Which of the following is not a condition statement in VBScript?

   a. Abc == 10

   b. abc < 10

   c. abc = 10

   d. none of the above

21. Which of the following is not a condition statement in JavaScript?

   a. Abc == 10

   b. Abc < 10

   c. Abc = 10

   d. none of the above

22. Which is not a logical operator in VBScript?

   a. Not

   b. And

   c. Or

   d. &&

23. Write an array declaration statement for the following situations:
    a. a list of ten customers' last names
    b. a list of 25 sales made during a typical day at a grocery store
    c. a list of seven grades on an exam
    d. a list of 10 assignments for a class

24. Examine the following IFTHENELSE statement and then answer the questions:

```
IF age < 21 Then
    strMsg = "You are a child!"
Else
    strMsg = "You are an adult!"
End If
```

What will strMsg contain in the following scenarios?

    a. age = 25
    b. age = 10
    c. age = 21
    d. age = 50

25. Write an IFTHENELSE statement for the following situations:
    a. Display (use Response.Write) an error message if the txtFirstName field on a form contains no data.
    b. Display an error message if the data entered in the txtSales field on a form does not contain a number.
    c. Display an error message if the data entered in the txtStartDate field on a form does not contain a date.
    d. Determine the number of weeks of vacation owed an employee, depending on years of service.

Years of Service	Vacation Weeks
< 1	0
1 – 4	2
5 – 9	3
> 10	4

26. Examine the following WHILE statement and then answer the questions:

```
Dim intCount
intCount = 1
Do While intCount < 10
   Response.Write intCount & "<p>"
   intCount = intCount + 1
Loop
```

Answer the following questions:

    a. What value does intCount contain just before entering the loop?
    b. What value does intCount contain after the loop has finished?
    c. What is displayed on the Web page after the loop has finished?

3

27. Using the following DO...WHILE statement:

```
Dim intCount
intCount = 1
Do While intCount < 10
  intCount = intCount + 1
  Response.Write intCount & "<p>"
Loop
```

Answer the following questions:

a. What value does intCount contain just before entering the loop?

b. What value does intCount contain after the loop has finished?

c. What is displayed on the Web page after the loop has finished?

28. Examine the following FOR.,.NEXT statement:

```
Dim intCount
For intCount = 1 to 4 Step 2
  Response.Write intCount & "<br>"
Next
```

Answer the following questions:

a. What value does intCount contain the first time through the loop?

b. What value does intCount contain after the loop finishes?

c. What is displayed on the Web page after the loop finishes?

29. Write a FOR..NEXT loop that will sum four salaries and find the average of the salaries. Use an array for the salaries.

HANDS-ON PROJECTS

Project 3-1

Modify the existing grades application in this chapter to support seven grades.

1. Open the default.asp file from the grades folder of Chapter_3 and add form elements to grades to make it seven grades.

2. Open the clsGrades.cls file from the grades folder of Chapter_3 and modify the code to handle seven grades.

3. Open the calc_grades.asp file from the grades folder of Chapter_3 and modify the code to handle the seven grades.

4. Test your new application in a browser.

Project 3-2

Write a Web application that computes and outputs the total pay for an employee for one week. Using an employee time sheet as input, you will determine regular hours for each day, overtime hours, and hourly wage rate for one employee. Do not forget to do server-side validation in this code.

1. You will use an array to store the regular hours for each day of the week.

   a. Create a folder called pay in your Chapter_3 folder of your Data Disk.

   b. Create a virtual directory for the pay folder.

   c. Create an HTML form called default_a.htm similar to the default.asp page in this chapter to request hours for Sunday, Monday, Tuesday, Wednesday, Thursday, Friday, and Saturday and the hourly wage rate. Save this file in the pay folder.

   d. Create an ASP script called calc_pay_a.asp that creates a FormValidation subroutine, creates an item in a collection for each day of the week that stores the hours worked each day, calculates the overtime hours from the regular hours, and calculates the total pay for an employee. Use a loop to calculate the total regular hours. Save this file in the pay folder.

   e. Test your new application in your browser.

2. You will use a collection to store the regular hours for each day of the week.

   a. Create an HTML form called default_b.htm similar to the default.asp page in this chapter to request hours for Sunday, Monday, Tuesday, Wednesday, Thursday, Friday, and Saturday and the hourly wage rate.

   b. Create an ASP script called calc_pay_b.asp that creates a FormValidation subroutine, creates an item in a collection for each day of the week that stores the hours worked each day, calculates the overtime hours from the regular hours, and calculates the total pay for an employee. Use a loop to calculate the total regular hours. Save this file in the pay folder.

   c. Test your new application in your browser.

Project 3-3

Mrs. Wu needs a simple Web application that will generate a times table for a particular number (0–12) that she can hand out to her students to practice with. Do not forget to use server-side validation for this project.

1. Create a folder called times in your Chapter_3 folder of your Data Disk.

2. Create a virtual directory for the times folder.

3. Create an HTML form called times.htm that asks for a number between 0 and 12. Save this file in the times folder.

4. Create an ASP script called calc_table.asp that generates a times table for a particular number up to 12. Use a loop to generate the table.

5. Test your new application.

Project 3-4

Write a Web application that simulates an invoice that requests the item, the quantity, the unit price for five items, and the sales tax. The Web application will respond with an invoice that calculates the total cost for each item and the grand total of all items.

1. Create a folder called invoice.

2. Create a virtual directory for the invoice folder in your Chapter_3 folder of your Data Disk.

3. Create an HTML form called invoice.htm that requests an item, the quantity (qty), and the unit price for five items, and the sales tax. Save this file in the invoice folder.

4. Create an ASP script called calculate.asp that calculates the total cost for each item and the grand total cost for all items. Use a loop to calculate the total cost for each item.

5. Test your new application.

Project 3-5

You have an application that has incorrect code. You will fix the errors, creating the object code as necessary.

1. Open your browser, and navigate to *http://localhost/Chapter_3/collection/invoice.htm*. Enter values in the text boxes, and then click the Calculate button. You should see a runtime error, as in Figure 3-5.

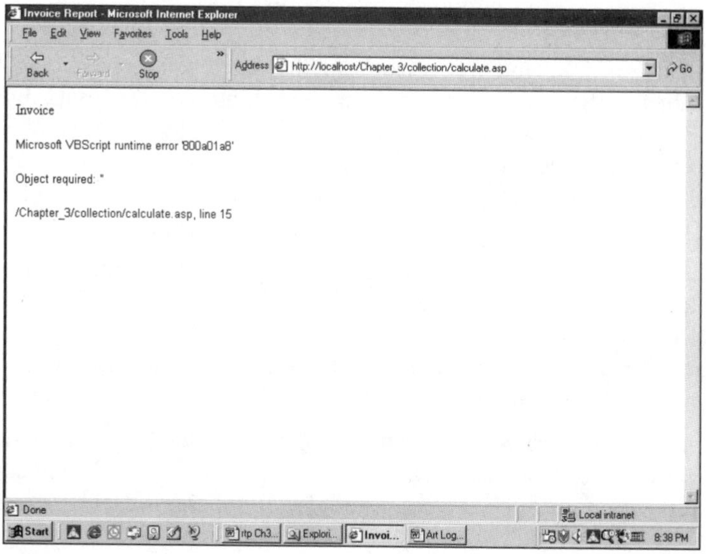

Figure 3-5 Runtime error

2. Close your browser.

3. Open calculate.asp in your text editor and add the following lines after the Dim statement:

```
set objItem = CreateObject("Scripting.Dictionary")
set objQty = CreateObject("Scripting.Dictionary")
set objUnit = CreateObject("Scripting.Dictionary")
```

4. Save the calculate.asp file. Open your browser, navigate to *http://localhost/Chapter_3/collection/invoice.htm*, add values to the text boxes, and then click the Calculate button. The results are shown in Figure 3-6.

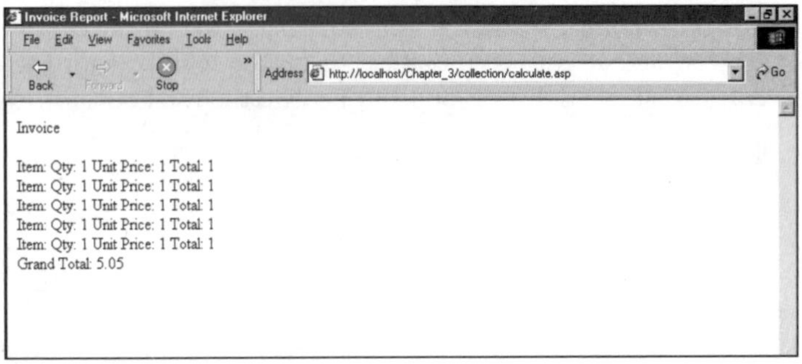

Figure 3-6   Expected results

CASE PROJECTS

1. The owner of Centreville Construction Company has hired you to create a Web application that will calculate the gross salary of all company employees. The application should accept the employee's name, hours worked, and hourly rate as input. An employee gets time and a half for any hours over 40 hours worked. Your job is to create an application that displays an employee's name, hours worked, regular pay, overtime pay, and total pay.

2. The people at Centreville Construction loved your work on the first project, and have asked you to solve another problem. The company needs a Web application that will allow an employee to enter the hours worked each day of the week. The application should then calculate the total hours the employee worked during the week. The application should create a report that an employee can print and sign, displaying the hours worked each day and the total hours worked for the week.

3. WHTV Channel 4 has hired you to create an application that prepares a daily temperature report for the last seven days. Input to the application should include the start date of the temperature readings and the seven days' temperatures. The application should display a temperature report for the seven days, along with the average temperature for the seven-day period.

THE FILESYSTEMOBJECT OBJECT

In this chapter, you will:

♦ Describe a drive, a folder, and a file

♦ Describe and use the different objects in the FileSystemObject object

♦ Describe the properties and methods of the FileSystemObject object

♦ Use the FileSystemObject object to save data on the server

♦ Understand the code that the use of the FileSystemObject object dictates

♦ Use the SiteGalaxy Upload component to upload files from a client to a server

Welcome to Chapter 4. We're glad that you're still with us, because this chapter is one of our favorites. It's where you will learn about and really begin to appreciate the power of objects in ASP. Specifically, you'll see how the FileSystemObject, with its attendant methods and properties, lets you dynamically gather information about drives, folders, and files that are on a server. Then, you'll explore where and how the FileSystemObject makes its mark in a multifile application. Last, you'll learn about a valuable component that no ASP programmer should be without—the SiteGalaxy Upload component.

REVIEW OF DRIVES, FOLDERS, AND FILES

If you are like most computer aficionados, you are quite familiar with the concepts of drives, folders, and files from your role as the *end user*. That being said, you may feel that it is not necessary to review the topics once again. However, this section will provide a review because we feel it is necessary for you, as a programmer, to begin looking at these concepts less as functional entities for the end user and more as role players in the system that you will be manipulating.

On the average PC, you can store folders and files on either a floppy disk drive or on a hard disk drive. The floppy disk drive is usually referred to by the drive letter "A:". The hard disk on a computer is usually referred to as the "C:" drive. In some cases, a hard drive may be divided into multiple storage areas (known as partitions), in which case each partition is assigned its own drive letter. Thus, one partition on a hard drive might be assigned the drive letter "C:" while the other is assigned the letter "D:". You can also use drive letters to represent CD-ROM drives or remote network drives (usually using drive letters F: –Z:). (A remote network drive, also called a **share**, is a pointer to a folder stored on another computer.)

The storage area on a hard or floppy drive is divided into directories, or **folders**, that you can use to organize your files. You can think of a computer as similar to a filing cabinet. The individual drawers of the filing cabinet are analogous to the various drives on a computer. The folders within each drawer are analogous to the directories, or folders, stored on a drive. As in a filing cabinet, the folders on a computer can contain files (sometimes called documents) or other folders.

 The top of the folder hierarchy is called the root folder or root, which are referred to by "a:\" and "c:\" in Windows for the floppy drive and hard drive, respectively.

Different types of computer files are distinguished by file extensions. For example, the file named "Letter.doc" would be a Word document, while the extension ".gif" indicates a graphics file. As a Web programmer, you use file extensions to indicate the type of data stored in a file. The exact format of the data in a file is determined by the application that uses it.

A file or folder can have one or more of the following attributes.

- **Normal**: A regular file that can be opened, modified, and saved
- **Read only**: A file that can be read, but not altered
- **Hidden**: A file that is hidden from the user; usually a system file
- **System**: A special file used by the operating system
- **Directory**: A file that is a folder
- **Archive**: A file that has been changed and needs to be backed up
- **Alias**: A file that is a shortcut to another file
- **Compressed**: A file that has been compressed by the operating system

There are three types of files: binary, ASCII, and Unicode. A **binary file** contains data that is stored in the form of 1's and 0's; you can't interpret or read a binary file simply by opening it in a text editor such as Notepad. Instead, you need to open it in the application for which it was designed. A Word document (.doc) is a binary file that can only be read by applications that understand this type of file. Most files with the .exe file extension are binary files.

An **ASCII** file stores data as a series of characters—that is, as text. You can read ASCII files in Notepad, because Notepad translates each 8-bit block to an ASCII character—that is, to a letter, number, or special character.

A **Unicode** file is a file that stores data as a series of characters—that is, as text. This type of file differs from ASCII in that it can store special characters from different languages; also, a Unicode file is stored in a 16-bit block.

FileSystemObject Object Overview

ASP applications often must have the ability to manipulate drives, folders, and files on a Web server. You can give your application this ability by using the CreateObject function to create an instance of the FileSystemObject object.

The FileSystemObject object itself provides functionality to the programmer. This object is also at the top of a hierarchy of functionality that is provided by a series of child objects. (These objects are housed in collections, which are properties of the FileSystemObject object.)

Once you create a FileSystemObject object, you incorporate the object into VBScript by using the following format:

Code Example

```
Dim objFileSystemObject
Set objFileSystemObject = CreateObject("Scripting.FileSystemObjec
t")
```

To incorporate a FileSystemObject in JavaScript, you would use this format:

Code Example

```
var objFileSystemObject;
objFileSystemObject = CreateObject("Scripting.FileSystemObject");
```

In both examples, the file system object is named objFileSystemObject.

Table 4-1 shows the properties and methods of the FileSystemObject object.

Table 4-1   Important Properties and Methods of the FileSystemObject Object

Property/Method	Name	Description
Property	Drives	Stores a collection of all Drive objects on the Web server
Method	CopyFile	Copies files
Method	CreateTextFile	Creates a text file on the server
Method	DeleteFile	Deletes a file
Method	FileExists	Determines whether a file exists
Method	MoveFile	Moves a file from one location to another
Method	OpenTextFile	Opens an existing file on the server
Method	CopyFolder	Copies a folder
Method	CreateFolder	Creates a folder
Method	DeleteFolder	Deletes a folder
Method	FolderExists	Determines whether a folder exists
Method	MoveFolder	Moves a folder from one location to another
Method	BuildPath	Manipulates a path
Method	GetDrive	Gets a Drive object
Method	GetFile	Gets a File object
Method	GetParentFolderName	Gets the parent folder's name
Method	GetFolder	Gets a Folder object
Method	OpenAsTextStream	Returns a TextStream object from a current file

Now that you are familiar with the high-level object and its functionality, we will take a look at the child objects.

Drive Object

A Drive object provides properties and methods to interact with a particular drive (such as A: or C:). Each Drive object is contained in the Drives collection. Table 4-2 shows the properties of the Drive object.

Table 4-2   Important Properties of the Drive Object

Name	Description
AvailableSpace	Returns the number of bytes available on the current drive
DriveLetter	Returns the drive letter of the current drive
DriveType	Returns the type of drive as follows: • 0 for Unknown • 1 for Removable (such as a Zip drive, or floppy drive) • 2 for Fixed (such as a hard drive) • 3 for Network (such as a network share) • 4 for CD-ROM • 5 for RAM disk (such as a virtual disk drive stored in RAM)
FileSystem	Returns the type of file system for the current drive. Types include NTFS, a special file system used by Windows NT; FAT, a special file system used on Windows 95/98/NT/2000; and CDFS, a special file system used on CD-ROM drives.
FreeSpace	Returns the free space on the current drive
IsReady	Returns true if a drive is ready or false if it is not
Path	Returns the path for the current drive
RootFolder	Returns the root folder of the current drive
SerialNumber	Returns the serial number of the drive
ShareName	Returns the network name of the network drive
TotalSize	Returns the total space (bytes) of the current drive
VolumeName	Returns the name of the volume of the current drive

Folder Object

A Folder object provides the properties and methods to interact with a folder on a computer. Table 4–3 shows the properties and methods of the Folder object.

Table 4-3   Properties and Methods of the Folder Object

Property/Method	Name	Description
Property	Attributes	Contains the attribute of the folder; attributes can be a combination of several of the following values: • 0 for Normal • 1 for Read-only • 2 for Hidden • 4 for System • 5 for Volume • 16 for Directory • 32 for Archive • 64 for Alias • 128 for Compressed
Property	DateCreated	Contains the date and time the folder was created

Table 4-3   Properties and Methods of the Folder Object (continued)

Property/Method	Name	Description
Property	DateLastAccessed	Contains the date and time the folder was last accessed
Property	DateLastModified	Contains the date and time the folder was last modified
Property	Drive	Contains the letter of the drive in which the folder is located
Property	IsRootFolder	Contains information indicating whether the folder is the root folder
Property	Name	Contains the name of the folder
Property	ParentFolder	Contains a folder object of the parent folder
Property	Path	Contains the path of the folder
Property	ShortName	Contains the 8.3 DOS name
Property	ShortPath	Contains the 8.3 DOS version of the path
Property	Size	Contains the size of all files and subfolders in this folder
Property	SubFolders	Contains the Folder collection of all SubFolders in this folder
Method	Copy	Copies the specified folder from one location to another location
Method	Delete	Deletes a specified folder
Method	Move	Moves a specified folder from one location to another
Property	Files	Contains a file collection in the current folder
Property	Folders	Contains a collection of all folders within a folder; contains a count and item properties as well as an AddFolders method

File Object

Each Folder object contains a property called Files. This property contains the collection of File objects. One File object represents one file on your server.

Table 4-4 shows the properties and methods of the File object.

Displaying File and Folder Information

Suppose you wanted an application to display all the files and folders in the root of drive A. This is a common administrative task that is well suited to the abilities of ASP and its specialized objects.

To display the files and folders, you would use the FileSystemObject, Drive, Folder, and File objects. In our example, we will use the objects in VBScript. To begin our sample scenario, we will prepare PWS to handle our "target" application, which will have its files and folders "investigated" by a second application.

Table 4-4   Properties and Methods of the File Object

Property/Method	Name	Description
Property	Attributes	Contains the attribute of a file in the form of one or more of the following values: • 0 for Normal • 1 for Read-only • 2 for Hidden • 4 for System • 5 for Volume • 16 for Directory • 32 for Archive • 64 for Alias • 128 for Compressed
Property	DateCreated	Contains the date and time the file was created
Property	DateLastAccessed	Contains the date and time the file was last accessed
Property	DateLastModified	Contains the date and time the file was last modified
Property	Drive	Contains the letter of the drive where the file is located
Property	Name	Contains the name of the file
Property	ParentFolder	Contains a folder object of the parent folder
Property	Path	Contains the path of the file
Property	ShortName	Contains the 8.3 DOS name
Property	ShortPath	Contains the 8.3 DOS version of the path
Property	Size	Returns the size, in bytes, of the specified file
Property	Type	Contains information about the type of file
Method	Copy	Copies the specified file from one location to another location
Method	Delete	Deletes a specified file
Method	Move	Moves a specified file from one location to another
Method	OpenAsTextStream	Opens a file and returns a TextStream object (discussed later in this chapter), a special object that allows an application to read, write, and append to a file

To make a virtual directory:

1. Open the **Personal Web Manager**, and click the **Advanced** icon on the left side of the window. The Advanced Options window opens.

2. Click the **Add** button. The Add Directory dialog box opens.

3. In the Alias text box, type **Chapter_4**. The alias is the name of the folder you are using.

4. In the Directory text box, type the pathname to the Chapter_4 folder.

5. Click the **OK** button, and then close the Personal Web Manager window.

Now that the application is on PWS, let's take a look at it so we know what we are dealing with.

To preview the Student Contacts Application:

1. Open your browser.

2. Type **http://localhost/Chapter_4/register/default.htm** in the Address text box, and then press **Enter.** Your screen should resemble Figure 4-1. You will now enter contact information for a new student.

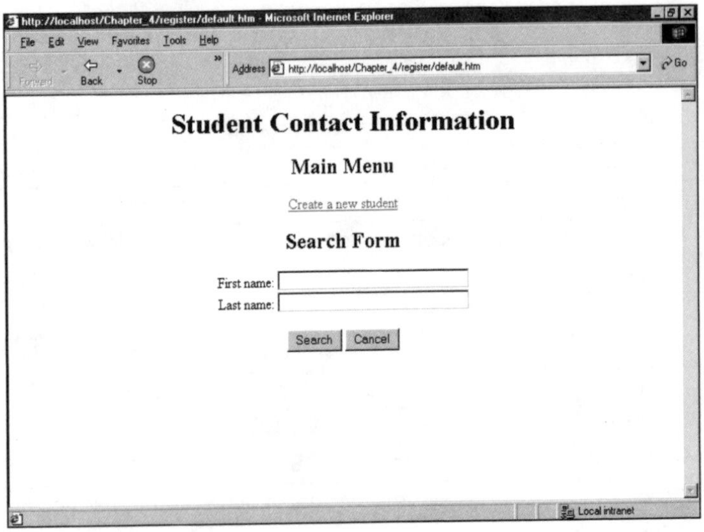

Figure 4-1   Student contact information

3. Click **Create a new student.** Your screen should now resemble Figure 4-2. Note the information that appears after the "?" in the Address text box. This information is called a query string. You will learn about query strings later in this chapter.

4. Enter the following information in the form:

   First name: **Lee**
   Last name: **Cheung**
   Home phone: **703-823-1234**
   Work phone: **703-323-3222**
   E-mail: **lcheung@jobs.com**

5. Click the **Save** button. The data is saved to a file.

6. The Student Contact Response page appears, as shown in Figure 4-3, verifying the information you provided. Now that you have entered information for a new student, you can try searching for information for a particular student.

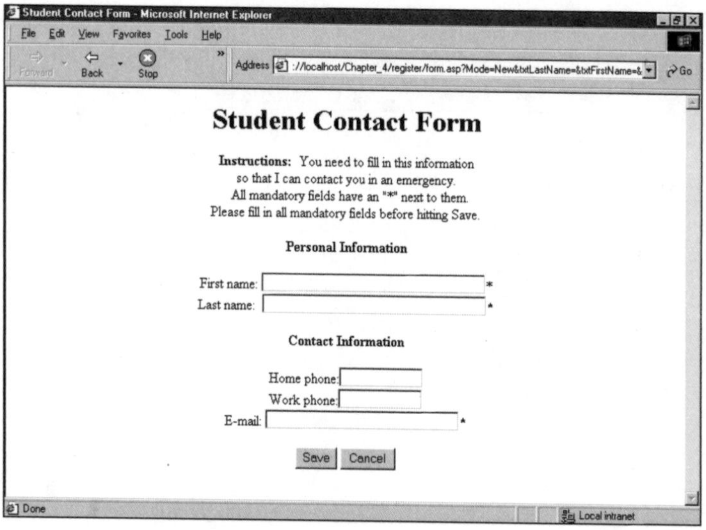

Figure 4-2   Student contact form

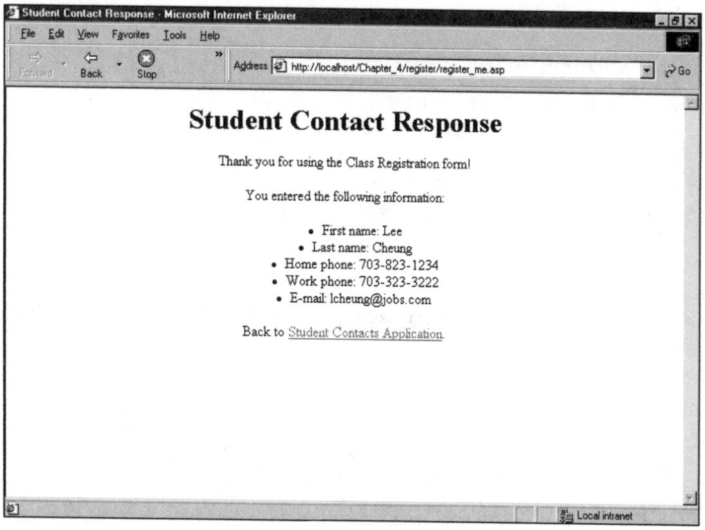

Figure 4-3   Confirmation of registration

7. Click **Student Contacts Application**.

8. In the Student Contacts Application form, enter the following:

   First name: **Lee**
   Last name: **Cheung**

9. Click the **Search** button. The record for the name you just entered is displayed in the Student Contacts Application form, as shown in Figure 4–4.

10. Close your browser.

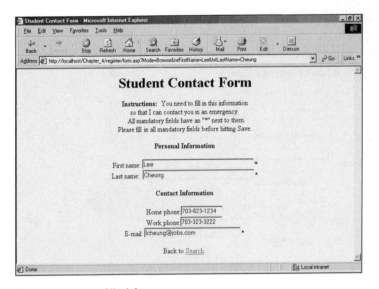

Figure 4-4   Prefilled form

Now's your chance to get a very overt look at the power of ASP.

1. Make sure your Data Disk is in drive A.

2. Create a new file in your text editor.

3. Type the following:

```
<%@ Language=VBScript %>
<% Response.Buffer = True %>


<HTML>
<HEAD>
<TITLE>Using FileSystemObject, Drive, Folder, and File
Objects</TITLE>
</HEAD>
<BODY>
<%
  Dim objFileSystemObject, objFile, objFolder, objDrive
  Set objFileSystemObject = CreateObject
  ("Scripting.FileSystemObject")

  'Get a drive object off your Data Disk
  Set objDrive = objFileSystemObject.GetDrive("a:")
%>
<TABLE border>
    <TR><TD>Path</TD><TD>Size</TD><TD>Parent Folder</TD>
    <TD>Name</TD><TD>f/d</TD></TR>
<%  For Each objFolder  In objDrive.RootFolder.SubFolders
%>
    <TR><TD><% =objFolder.Path %></TD>
        <TD><% =objFolder.Size %></TD>
        <TD><% =objFolder.ParentFolder %></TD>
        <TD><% =objFolder.Name %></TD>
        <TD>d</TD></TR>
```

```
<%  Next %>

<%  For Each objFile In objDrive.RootFolder.Files %>
    <TR><TD><% =objFile.Path %></TD>
            <TD><% =objFile.Size %></TD>
            <TD><% =objFile.ParentFolder %></TD>
            <TD><% =objFile.name %></TD>
            <TD>f </TD></TR>
<%  Next %>
    </TABLE>

</BODY>
</HTML>
```

4. Save the file as **example1.asp** in the Chapter_4 folder of your Data Disk. Save it again as **example2.asp** in the root folder of your Data Disk.

5. Open your browser.

6. In the Address text box, type **http://localhost/Chapter_4/example1.asp**, and then press **Enter**.

7. Verify the results. You should see a list of the files and folders on the root directory of your Data Disk, as shown in Figure 4-5.

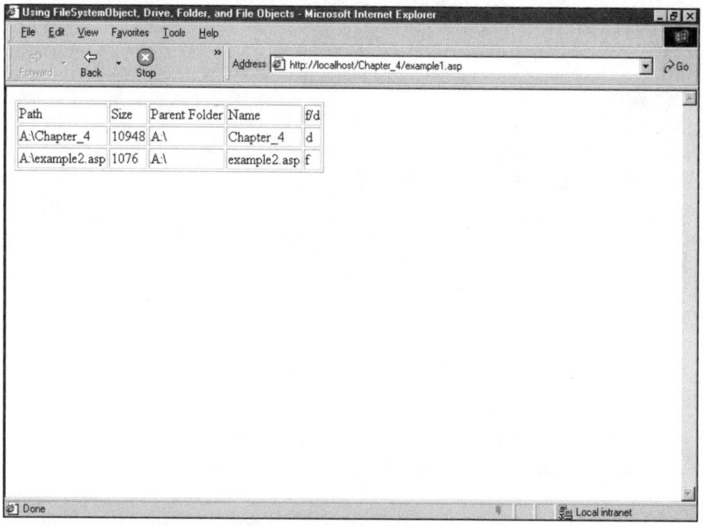

Figure 4-5 Root directory information

8. Close your browser.

Now that you have seen an example in action, you can review the code you just typed.

Code Example

```
1 <%@ Language=VBScript %>
2 <% Response.Buffer = True %>
```

```
3
4 <HTML>
5 <HEAD>
6 <TITLE>Using FileSystemObject, Drive, Folder, and File
Objects</TITLE>
7 </HEAD>
8 <BODY>
9 <%
10  Dim objFileSystemObject, objFile, objFolder, objDrive
11  Set objFileSystemObject = CreateObject
("Scripting.FileSystemObject")
12
13 'Get a drive object off your Data Disk
14  Set objDrive = objFileSystemObject.GetDrive("a:")
15 %>
16 <TABLE border>
17     <TR><TD>Path</TD><TD>Size</TD><TD>Parent Folder</TD><TD>
Name</TD><TD>f/d</TD></TR>
18 <%  For Each objFolder  In objDrive.RootFolder.SubFolders %>
19    <TR><TD><% =objFolder.Path %></TD>
20          <TD><% =objFolder.Size %></TD>
21          <TD><% =objFolder.ParentFolder %></TD>
22          <TD><% =objFolder.Name %></TD>
23          <TD>d</TD></TR>
24 <%  Next %>
25
26 <%  For Each objFile In objDrive.RootFolder.Files %>
27    <TR><TD><% =objFile.Path %></TD>
28          <TD><% =objFile.Size %></TD>
29          <TD><% =objFile.ParentFolder %></TD>
30          <TD><% =objFile.name %></TD>
31          <TD>f </TD></TR>
32 <%  Next %>
33  </TABLE>
34
35 </BODY>
36 </HTML>
```

Code Dissection

- Lines 10 and 11 show how to declare a FileSystemObject. In this case, the FileSystemObject is named objFileSystemObject.

- Line 14 returns a Drive object for drive A.

- The code after line 14 uses HTML tables. To declare a table you use the <TABLE>…</TABLE> tags. The border keyword in the <TABLE> tag creates a border around the table. <TR>…</TR> defines a row in a table. <TD>…</TD> defines a column in a row.

- Line 17 provides the header row that displays the titles in the columns.

- Lines 18–24 show how to display information about all folders in the folders collection . The For loop construct `For Each <item> In <collection>` shows a simple way to iterate through a collection.

- Lines 26–32 show how to loop through a collection of file objects and display information about a file.

Opening New and Existing Files

Now that you understand how to display information in an application using the FileSystemObject object, the Drive object, Folder object, and File object, you need to learn the particulars of how to open new files and existing files using the FileSystemObject. This will allow you to manipulate the files to suit your needs.

The syntax for creating a new file in VBScript and JavaScript is as follows:

Syntax Example

objFileSystemObject.CreateTextFile(filename, [, overwrite [, unicode]])

Syntax Dissection

- For the filename argument, you need to specify a filename and full path for the new file. For example, you might specify c:\temp\filename.ext.

- Set the overwrite argument to True if you want the new file to overwrite any existing file with the same name; set this argument to false if you do not want to overwrite an existing file.

- Set the unicode argument to true if you are using a Unicode or false if you are using ASCII.

- The overwrite and unicode arguments are optional.

The following example creates a new file named newfile.txt in VBScript:

Code Example

```
'Create the text file
objFileSystemObject.CreateTextFile("c:\temp\newfile.txt")
```

The syntax for opening an existing file in VBScript and JavaScript is as follows:

Syntax Example

objFileSystemObject.OpenTextFile(filename, [, iomode [, create [, format]]])

Syntax Dissection

- The iomode argument specifies how the application will interact with the file. To open a file as read-only (ForReading), use 1 for this argument. To open and allow the application to write to the file (ForWriting), use 2 for this argument. To open and then add to (append to) an existing file (ForAppending), use 8 for this argument.

- Set the create argument to true to create a new file if the specified file does not exist and you want the application to create it.

- Use the format argument to specify the type of text file: use −1 for Unicode, 0 for ASCII, or −2 for the system default. (Unicode is a 16-bit character format instead of a 8-bit character format like ASCII.)

- Notice that iomode, create, and format are enclosed in brackets. Brackets signify that these arguments are optional.

The following example opens an existing file named newfile.txt in VBScript.

Code Example

VBScript

```
Open an existing file for write only
objFileSystemObject.OpenTextFile("c:\temp\newfile.txt",2)
```

The TextStream Object Steps In

Well, you now know how to display folders and files, create new files, and even open existing files. That's useful, to a point. What you want to be able to do is manipulate the contents of these files. That's where the **TextStream** object comes in. With it, your application can open, read, write, and close a file on a server.

As always, our objects come with a plethora of useful methods and properties, and the TextStream object is no exception. See Table 4-5 for details.

Table 4-5   Important Properties and Methods of the TextStream Object

Property/Method	Name	Description
Property	AtEndOfLine	Contains true if at the end of a line, and false if not; the textstream must be in read mode
Property	AtEndOfStream	Contains true at the end of a file, and false if not; if not, the textstream must be in read-only mode
Method	Close	Closes an open TextStream
Method	Read(numchars)	Reads a number of characters in a file
Method	ReadAll	Reads all characters in a file in a string
Method	ReadLine	Reads an entire line of a file
Method	Skip(numchars)	Skips a number of characters in a file
Method	SkipLine	Skips an entire line of a file

Table 4-5   Important Properties and Methods of the TextStream Object (continued)

Property/Method	Name	Description
Method	Write(string)	Writes a string to a file
Method	WriteLine([string])	Writes an optional string to file and a new line character
Method	WriteBlankLines(n)	Writes a number of (n) newlines to a file

4

REVIEWING THE STUDENT CONTACTS APPLICATION

The FileSystemObject object was useful, no doubt. With it, we saw how we could write code that produced the dynamic drive, folder, and file information that we wanted to see. With just our browser, we obtained real-time information about a root directory and its contents.

At the core of our example was an application. Besides being our guinea pig in the showcasing of the FileSystemObject object, this application had attributes in its files that are a direct result of the use of the FileSystemObject. This section will highlight those attributes.

The QueryString Property of the Request Object

We start by going back to a subject that we briefly mentioned during the hands-on steps: the query string. During those steps, we directed your attention to the Address text box, which appeared as you see in Figure 4-6.

::/localhost/Chapter_4/register/form.asp?Mode=New&txtLastName=&txtFirstName=&

Figure 4-6   Query string

The URL you generated consisted of everything before the question mark. The question mark in the URL begins a query string. A **query string** is a collection of variable and value pairs that allow an application to pass data between Web pages. For example, in the URL above, one variable and value pair is "Mode=New", where Mode is the variable and New is the value of the variable. Depending on the application you are creating, you will use one or many variable/value pairs in your query strings.

 According to the HTML standards, query strings can be only about 1000 characters long.

You can create your own query string using one of two methods. First, you can place (by hand) a question mark right after the URL, followed by one or more control items (e.g., http://localhost/Chapter_4/register/form.asp?Mode=Browse&Last_name=Morneau&First _name=Keith). Alternately, you can create a form that contains the GET method, which then stores data in the QueryString collection. Typically, you use a GET method for a very simple form such as a search form, which requests keywords to search for. You should not use a GET method on a form for large amounts of data. However, it is common practice to use the GET method on search forms and in situations in which the application must send data to another Web page as a link.

We generated a query string because we knew our application only needed to send temporary data between the Web pages. The data was temporary because it was only needed while the application searched for the matching record. There was no need to store temporary data in the Session or Application objects, and doing so could have slowed our application's overall performance. (Keep in mind that data stored in the Session and Application objects typically affects the entire Session or the entire Application.)

 Use the GET method of an HTML form for data you do not need to store in a database or file and that is only needed for short periods of time. Use the POST method of an HTML form for data you must store into a database or file.

Table 4-6 illustrates examples of query strings.

Table 4-6   Examples of Query Strings

Example	Explanation
`form.asp?usr=Keith+Morneau&` `password=nobody`	In a control's value, a + sign replaces a space in the string. ASP converts the + sign to a regular space when creating the QueryString collection.
`form.asp?address=123` `Street%0D%0A`	URL encoding converts special ASCII characters, such as a carriage return and line feed, into hexadecimal values such as %0D (which is 13 in decimal notation) and %0A (which is 10 in decimal notation). You represent hexadecimal numbers in a query string by using %*hex*, where hex is replaced with a hexadecimal number. ASP converts these URL-encoded characters back into their normal representations.

Default.htm

This page contains the search form that the user can use to find contact information for an existing student. It also includes the link that the user can click in order to enter information for a new student. The HTML for the default.htm page is shown below:

Code Example

```
1 <HTML>
2 <HEAD>
3
4 </HEAD>
5 <BODY>
6 <FORM id="frmSearch" name="frmSearch" action="form.asp"
method="get">
7 <CENTER><H1>Students Contact Information</H1>
8 <CENTER><H2>Main Menu</H2></CENTER>
9 <CENTER>
10 <A href="form.asp?Mode=New&txtLastName=&txtFirstName=&">Create
a new student
```

```
11 </A>
12 </CENTER>
13
14 <CENTER><H2>Search Form</H2></CENTER>
15
16 <CENTER>
17 <P>
18 <INPUT type="hidden" name="Mode" value="Browse">
19 First name: <INPUT type="text" name="txtFirstName" size="30">
<BR>
20 Last name: <INPUT type="text" name="txtLastName" size="30">
21 </P>
22 </CENTER>
23
24 <CENTER>
25 <P><INPUT id="cmdSubmit"  type="submit" value="Search">
26 <INPUT id="cmdReset"  type="reset" value="Cancel"> </p>
27 </CENTER>
28
29 </FORM>
30
31 </BODY>
32 </HTML>
```

Code Dissection

- Line 6 employs the GET method, which causes ASP to create a QueryString when the data is passed to the server.

- Line 18 contains an HTML form element that is hidden from the user. Hidden HTML form elements are useful when you do not want the user to see an HTML element on the form, but you want to send data to the server. The hidden form element in line 18 is the Mode variable, which tells an HTML page whether or not to allow the user to edit data on the form. In this case, the hidden form element has a value of "Browse", which tells the student contact form page to find information for an existing student and display the information to the user without allowing the user to edit it.

- If you do not want an HTML form element to be passed to the server, do not include the name property when defining the element. For example, lines 25 and 26 do not contain a name property, because there is no need to pass the Submit and Reset buttons to the server.

ClsForm.cls

The ClsForm.cls class provides the main functionality of the student contact form. The script code in this file creates a form class that contains the reusable properties and methods for processing the input.

It contains three properties:

- **strMode**: Specifies the state of the form. The state of a form is dictated by the contents of the Mode variable. The form is in Browse state when the Mode variable contains Browse, and in New state when the Mode variable contains New. The Browse state tells a script to only display student data and not allow changes to the data. The New state tells a script that the form will be cleared to allow for entry of a new student.

- **colFormElements**: A collection that stores the information to be displayed on the form

- **strServerFilePath**: The path to the physical location where the file is stored

In addition, the ClsForm.cls class contains two methods. The Search method searches a file to find a match based on first and last name. The Save method saves the information from a form to a file.

To use the Save method, you will need to know the physical path—that is, where the file is located on the server. The **physical path** specifies the precise location of a file, including the drive letter and all the relevant folders and subfolders. For example, if a file named register were stored in a folder named Chapter_4, which in turn was stored in a folder named wwwroot, which in turn was stored in a folder named inetpub, which was stored on drive C, the file's physical path would be as follows: c:\inetpub\wwwroot\Chapter_4\register. When you access a Web page via PWS, however, you are using a logical path. The **logical path** is the URL that the user types in the browser; it does not point to the physical location of a file; instead, it provides a path from the virtual directory to the file.

Well, how do we reconcile the two? Fortunately, in ASP, the Server.Mappath function translates a logical path within your code into a physical path. For instance, Server.Mappath ("/Chapter_4/Register") takes a logical path (/Chapter_4/Register) and translates it into a physical path (a:\Chapter_4\Register) on the server. Essentially, the Server.Mappath function adds the a:\ to the physical path.

The code for the clsForm.class is as follows:

Code Example

```
1 <%
2 CLASS clsForm
3
4 Private strMode
5 Public colFormElements
6 Private strServerFilePath
7
8 Public Sub Class_Initialize
9
10   strMode = "Browse"
11   set colFormElements = CreateObject("Scripting.Dictionary")
12   strServerFilePath = Server.Mappath("/Chapter_4/register")
& "\students.txt"
```

```
13  Call CreateDict
14
15 End Sub
16
17 Public Function Search(strFirstName,strLastName)
18
19    Dim objFile,objFileSystemObject,objFS,strDummy1,strDummy2,
strDummy3,strFirst,strLast
20    set objFileSystemObject = CreateObject("Scripting.File
SystemObject")
21    set objFile = objFileSystemObject.GetFile(strServerFilePath)
22    set objFS = objFile.OpenAsTextStream(1, -2)
23    Do While Not objFS.AtEndOfStream
24      strFirst = UCASE(objFS.ReadLine)
25      strLast = UCASE(objFS.ReadLine)
26      if (UCASE(strFirstName) = strFirst) and
(UCASE(strLastName = strLast) Then
27         strMode = "Browse"
28         colFormElements.RemoveAll
29         colFormElements.Add "txtFirstName", strFirstName
30         colFormElements.Add "txtLastName", strLastName
31         colFormElements.Add "txtWorkPhone", objFS.ReadLine
32         colFormElements.Add "txtHomePhone", objFS.ReadLine
33         colFormElements.Add "txtemail", objFS.ReadLine
34         Search = True
35         objFS.close
36         Exit Function
37      'Else
38         'strMode = "New"
39         'colFormElements.RemoveAll
40         'colFormElements.Add "txtFirstName", strFirstName
41         'colFormElements.Add "txtLastName", strLastName
42         'colFormElements.Add "txtWorkPhone", ""
43         'colFormElements.Add "txtHomePhone", ""
44         'colFormElements.Add "txtemail", ""
45         'strDummy1 = objFS.ReadLine
46         'strDummy2 = objFS.ReadLine
47         'strDummy3 = objFS.ReadLine
48      End If
49    Loop
50    Search = False
51    objFS.close
52 End Function
53
54
55 Private Sub CreateDict
56
57  Dim item
58
59  For Each item in Request.Form
```

```
60       colFormElements.Add item, Request.Form(item)
61    Next
62
63 End Sub
64
65 Public Sub Save
66
67    Dim objForm, objFileSystemObject, objFile, objFS
68  set objFileSystemObject = CreateObject("Scripting.FileSystem
Object")
69
70    If Not objFileSystemObject.FileExists(strServerFilePath)
Then
71
72     set objFS =  objFileSystemObject.CreateTextFile
(strServerFilePath)
73
74  else
75
76     set objFile = objFileSystemObject.GetFile(strServerFile
Path)
77     set objFS = objFile.OpenAsTextStream(8, -2)
78
79  End If
80
81   For Each strItem in colFormElements
82     objFS.WriteLine trim(colFormElements.Item(strItem))
83   Next
84
85   objFS.Close
86   set objFS = Nothing
87  set objFileSystemObject = Nothing
88
89 End Sub
90
91 'Create a property called Mode
92 Public Property Get Mode
93
94   Mode = strMode
95
96 End Property
97
98 Public Property Let Mode(newMode)
99
100   strMode = newMode
101
102 End Property
103
104 'Create a property called ServerPath
105 Public Property Get ServerPath
106
```

```
107    ServerPath = strServerFilePath
108
109 End Property
110
111 Public Property Let ServerPath(newServerPath)
112
113   strServerFilePath = newServerPath
114
115 End Property
116
117 END CLASS
118
119 %>
```

4

Code Dissection

- Line 12 specifies the physical path for the students.txt file. The code Server.Mappath("/Chapter_4/Register") is a function that takes a logical path (/Chapter_4/Register) and translates it into a physical path (a:\Chapter_4\Register) on the server.

- Line 12: Server is an internal object in ASP that you can use to determine physical paths. This object also allows you to create an instance of an object as follows: `Server.CreateObject`. You have seen the CreateObject function previously.

- Lines 17–52 incorporate the Search function. The application needs to get the file first and open the file as input, `set objFS = objFile.OpenAsTextStream(1, −2)`, where the first argument is the iodmode and the second argument is the format. 1 is for reading and −2 is the default character format. Once the file is opened, you can loop through the file until you reach the end of file marker. Each line of the file represents a different element on the form. If the student is found, the application creates a collection with the appropriate data. If the collection is not found, the application sends the first and last name into the collection and clears out the other elements. The ReadLine function reads a line from the opened file.

- Lines 55–63 incorporate the CreateDict subroutine. This subroutine creates a collection with the form data only if the Request object contains form data.

- Lines 65–90 illustrate the Save subroutine. The application checks to see if the file exists. The logic of this subroutine goes something like this: If the file exists, then get the file and open it in Append mode. If it does not, create a new file. Write the elements from the collection (which contains information entered into the form) into the file one line at a time. When done, close the file.

Form.asp

Once again, think back to when you typed in a name in the application and then later searched for that name. Your search caused the student contact form to reappear with the informational text boxes already filled in. For that simple convenience, you can thank the form.asp script.

The form.asp script uses the clsForm class to search for information for existing students or to save information for a new student. This script also uses the query string to pass search information between the search form to the form.asp page. First, the form.asp script creates a collection of form data that includes blank fields (if the user clicks on Create a New Student in the Student Contacts Application form) or fields that are filled by a successful search (if the user fills in the first name and last name, clicks Search, and the data is found in the file). The form.asp script then displays the student contact form either with blank fields or (in the case of a search) with fields filled in with data from the collection. Whether the fields are blank or filled in depends on the script's current state. In Browse state, the script does a search and fills in the fields. In New mode, the script displays a blank form, into which the user can then enter contact information. This script illustrates how to use ASP to achieve multiple goals (searching for existing data or adding new data) with one form.

The code for the form.asp file is as follows:

Code Example

```
1 <%@ Language=VBScript%>
2 <%Option Explicit%>
3 <%Response.buffer=true%>
4 <!-- #include file="clsForm.cls" -->
5 <html>
6
7 <head>
8 <title>Student Contact</title>
9 <!--
10     *************************************************
11     *** Form Name:      frmRegister             ***
12     *** Author:         Keith Morneau           ***
13     *** Date:           8/6/00                  ***
14     *** Description:                            ***
15     ***    This form allows user to enter       ***
16     ***    the student information.             ***
17     ***                                         ***
18     *** Revisions:                             ***
19     *************************************************
20 -->
21 <%
22  Dim objForm,objFileSystemObject
23  set objForm = new clsForm
24
25  set objFileSystemObject = CreateObject("Scripting.FileSystemO
bject")
26  objForm.ServerPath = Server.Mappath("/Chapter_4/Register")&
"\students.txt"
27  If objFileSystemObject.FileExists(objForm.ServerPath) Then
28     objForm.Mode = Request.QueryString("Mode")
29     If Request.QueryString("Mode") = "Browse" then
30        If Request.QueryString("txtFirstName")<>"" AND Request.
QueryString("txtLastName")<>"" Then
```

4

```
31          If Not objForm.Search(Request.QueryString("txtFirstName
"),Request.QueryString("txtLastName")) then
32            Response.Redirect("form.asp?Mode=New&txtFirstName=&txt
LastName=")
33          End If
34        End If
35      End If
36      'Else
37      'objForm.Mode = "New"
38      'objForm.colFormElements.RemoveAll
39      'objForm.colFormElements.Add "txtFirstName", ""
40      'objForm.colFormElements.Add "txtLastName", ""
41      'objForm.colFormElements.Add "txtWorkPhone", ""
42      'objForm.colFormElements.Add "txtHomePhone", ""
43      'objForm.colFormElements.Add "txtemail", ""
44    End If
45
46    set objFileSystemObject = Nothing
47    %>
48
49    </head>
50
51    <body>
52
53    <h1 align="center">Student Contact</h1>
54
55    <p align="center"><strong>Instructions:</strong> 
56    You need to fill in this information
57    </p>
58
59
60    <form id="frmRegister" name="frmRegister" action="register_me.
asp" method="post">
61
62    <center><p><b>Personal Information</b></p></center>
63
64    <center><p>First name: <input id="txtFirstName" name="txtFirst
Name" size="35" value="<% = objForm.colFormElements.Item("txtFirst
Name")%>" >*<br>
  Last name: 
65
66    <input id="txtLastName" name="txtLastName" size="35" value="
<% = objForm.colFormElements.Item("txtLastName")%>"><strong>*</
strong> </label></p>
68    </center>
69
70    <center><p><b>Contact Information</b></p>
71    </center>
72
```

```
73 <center><p>Home phone:<input type="text" name="txtHomePhone"
size="12" value="<% = objForm.colFormElements.Item("txtHomePhone"
)
%>"><br>
74
75 Work phone:<input type="text" name="txtWorkPhone" size="12"
value="<% = objForm.colFormElements.Item("txtWorkPhone")%>"><br>
76
77 E-mail: <input type="text" name="txtemail" size="30" value="
<% = objForm.colFormElements.Item("txtemail")%>"><strong>*</
strong></p>
78 </center>
79
80 <%If (objForm.Mode <> "Browse") Then %>
81 <center><p><input id="cmdSubmit" type="submit" value="Save">
82 <input id="cmdReset" type="reset" value="Cancel">
</p></center>
83 <%Else %>
84 <center>Back to <a href="default.htm">Search</a>.</center>
85 <% End If %>
86 </form>
87
88 </body>
89 </html>
```

Code Dissection

- Lines 21–47 shows how to use the QueryString collection of the Request object. This script first checks to see if the students.txt file exists. If the file does exist, and if the search elements, the First Name and Last Name text boxes were filled in, then the script searches for the student. If the file does not exist, then the contact information must relate to a new student. In this case, the script creates a collection that includes blank fields to be used by the form.

- Lines 38–43: The Student Contact Information form itself illustrates how to use the collection to assign the initial values for the last name, first name, home phone number, work phone number, and e-mail fields.

- The last part (lines 80–85) of the HTML document specifies that if the Student Contact Information form is in browse mode, the Save or Cancel button should not be displayed on the form. Instead, the form should include a link the user can click to return to the Student Contacts Application screen. In other words, the Student Contacts form allows the user to view the data without allowing the user to change it.

register_me.asp

The register_me.asp script file takes the data from the form.asp script and saves the information to a file named students.txt if all the mandatory fields are filled in. If some of the mandatory fields are empty, then the script displays an error page. The Register_me.asp page is similar to other pages you have seen thus far. You can examine it yourself in Notepad. You'll find it in the Chapter_4 folder on your Data Disk.

UPLOADING FILES TO THE SERVER—HOW IT'S REALLY DONE

To complete the last section of this chapter, you will need to have installed the SiteGalaxy ASP Upload component, as outlined in the Front Matter of this book.

In this chapter, you have explored objects and their functionalities; you have also learned how an application can take data from a form on a client and save this data to a file on the server. To rephrase this, the application took generated information (not a file) and placed it in an existing file on the server.

Sometimes, however, in the real world of ASP programming, you (as a programmer or as an end user) are going to want to take an entire file from a client computer and save it to a directory on a server. Once the file is on the server, it can be used by a Web application or retrieved later by another individual. Regardless of the end use you have in mind, you'll find the SiteGalaxy Upload freeware component to be a handy device.

SiteGalaxy Upload Component

The SiteGalaxy Upload component uses a special MIME type, multipart/form, to allow the SiteGalaxy component to upload files from a client to the server. The SiteGalaxy Upload component includes two objects:

- **Form:** A collection of form elements returned by the client. The Item property of the Form object returns a FileField object if an element is supplied to Form object by the browser.

- **FileField:** An object that supplies information about a file passed to the server by the client

Table 4–7 shows the properties and methods of the Form object. (In this table, "Read-only" means that the property can be viewed but not changed.)

Table 4-7   Important Properties and Methods of the Form Object

Property/Method	Name	Description
Property	Item or Item(element)	Contains the collection of form elements submitted by the user. If an element (that is, a form element) is supplied in the parentheses, this property returns a FileField object.
Property	ContentDisposition	Contains a "form-data" string for "multipart/form-data" type HTML forms. You can use this property in your code to verify the correct MIME type. Read-only.
Property	Count	Contains the number of form elements in the collection. Read-only.
Property	MimeType	Contains the Mime type property of the file field. Read-only.
Property	MimeSubtype	Contains the Mime subtype property of the file field. Read-only.
Property	Size	Contains the Size property of the file field. Read-only.

Table 4–8 shows the properties and methods of the FileField object.

Table 4-8   Properties and Methods of the FileField Object

Property/Method	Name	Description
Property	FilePath	Contains the filename that the client is sending in the body of the request. Default value is read-only.
Property	MimeType	Contains the MIME type of the file (e.g., "image"). Read-only.
Property	MimeSubtype	Contains the MIME subtype of the file (e.g., "gif"). Read-only.
Property	Size	Contains the size in bytes of the file's data. Read-only.
Property	SaveAs(filename)	Saves the file on the server under the filename.
Property	SaveAsBlob(object)	Saves the file data in a database

You will now see some of the properties and methods of the SiteGalaxy Upload component in action in the following VBScript example.

Using the SiteGalaxy Upload Component

Suppose you have been asked to create an application that will make it possible for the students in a class to submit assignments electronically. In the past, the instructor accepted files sent as e-mail attachments But now, with class size on the increase, the instructor would prefer that students be able to go to a Web site, and then upload assignments from their computers directly to the Web site. This approach will make it easier for the instructor to organize the assignment files he or she receives.

To create the code to upload a file:

1. Start your text editor and create a new file.

2. Type the following VBScript code:

VBScript

```
<HTML>
<HEAD>
<TITLE>Upload Form Example</TITLE>
</HEAD>
<BODY>
<FORM action="submit_assignment.asp" id="frmAssignment"
method=post encType="multipart/form-data">
Select an assignment:
    <INPUT id=txtassignfile name=txtassignfile type=file>
    <BR>
    <INPUT id=cmdsubmitdisk name=cmdsubmitdisk
    type=submit value="Save to disk"></TD>
</FORM>
</BODY>
</HTML>
```

3. Save this file as **assignment.htm** in the Chapter_4 folder of your Data Disk.

4. Create a new file in your text editor.

5. Type the following VBScript code:

VBScript

```
<%@ Language=VBScript %>
<%Response.Buffer = True%>
<HTML>
<HEAD>
<TITLE>Uploading File Example</TITLE>
<%    Dim objuploadform, objfs, objfso, objfile, strfn

    set objuploadform = Server.CreateObject("SiteGalaxy
    Upload.Form")

    if objuploadform("cmdsubmitdisk") <> "" then
        ' save to disk
        set objfs = server.CreateObject("Scripting.File
        SystemObject")
        strfn = server.mappath("/Chapter_4") & "\" &
        objfs.GetFileName(objuploadform("txtassignfile")
        .FilePath)
        set objfs = Nothing

        objuploadform("txtassignfile").SaveAs(strfn)
    end if
```

```
%>
</HEAD>
<BODY>
<CENTER><H1>Submit Assignment Example</H1>
<P>Thank you for submitting your assignment,<BR>
 <%=objuploadform("txtassignfile").FilePath%>!</CENTER></p>
</BODY>
</HTML>
```

6. Save this file as **submit_assignment.asp** in Chapter_4 folder of your Data Disk.

7. Close your text editor, and then start your browser.

8. Type **http://localhost/Chapter_4/assignment.htm** in the Address text box, and then press **Enter**.

9. Click the **Browse** button.

10. Select the **C:** drive in the Look in list box, and then select **Autoexec.bat**.

11. Click the **Open** button.

12. Click the **Save to disk** button on the form to save the file to the Chapter_4 folder of your Data Disk. You will see a confirmation, as shown in Figure 4-7.

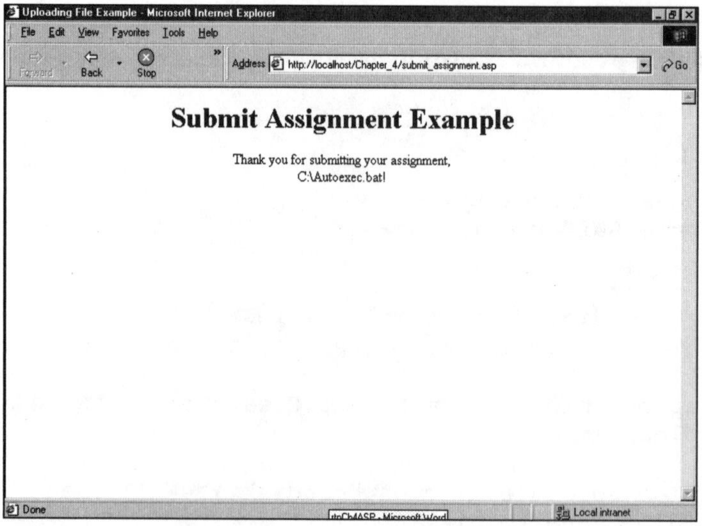

Figure 4-7 Assignment submitted

13. Verify that the file was saved to the Chapter_4 folder of your Data Disk.

14. Close your browser.

The application you just created uploaded a file to the Chapter_4 folder of your Data Disk. Now take a moment to examine the application's code. We begin with assignment.htm.

Code Example

```
1 <HTML>
2 <HEAD>
3 <TITLE>Upload Form Example</TITLE>
4 </HEAD>
5 <BODY>
6 <FORM action="submit_assignment.asp" id="frmAssignment" method=
post encType="multipart/form-data">
7 Select an assignment:
8     <INPUT id=txtassignfile name=txtassignfile type=file><BR>
9     <INPUT id=cmdsubmitdisk name=cmdsubmitdisk type=submit
value="Save to disk"></TD>
10 </FORM>
11 </BODY>
12 </HTML>
```

Code Dissection

- Line 6. The only difference between this form and the forms you have created previously is the encType property used in this line. The multipart/form-data is the MIME encoding type used to send files to the server.

- Line 8 supplies the input type of file that allows users to select the file they want to upload.

Then, we move right into submit_assignment.asp:

Code Example

```
1 <%@ Language=VBScript %>
2 <%Response.Buffer = True%>
3 <HTML>
4 <HEAD>
5 <TITLE>Uploading File Example</TITLE>
6 <%    Dim objuploadform, objfs, objfso, objfile, strfn
7
8    set objuploadform = Server.CreateObject("SiteGalaxyUpload.
Form")
9
10   if objuploadform("cmdsubmitdisk") <> "" then
11        ' save to disk
12        set objfs = Server.CreateObject("Scripting.FileSystem
Object")
13        strfn = server.mappath("/Chapter_4") & "\" & objfs.Get
FileName(objuploadform("txtassignfile").FilePath)
14        set objfs = Nothing
15
16        objuploadform("txtassignfile").SaveAs(strfn)
17    end if
18 %>
```

```
19 </HEAD>
20 <BODY>
21 <CENTER><H1>Submit Assignment Example</H1>
22 <P>Thank you for submitting your assignment,<BR>
23 <%=objuploadform("txtassignfile").FilePath%>!</center></p>
24 </BODY>
25 </HTML>
```

Code Dissection

- This code presents an alternative to the Request.Form collection, which you have previously used to retrieve form data. The Form collection provides the values of the form elements used in the assignment form.

- Line 8 declares a form object using the SiteGalaxy component

- Lines 12 and 13 supply the appropriate filename to the SiteGalaxy component.

- Line 16 shows how to save file data to the server.

As you can see, the component is quite useful in allowing the uploading of files of a dynamic nature. Instead of a static upload via FTP, in which the placement of the file is a terminal action, the end user can upload files that trigger events as dictated by the code of the ASP programmer.

CHAPTER SUMMARY

- On the average PC, you can store folders and files on either a floppy disk drive or a hard disk drive. The floppy disk drive is usually referred to by the drive letter "A:". The hard disk on a computer is usually referred to as the "C:" drive. The storage area on a hard or floppy drive is divided into directories, or folders, that you can use to organize your files. As a Web programmer, you use file extensions to indicate the type of data stored in a file. The exact format of the data in a file is determined by the application that uses it. There are three types of files: binary, ASCII, and Unicode.

- The FileSystemObject object itself provides functionality to the programmer. This object is also at the top of a hierarchy of functionality that is provided by a series of child objects.

- A Drive object provides properties and methods to interact with a particular drive (such as A or C). Each Drive object is contained in the Drives collection. A Folder object provides the properties and methods to interact with a folder on a computer. Each Folder object contains a property called Files. This property contains the collection of File objects. One File object represents one file on your server.

- You can use the FileSystemObject to create new files and existing files. You use the **TextStream** object to manipulate the information contained in the files.

❑ A query string is a collection of variable and value pairs that allow an application to pass data between Web pages. Depending on the application you are creating, you will use one or many variable/value pairs in your query strings.

❑ Hidden HTML form elements are useful when you do not want the user to see an HTML element on the form, but you want to send data to the server. In the ClsForm.cls class, you will find two methods: the Search method searches a file to find a match based on first and last name, and the Save method saves the information from a form to a file. In your application in this chapter, the form.asp script used the clsForm class to search for information for existing students and to save information for a new student.

❑ The SiteGalaxy Upload freeware component uses a special MIME type, multipart/form-data, to allow the SiteGalaxy component to upload files from the client to the server.

4

REVIEW QUESTIONS

1. Drives are directories that allow you to organize your data. True or False?
2. Folders are represented by the letters A: or C:. True or False?
3. A remote drive is also called a(n) _____.
   a. a:
   b. share
   c. directory
   d. none of the above
4. A: is a _____ and is the name used in Windows to access a floppy disk drive.
   a. folder
   b. file
   c. drive letter
   d. none of the above
5. A(n) _____ file stores data as 1's and 0's.
   a. binary
   b. ASCII
   c. Unicode
   d. none of the above
6. A(n) _____ file stores data as 8-bit characters.
   a. binary
   b. ASCII
   c. Unicode
   d. none of the above

7. A(n) _____ file store data as 16-bit characters.

   a. binary

   b. ASCII

   c. Unicode

   d. none of the above

8. The FileSystemObject is part of what ASP component?

   a. SiteGalaxy

   b. Scripting

   c. Request

   d. Response

9. Query strings use a _____ sign to represent a space.

   a. +

   b. −

   c. /

   d. *

10. Query strings use a _____ symbol to separate control name and value pairs.

    a. ^

    b. %

    c. &

    d. !

11. What method of the Server object allows you to map logical paths to physical paths?

    a. CreateObject

    b. ContentType

    c. Mappath

    d. none of the above

12. _____ specifies the data type being transmitted to or received from the server.

    a. ASCII

    b. Unicode

    c. MIME

    d. Extension

13. The _____ method of a form uses the QueryString collection.

    a. POST

    b. GET

  c. ACTION

  d. none of the above

14. The _____ method of a form uses the Form collection.

  a. POST

  b. GET

  c. ACTION

  d. none of the above

15. SiteGalaxy's component is used to _____ files from the client to the server.

  a. upload

  b. download

  c. upload and download

  d. none of the above

16. What is the likely MIME type and subtype for a jpg image?

  a. image/gif

  b. text/html

  c. image/jpeg

  d. image/jpg

17. What is the likely MIME type and subtype for a standard HTML document?

  a. image/gif

  b. text/html

  c. image/jpeg

  d. image/jpg

18. Another name for a directory is a _____.

  a. file

  b. remote directory

  c. folder

  d. none of the above

19. When an application wants to store data from an HTML form to a file, you should use the _____ method.

  a. GET

  b. POST

  c. BROWSE

  d. none of the above

20. The largest length of a query string is ―――――――― characters.

    a. 255

    b. 155

    c. 1000

    d. 2000

HANDS-ON PROJECTS

Project 4-1

Modify the example1.asp script in the Chapter_4 folder of your Data Disk to add a form that includes a drive and folder text box. Modify the script to display the files and file sizes for the drive and folder the user enters on the form.

1. Create a folder called dir.

2. Create a virtual directory for folder dir.

3. Create an HTML form called default.htm in the dir folder with a drive and folder text box and submit and reset buttons.

4. Create an ASP script called example1.asp in the dir folder with the following code:

```
<%@ Language=VBScript %>
<% Response.Buffer = True %>

<HTML>
<HEAD>
<TITLE>Using FileSystemObject, Drive, Folder, and File
Objects</TITLE>
</HEAD>
<BODY>
<%
   Dim objFileSystemObject, objFile, objFolder, objDrive
   Set objFileSystemObject = CreateObject("Scripting.File
SystemObject")

  'Get a drive object off your Data Disk
   Set objDrive = objFileSystemObject.GetDrive(Request.Form
("txtDrive"))
   Response.Clear
%>
<H2>Files in path <%=Request.Form("txtDrive") & "\" _
& Request.Form("txtFolder")%></H2>
<TABLE border>
    <TR><TD>Path</TD><TD>Size</TD></TR>

<%  For Each objFile In _
```

```
objDrive.RootFolder.SubFolders.Item(Request.Form("txtFolder"
)).Files %>
    <TR><TD><% =objFile.Name%></TD>
            <TD><% =objFile.Size%></TD></TR>
<% Next %>
  </TABLE>

</BODY>
</HTML>
```

5. Test your new application with valid values.

Project 4-2

Modify Project 4-1 to save the information to a file and display the files for the drive and folder the user enters on the form.

1. Edit example1.asp from the dir folder so that it matches the following code:

```
<%@ Language=VBScript %>
<% Response.Buffer = True %>
<HTML>
<HEAD>
<TITLE>Using FileSystemObject, Drive, Folder, and File
Objects</TITLE>
</HEAD>
<BODY>
<%
  Dim objForm, objFileSystemObject, objFile, objFileS, objFS,
  strServerFilePath
  Set objFileSystemObject = CreateObject("Scripting.File
  SystemObject")

  'Get a drive object off your Data Disk
  Set objDrive = objFileSystemObject.GetDrive(Request.Form
("txtDrive"))
  Response.Clear

  strServerFilePath = Server.Mappath("/dir") & "\files.txt"
  If Not objFileSystemObject.FileExists(strServerFilePath)
  Then

    set objFS = objFileSystemObject.CreateTextFile(strServer
FilePath)

  else

    set objFileS = objFileSystemObject.GetFile(strServerFile
Path)
    set objFS = objFileS.OpenAsTextStream(8, -2)

  End If
%>
```

```
<H2>Files in path <%=Request.Form("txtDrive") & "\" &
Request.Form("txtFolder")%></H2>
<TABLE border>
    <TR><TD>Path</TD><TD>Size</TD></TR>

<%  For Each objFile In objDrive.RootFolder.SubFolders.Item
(Request.Form("txtFolder")).Files

  objFS.WriteLine objFile.Name & " " & objFile.size
%>

    <TR><TD><% =objFile.Name%></TD>
    <TD><% =objFile.Size%></TD></TR>
<%  Next %>
  </TABLE>

<%  objFS.Close
  set objFS = Nothing
  set objFileSystemObject = Nothing %>
</BODY>
</HTML>
```

2. Test the new application by viewing the results in the browser and the files.txt file in the dir folder.

In the following hands-on projects, remember to include server-side form validation for each Web application.

Project 4-3

Write a Web application that requests an employee's name and salary, and then saves that data to a file. Provide a search functionality for this application.

1. Create a folder called salary.

2. Create a virtual directory for folder salary.

3. Create an HTML form called Default.htm in the salary folder similar to the default.htm form in this chapter. Make sure to change the contents of the form to match this problem.

4. Create an HTML form called Form.asp in the salary folder similar to the form.asp form in this chapter. Make sure to change the contents of the form to match this problem.

5. Create a clsForm.cls class in the salary folder similar to the clsForm.cls class in this chapter. Make sure to modify the file to match the problem.

6. Create an ASP script called save_me.asp similar to the register_me.asp script in this chapter.

7. Test the application in your browser.

Project 4-4

Write a Web application that requests a department code and the name of an employee within that department, and then saves that data to a file. Assume that the following are valid department codes:

ACCT Accounting

ENG   Engineering

MKT   Marketing

HR   Human Resources

The application should prevent the user from entering invalid department codes.

1. Create a folder called dept.

2. Create a virtual directory for folder dept.

3. Create an HTML form called Default.htm in the dept folder similar to the default.htm form in this chapter. Make sure to change the contents of the form to match this problem.

4. Create an HTML form called Form.asp in the dept folder similar to the form.asp form in this chapter. Make sure to change the contents of the form to match this problem.

5. Create a clsForm.cls class in the dept folder similar to the clsForm.cls class in this chapter. Make sure to modify the file to match the problem.

6. Create an ASP script called save_me.asp similar to the register_me.asp script in this chapter. Make sure to check for appropriate department codes in the FormValidation subroutine.

7. Test the application in your browser.

Project 4-5

Write a Web application that accepts employee time reports as files and stores them in a directory called time_reports on your Data Disk. The application should store each employee's time report in the time_reports directory.

1. Create a folder called time_reports.

2. Create a virtual directory of the time_reports folder.

3. Create a file default.htm similar to default.htm file in the SiteGalaxy Upload section.

4. Create a file submit_time.asp similar to the submit_assignments.asp script in the SiteGalaxy Upload section.

5. Test the application with your browser.

CASE PROJECTS

1. WHTV Channel 4 has hired you to create an application that allows you to report the daily temperature. A form should request the date of the temperature reading and the temperature, and then save this information to a file. The application should also create a temperature report for all entries in the file and indicate the average temperature.

2. Dr. Charles Way, a dentist, sends his clients a coupon for a free dinner on their birthdays. He has hired you to create a Web application that accepts the customer name, address, and birthday as input, and then saves this data to a file. In addition, the application should create coupons for all customers in the file when requested.

3. The inventory manager at Shoppers, Inc. has hired you to create a Web application that will calculate the average price of all the items in inventory. This application should require the user to enter the inventory number, the quantity in stock, and the price for each item in inventory. The application should then save this data to a file. The application should also include a display average link that displays the average price when clicked.

5

SQL AND DATABASES FOR DATA-DRIVEN APPLICATIONS

> **In this chapter, you will:**
> - Learn why ASP programmers need to write code that interacts with databases
> - Learn about the DBMSs in the industry
> - Learn how a database structure is created
> - Create a Web application to interact with a database
> - Query a database with SQL
> - Learn the intricacies of the SELECT statement
> - Learn how the INSERT, UPDATE, and DELETE statements work in SQL

In this chapter, and in Chapter 6, you will become very proficient in using, manipulating, and adapting databases to your own uses. In this chapter, you will learn how SQL allows your code to tread a "path" from a client to a server to a database, and then back again. In Chapter 6, you will learn how to prepare that path for other programmers.

DATABASE OVERVIEW

In this section, you will learn the background of databases. To begin the process, we will orient you to the database "players" in the market today so that you can understand the benefits and limitations each brings to the ASP programmer. Then, we'll review basic database concepts.

The DBMSs in the Industry

The term **database management system (DBMS)** refers to any database product, including Access and SQL Server by Microsoft, and Oracle by the Oracle Corporation. A DBMS provides storage functionality (that is, a means for storing data on a computer), as well as query, form, and report functionality.

You can interact with most databases using a standard language—SQL. At the same time, you should keep in mind that the various databases available today do have their own little quirks; you will learn about these details when using the database system itself. This book will focus on three DBMSs: Access, SQL Server, and Oracle.

Microsoft Access is a personal DBMS used for small databases (less than 1 GB). Access is designed for use on client and server computers. However, when run on a server, it does not offer the processing power of SQL Server and Oracle because it does not run as a separate application. Instead, Access runs on the client and accesses the database on the server, as any application would access a file.

For large databases that require 24-hours-a-day, 7-days-a-week access by many people, SQL Server and Oracle are the more appropriate choices. These products can accommodate extremely large databases that can span **terabytes** of disk storage. SQL Server and Oracle are also client/server database management systems, designed specifically to run on a database server. To the ASP programmer, this means that most commercial Web applications will be created with Oracle or SQL Server.

You need to consider the following when choosing a DBMS:

- **Volume of data**: The right choice depends on your present and future storage requirements. When they are first installed, most DBMSs store no data. However, keep in mind that in some situations existing data must be converted for use with the new DBMS. In that case, you need to consider the amount of storage and the size of the old database. And of course you need to consider how your storage requirements will change over time. For databases that will remain relatively small, choose Access. Choose SQL Server or Oracle for large databases.

- **Number of transactions per time increment**: If many users must access the database at the same time, and each user must perform numerous transactions, then SQL Server or Oracle is the perfect choice. If you expect only a couple of users with very few transactions, then Access is best. Again, be sure to consider how your needs might change in the future before making your choice.

- **Number of users and number of connections or sessions**: You need to consider the number of users who will be accessing the system. For systems serving a high number of users, choose SQL Server or Oracle. Otherwise, choose Access.

- **Extensibility requirements**: In the world of databases, the term **extensibility** refers to the ability of a system to grow to meet the needs of the user. Both SQL Server and Oracle can expand from small databases to extremely large databases. However, if you know that your database will not grow at all, then Access is a good choice.

- **Reporting requirements**: If you need to run lots of reports on a system quickly, then SQL Server or Oracle is your choice. If you only have to run a few reports occasionally, then Access is an acceptable choice.

Choosing the wrong DBMS puts your entire project at risk. Because Access is readily available as part of Microsoft Office (and so involves no additional cost), many developers choose Access when they really should use Oracle or SQL Server. However, they will pay in the end if they choose Access and then find that any of the considerations discussed in the preceding list change.

Because most readers are likely to have access to Microsoft Office 2000, this chapter will illustrate its concepts via Microsoft Access 2000. However, this book's coverage of Microsoft Access 2000 will be very limited and will only present enough information to allow you to use its most basic features. Because the basic structure of databases is similar, however, even this basic instruction will allow you to apply what you learn in this chapter to other large-scale DBMSs, such as SQL Server and Oracle.

Database Concepts

In this book, it is assumed that you are already familiar with the basic concepts related to databases. The following sections review those concepts. They are not intended as an exhaustive introduction to databases; if you must investigate databases extensively, you need to take a class devoted exclusively to databases or review an appropriate text.

Tables, Rows, and Columns

A **database** is a collection of information organized into tables. A **table** is a two-dimensional structure made up of rows and columns. Figure 5-1 illustrates the database that stores the following information: contact information for instructors, contact information for students, general class schedule information, and class schedule information for individual students. This information is organized into five tables:

- INSTRUCTORS: Contains contact information for each instructor

- STUDENTS: Contains contact information for each student

- CLASSES: Contains class information for each class

- CLASS_SCHEDULES: Contains a list of all available classes

- STUDENT_SCHEDULES: Contains a list of registered classes for each student

TABLE NAME	FIELD NAME
INSTRUCTORS	INSTRUCTOR_ID
	FIRST_NAME
	LAST_NAME
	PHONE_NUMBER
	E-MAIL
	WEB_ADDRESS
STUDENTS	STUDENT_ID
	FIRST_NAME
	LAST_NAME
	HOME_PHONE
	WORK_PHONE
	E_MAIL
CLASS_SCHEDULES	CLASS_SCHEDULE_ID
	TERM
	YEAR
	SECTION
	CLASS_ID, STUDENT_ID
STUDENT_SCHEDULES	STUDENT_SCHEDULE_ID
	STUDENT_ID,
	CLASS_SCHEDULE_ID

Figure 5-1   Structure of a database

Figure 5-1 shows columns (or fields) in each table. A **column** (or **field**) is a category of data. For instance, the INSTRUCTORS table includes the INSTRUCTOR_ID field, the LAST_NAME field, the FIRST_NAME field, and so on. A **row** or **record** is a set of columns or a collection of related data items. For example, one row of the STUDENTS table might be {1 Keith, Morneau, 7033232197, 7033232197, kmorneau@nv.cc.va.us }.

Relational Databases and Keys

A **primary key** is a column that contains information that uniquely identifies each row in a table. Typically, a key contains an identification number, or some other value that is unique for each row. For instance, in Figure 5-1, the INSTRUCTOR_ID column is the key for the INSTRUCTORS table.

The term **relational database** refers to databases made up of multiple tables, which are linked, or related, to one another by common columns. (The database in Figure 5-1 is actually a relational database.) You can search for information in a relational database by using information in one table's primary key to find information in another table. A **foreign key** is a column in one table that corresponds to a primary key in another table. In order for you to search for information in a database, the primary key of one table must match a foreign key in another table.

To understand how this all works, let's look at Figure 5-2. The INSTRUCTORS table is linked to the CLASS_SCHEDULES table by the common column INSTRUCTOR_ID. Note that the INSTRUCTOR_ID column is the primary key for the INSTRUCTORS table. When it appears in the CLASS_SCHEDULES table, it is considered a foreign key.

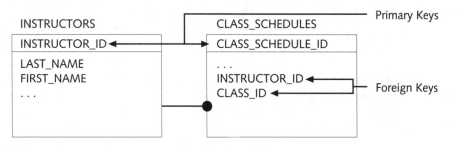

Figure 5-2   Primary keys and foreign keys

Keep in mind that data inserted into a primary key column must be unique. For instance, in the INSTRUCTORS table, each entry into the INSTRUCTOR_ID column must be unique. The first record entered into this database might have an INSTRUCTOR_ID of 1. The second instructor would have an INSTRUCTOR_ID of 2, and so on. The fact that each record has one unique field makes it much faster and easier to retrieve data from a table.

Not everyone agrees on how to create a primary key in a table. Some experts argue that a primary key can consist of more than one column, just as long as the two columns together make a row unique. For example, in the INSTRUCTORS table, LAST_NAME and FIRST_NAME could be the primary key. Such a scenario can be problematic if, for instance, two students happen to have the same name, or if a student changes his or her name. If the latter occurred, you would have to update every row that contained the student's old last name. In a large database, such updates could be time-consuming.

For simplicity's sake, then, a primary key typically uses a number counter that increments by one each time a new row is created in a table. Why a number? A number processes faster than an alphanumeric character. In large tables, this will make a difference. This number is arbitrary—not at all related to the table itself; therefore, unlike a field such as LAST_NAME, it won't have to be changed to reflect a change of data. By convention, a primary key name should consist of the table name (singular) with an underscore and ID. This will make it easy for you to identify the keys in your database.

Relationships

Tables within a database can have several different types of relationships:

- **One-to-One Relationship:** A relationship in which one row in one table has one (and only one) matching row in another table. The term **match** refers to the connection between the primary key and foreign key columns of two tables. You will not see many of these relationships in your database designs. For example, if a student could only register for one class at a time, this would be an example of a one-to-one relationship, represented by a straight line on a diagram, as shown in Figure 5-3.

- **One-to-Many Relationship:** A relationship in which a row in one table has many matching rows in a second table. At the same time, the second table matches only one row of the first table. For example, a student can register for one or more of the classes listed in the CLASS_SCHEDULES, as shown in Figure 5-3. Realistically, a student can register for many classes. This means that a row in the STUDENTS table will match up to many rows of the STUDENT_SCHEDULES table. (The solid circle end of the line represents the many part of the relationship.)

- **Many-to-Many Relationship:** A relationship in which one row in the first table matches many rows in the second table, and one row in the second table matches many rows in the first table. For example, a student can register for many classes. A class can have many students. You would need to put a foreign key of STUDENT_ID in the CLASSES table and a foreign key of CLASS_ID in the STUDENTS table for this relationship. If you do this, you create a circular reference between STUDENTS and CLASSES. A row of one table matches a row of a second table, and a row of the second table matches a row of the first table. Well, the student in the STUDENTS table can only occur once, and the class data can only occur in the CLASSES table once. The problem is that each table would need to duplicate student and class data more than once, which cannot be done. Therefore, a many-to-many relationship is not allowed in relational databases and will not be discussed further in this chapter.

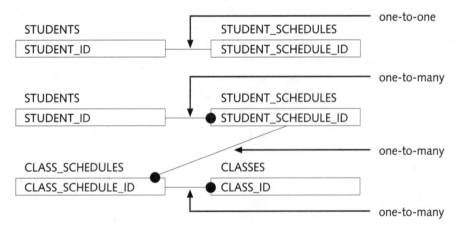

Figure 5-3 Relationships

Data Types

Each column in a database is assigned a particular type of data. For example, the LAST_NAME column of the STUDENTS table might have a data type of text with a size of 70 characters. Table 5-1 summarizes all the available data types for Microsoft Access, their uses, and their storage sizes.

Table 5-1   Data Types in Microsoft Access

Data Type	Uses
Text	Text or combinations of text and numbers, such as names, addresses, and phone numbers. Can be up to 255 characters, with each character equal to one byte. The FieldSize property determines the size of the field.
Memo	Lengthy text and numbers, such as notes or descriptions. Can be up to 64,000 characters (or bytes).
Number	Numeric data except for money (which requires the Currency type). The FieldSize property determines the specific Number type, which can be 1, 2, 4, or 8 bytes. Use the long (4 bytes) FieldSize for foreign keys.
Date/Time	Dates and times. The size is 8 bytes.
Currency	Currency values and money. Used to avoid rounding off errors during calculations. This data type is accurate to 15 digits to the left of the decimal point and 4 digits to the right. The size is 8 bytes.
AutoNumber	Primary keys, which require a one-up counter. The size is 4 bytes.
Yes/No	Fields that will contain only one of two values, such as Yes/No, True/False, or On/Off. The size is 1 bit.
OLE object	Objects like Microsoft Word, Microsoft Excel, pictures, sounds, or other binary data

Assigning data types is the most important decision you will make when designing a database application. If you choose the wrong data type or field size, the system will be sluggish and you'll waste disk space. For small databases, this is not an issue. But, for a medium-sized to large database, the poor performance will be noticeable to you and your users. We'll discuss this in more detail in Chapter 7.

 In this book, table and column names are given in all capital letters. Note that table names should always be plural, to reflect the fact that they contain multiple rows and columns of data.

DESIGNING A DATABASE STRUCTURE

New programmers find that examining the structure of an already-created database is a useful learning tool. It grounds them in the details of the end result and gives them the big picture; this is the basis for many learning experiences. For instance, most of us as children encountered books—how they looked, the components of them, and how more experienced readers used them—long before we understood their intricacies. The same learning structure transfers smoothly to the realm of databases: now that you've seen a final database structure and its logic, it's time to figure out how both came to be.

The following steps allowed one of the authors of this book to create the database that has been discussed so far in this chapter:

1. In this book, table and column names are given in all capital letters. It's most efficient to create a diagram in the form of an **ERD (entity relationship diagram)**. In an ERD, each table is represented by a box, with the table's name over the top (e.g., INSTRUCTORS in Figure 5-1). The rectangle at the top of the box lists the primary key and the primary key's data type (e.g., INSTRUCTOR_ID, for the INSTRUCTORS table in Figure 5-1). The remainder of the box contains the table's columns and data types.

2. Eliminate redundant information and other problems with database design, a process known as **normalizing** the data. There are three stages to normalizing data. The three stages are:

   - **First Normal Form**: All columns in the table contain atomic values—that is, each field contains only one item of data. For example, a FULL_NAME column name would actually contain two items of data—a first name and a last name. To normalize a FULL_NAME column, you would break it into two columns, a FIRST_NAME column and a LAST_NAME column.

   - **Second Normal Form**: The table is in first normal form and every column in the table depends on the entire primary key, not just part of the key. Achieving second normal form is problematic in tables in which the primary key is made up of more than one column. For instance, suppose a table consists of FIRST_NAME, LAST_NAME, and PHONE_NUMBER columns, and that the primary key is composed of the FIRST_NAME and LAST_NAME columns. Because many people share the same first or last name, such a table would be likely to contain records in which part of the primary key was not unique. (That is, some records might contain identical entries in the FIRST_NAME field, while others might contain identical entires in the LAST_NAME field.) One way to eliminate this problem (that is, to normalize the data) is to add a second phone column (such as a WORK_PHONE column) to the table.

   - **Third Normal Form**: A table is in second normal form and every column in the table depends on the entire primary key, and none of the non-key columns depend on each other. For example, let's say you create a table that contains FIRST_NAME, LAST_NAME, JOB_TITLE, and PAY_RATE columns. Suppose that LAST_NAME and FIRST_NAME are primary keys, and that your company pay rates depend on job titles. Currently, this table depends upon FIRST_NAME and LAST_NAME, not JOB_TITLE. This table would be a problem because PAY_RATE depends upon the JOB_TITLE. To normalize the data in this table, you would need to create a table of job titles and pay rates that depended upon the job title column. In addition, you would need to create a table that listed all the company's employees, that connected to the job titles and pay rates table. After creating these new tables, you could update an employee's salary simply by changing that employee's job title.

3. Evaluate your normalization and consider **denormalizing**—that is, keeping redundant data in your database structure. Keeping redundant data is sometimes preferable to completely normalizing data, because normalizing often results in creating additional tables and relationships between tables, which can cause the database to perform sluggishly.

4. Create relationships between the tables in the database structure, as described earlier in this chapter.

5. Create any constraints needed on the columns in your database structure. A **constraint** is a rule governing the contents of a column. For instance, you might specify that a LAST_NAME column cannot contain a blank value. In any DBMS, a NULL in a column means that field is empty.

Table 5-2 illustrates the database structure for the class-tracking application in this chapter, as it would be implemented in Microsoft Access. Keep in mind that in a different DBMS, the database structure would differ.

Table 5-2   Microsoft Access Database Design with Constraints

Table Name	Field Name	Data Type	Field Size	Constraint
INSTRUCTORS	INSTRUCTOR_ID	AUTO-NUMBER	LONG INTEGER	NOT NULL (cannot be blank)
	FIRST_NAME	TEXT	35	NOT NULL
	LAST_NAME	TEXT	35	NOT NULL
	PHONE_NUMBER	TEXT	10	NOT NULL
	E-MAIL	TEXT	255	
	WEB_ADDRESS	TEXT	255	
STUDENTS	STUDENT_ID	AUTO-NUMBER	LONG INTEGER	NOT NULL
	FIRST_NAME	TEXT	35	NOT NULL
	LAST_NAME	TEXT	35	NOT NULL
	HOME_PHONE	TEXT	10	EITHER PHONE NUMBER MUST BE FILLED IN

Table 5-2   Microsoft Access Database Design with Constraints (continued)

Table Name	Field Name	Data Type	Field Size	Constraint
STUDENTS (continued)	WORK_PHONE	TEXT	10	EITHER PHONE NUMBER MUST BE FILLED IN
	E_MAIL	TEXT	255	
CLASS_SCHEDULES	CLASS_SCHEDULE_ID	AUTO-NUMBER	LONG INTEGER	NOT NULL
	TERM	TEXT	10	NOT NULL
	YEAR	TEXT	4	NOT NULL
	SECTION	TEXT	10	NOT NULL
	CLASS_ID, STUDENT_ID	NUMBER	LONG INTEGER	NOT NULL
STUDENT_SCHEDULES	STUDENT_SCHEDULE_ID	AUTO-NUMBER	LONG INTEGER	NOT NULL
	STUDENT_ID, CLASS_SCHEDULE_ID	NUMBER	LONG INTEGER	NOT NULL

After designing the database structure, the programmer can then actually begin creating it in a DBMS. In this book it is assumed that you already know the basics of creating a database in Access. Specifically, you should know how to create tables and columns, and how to insert, update, and delete data. If you need further review, visit *www.course.com* to search for a book appropriate to your level of interest.

CREATING THE WEB APPLICATION TO INTERACT WITH THE DATABASE

Now to the fun part—creating a Web application that will interact with the Microsoft Access Database that has been provided on your Data Disk. Once we create the application—which will allow you to make a simple request to view data—we will develop the SQL code that will allow your Web application to fully interact with the database.

 Yes, we know that you could simply open the database in Access and manipulate it within the Access application; however, that isn't nearly as clever as doing it via SQL. Besides, aren't you reading this book to become adept at creating Web applications?

To create the SQL Web application:

1. Go to PWS and prepare a virtual directory named **Chapter_5** that corresponds to the Chapter_5 folder on your Data Disk.

2. Open your text editor, type the following code, and save the file as **SQL.htm** in the Chapter_5 folder:

```
<html>
<head>
<title>SQL Entry Form</title>
</head>
<body>
<h1 align="center">SQL Entry Form</h1>
<form id="frmSQL" name="frmSQL" action="execute_sql.asp"
method="post">
<center><p><b>Enter an SQL Statement:</b></p></center>
<center><p><TEXTAREA id="txtSQL" name="txtSQL" COLS=40
ROWS=5></TEXTAREA><br>
<center><p><input id="cmdSubmit" name="cmdSubmit" type=
"submit" value="Execute">
<input id="cmdReset" name="cmdReset" type="reset" value=
"Reset"> </p>
</center>
</form>
</body>
</html>
```

3. Create a file called **execute_sql.asp** in the Chapter_5 folder of your Data Disk, using the following code:

```
<%@ Language=VBScript %>
<% Response.Buffer = True %>
<html>
<head>
<title>SQL Query Response</title>
<body>
<%
  Dim objRS,objConn
  Set objRS = Server.CreateObject("ADODB.Recordset")
  set objConn = Server.CreateObject("ADODB.Connection")
  If cstr(Request.Form("txtSQL"))="" Then
    Response.Write("<CENTER><H3>WARNING!</H3>")
    Response.Write("<P>You must enter a query to run!" &_
"</CENTER>")
    Response.End
  Else
    objConn.Open "DRIVER={Microsoft Access Driver (*.mdb)};
    " &_
"DBQ=" & server.mappath("/Chapter_5") & "\" & "Course.mdb"
      '"PROVIDER=MSDASQL;DRIVER={SQL Server};SERVER=NOVASMS;
      'DATABASE=ctis;UID=kmorneau;PWD=Tpwivetr"
    set objRS = objConn.Execute(" "&_
cstr(Request.Form("txtSQL")),intRecordsAffected)
    if intRecordsAffected < 0 Then
    objRS.MoveFirst %>
    <CENTER><H2>SQL Query Response</H2>
```

```
            <b>SQL Statement:</b> <%=cstr(Request.Form("txtSQL"))%>
      <p>
            <TABLE BORDER=1 COLS=<%=objRS.Fields.Count%>>
              <TR>
                <% For each objField in objRS.Fields %>
                  <TH> <%=objField.Name %> </TH>
                <% Next %>
              </TR>
             <% Do while Not objRS.EOF %>
               <TR>
                 <% For Each objField in objRS.Fields %>
                   <TD align=right>
                       <% If IsNull(objField) Then
                              Response.Write(" ")
                          else
                              Response.Write(objField.Value)
                          End If
                       %>
                          </TD>
                  <% Next
                     objRS.MoveNext %>
                  </TR>
             <% Loop %>
           </TABLE>
          <% objRS.close
             set objRS = Nothing
             end if
             Response.Write("<p>" & intRecordsAffected & " records
      affected!")
             Response.Write("<p>Return to <a href=sql.htm>SQL Entry
       Form</a>")
             End IF
          %>
      </CENTER>
      </body>
      </html>
```

4. Save your work, close the text editor, open your browser, and navigate to
   http://localhost/Chapter_5/sql.htm. Your screen should resemble Figure 5-4.

5. Type **SELECT * FROM STUDENTS** into the text box, and then click the
   Execute button. Your screen should resemble Figure 5-5.

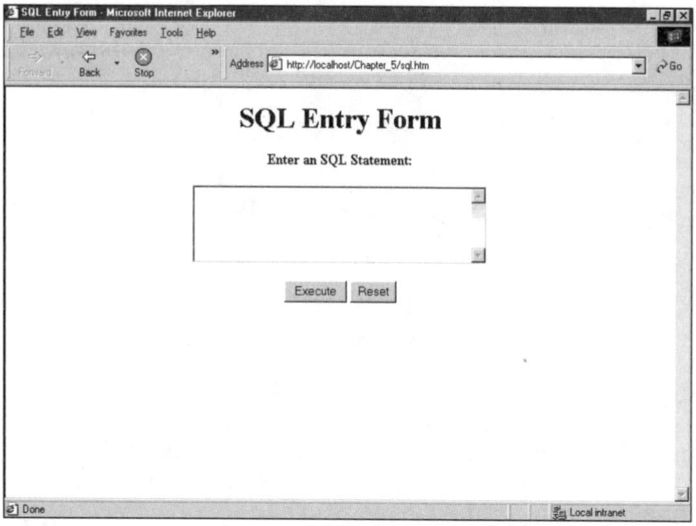

Figure 5-4 SQL Entry Form

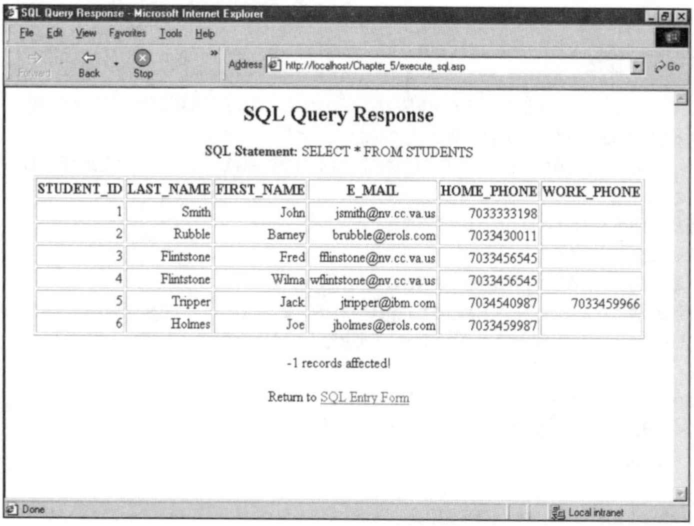

STUDENT_ID	LAST_NAME	FIRST_NAME	E_MAIL	HOME_PHONE	WORK_PHONE
1	Smith	John	jsmith@nv.cc.va.us	7033333198	
2	Rubble	Barney	brubble@erols.com	7033430011	
3	Flintstone	Fred	fflinstone@nv.cc.va.us	7033456545	
4	Flintstone	Wilma	wflintstone@nv.cc.va.us	7033456545	
5	Tripper	Jack	jtripper@ibm.com	7034540987	7033459966
6	Holmes	Joe	jholmes@erols.com	7033459987	

Figure 5-5 Query response

6. Click the **SQL Entry Form** link to bring you back to the SQL Entry Form.
7. Close your browser.

You have just created a Web application that made a selection from the database (the details of the selection will be covered in the next section of the chapter). For now, we'll review the essential concepts of the code:

Code Example

```
1 <%@ Language=VBScript %>
2 <% Response.Buffer = True %>
3 <html>
4 <head>
5 <title>SQL Query Response</title>
6 <body>
7 <%
8 Dim objRS,objConn
9 Set objRS = Server.CreateObject("ADODB.Recordset")
10 set objConn = Server.CreateObject("ADODB.Connection")
11
12 If cstr(Request.Form("txtSQL"))="" Then
13 Response.Write("<CENTER><H3>WARNING!</H3>")
14 Response.Write("<P>You must enter a query to run!</CENTER>")
15 Response.End
16 Else
17 objConn.Open "DRIVER={Microsoft Access Driver (*.mdb)}; DBQ="
& server.mappath("/Chapter_5") & "\" & "course.mdb"
18   '"PROVIDER=MSDASQL;DRIVER={SQL Server};SERVER=NOVASMS;
DATABASE=ctis;UID=kmorneau;PWD=Tpwivetr"
19   set objRS = objConn.Execute(cstr(Request.Form("txtSQL")),
intRecordsAffected)
20 if intRecordsAffected < 0 Then
21 objRS.MoveFirst %>
22 <CENTER><H2>SQL Query Response</H2>
23 <b>SQL Statement:</b> <%=cstr(Request.Form("txtSQL"))%><p>
24 <TABLE BORDER=1 COLS=<%=objRS.Fields.Count%>>
25  <TR>
26  <% For each objField in objRS.Fields %>
27        <TH> <%=objField.Name %> </TH>
28      <% Next %>
29    </TR>
30    <% Do while Not objRS.EOF %>
31     <TR>
32       <% For Each objField in objRS.Fields %>
33        <TD align=right>
34           <% If IsNull(objField) Then
35               Response.Write(" ")
36             else
37                Response.Write(objField.Value)
38             End If
39         %>
40            </TD>
41       <% Next
42           objRS.MoveNext %>
```

```
43            </TR>
44       <%  Loop %>
45       </TABLE>
46
47    <% objRS.close
48       set objRS = Nothing
49       end if
50       Response.Write("<p>" & intRecordsAffected & " records
affected!")
51       Response.Write("<p>Return to <a href=sql.htm>SQL Entry
Form</a>")
52    End IF
53     %>
54 </CENTER>
55 </body>
56 </html>
```

Code Dissection

- Lines 8 through 11 and lines 17 and 18 created an instance of the recordset and connection objects through ADO.

- Line 19 sent a query to the database, and a recordset was returned.

- Lines 21 through 46 manipulated the rows in the recordset.

- Line 47 and 48 closed the connection to the database.

Querying Databases with SQL

Well, we have our database, and we have a Web application to interact with the database. Now it's time to get a little fancy and learn how to fully manipulate the data.

SQL consists of commands that allow you to manipulate databases using a predefined syntax, or set of rules. In this part of the chapter, you will learn the details of the SELECT, INSERT, UPDATE, and DELETE statements. Each of these statements is a query in SQL.

SELECT Statement

The syntax of a basic SELECT statement is:

Syntax Example

SELECT	column_list
FROM	table_name
[WHERE	condition]
[ORDER BY	column_name **[DESC]]**

Syntax Dissection

- The column_list consists of the name of the columns you want to display in the query, separated by commas. Each column name should be preceded by the name of the table that contains it. So for example, you might include the following as a column_list: `INSTRUCTORS.LAST_NAME, INSTRUCTORS.FIRST_NAME`. Here, INSTRUCTORS is the table name and LAST_NAME is the column name.

- The table_name is a list of tables from which you want to retrieve data. The names of the tables should be separated by commas—for instance, `INSTRUCTORS, STUDENTS`.

- The condition is a statement that returns true or false, similar to an IFTHENELSE statement.

- The column_name specifies by which columns you want to sort the results. As with column_list, the column names should be separated by commas.

The order of the items in the SELECT statement is important, because a DBMS looks for clauses in a particular order. Specifically, the SELECT clause comes before the FROM clause, which comes before the WHERE clause. The items in brackets are optional. You use a WHERE clause when you only want to see rows that meet a specific condition. You use the ORDER BY clause when you want to sort the results of a query based on certain columns.

The simplest form of the SELECT statement would retrieve every row of a single table. However, such a SELECT statement is seldom used in real-world applications, except when testing a database. Nonetheless, studying an overview of the form is an excellent idea. Thus, consider the following example, which retrieves every row in the STUDENTS table:

Code Example

```
SELECT     *
FROM       STUDENTS
```

Code Dissection

- The column-list argument takes the form of an asterisk (*), which indicates that the query should select all columns in the table.

- The Table Name argument, in this case STUDENT, indicates the name of the table to be queried. The resulting query will return all rows from the STUDENTS table.

- Note that this example does not include the optional parts of the syntax.

This is the query that you ran in the previous section of the chapter. The SQL query you executed returned a results set in the form of an HTML table, and the column names appeared as titles in the table. The actual rows from the table were displayed in the table itself.

The SELECT Statement's Col-List Argument

A basic SELECT statement is useful in and of itself, and as a building block for more complicated SELECT statements that allow you to extract specific pieces of information from a database. For instance, you now have the knowledge to use the col-list argument of the SELECT clause, which will allow you to select the columns you want in your query.

Table 5-3 Using the Column-List Argument of the SELECT Clause

To do the following:	Use this code:
Return all columns and all rows in a table	SELECT * FROM STUDENTS
Return only certain columns in a table; for example, a query that displays all rows with only the LAST_NAME and FIRST_NAME columns from the STUDENTS table.	SELECT LAST_NAME,FIRST_NAME FROM STUDENTS;
Return only unique values within a column. Use the keyword DISTINCT to prevent duplicate data from displaying in the query.	SELECT DISTINCT LAST_NAME FROM STUDENTS;

The SELECT Statement's WHERE Clause

The SELECT statement has further functionality in that you can add a WHERE clause to a SELECT statement to define conditions that must be met before a row will be included in the query results. For example, you might add a WHERE clause that specifies that the query should return only records for students with a last name of Morneau. Because the WHERE clause must consist of a column with a comparison operator and a value, when the condition returns TRUE, the row belongs to the result set. Table 5-4 shows some sample WHERE clauses.

Table 5-4 Sample WHERE Clauses

Column	Comparison Operator	Value	Description
LAST_NAME	=	'Holmes'	Exact Match; equal to
POINTS_EARNED	>	50	Greater than
POINTS_EARNED	<	50	Less than
GRADE_DATE	<=	'10/30/98'	Less than or equal to
GRADE_DATE	>=	'10/30/98'	Greater than or equal to
LAST_NAME	<>	'Holmes'	Not equal to

Table 5-4   Sample WHERE Clauses (continued)

Column	Comparison Operator	Value	Description
MAX_POINTS * (WEIGHT/100)	=	20	Equal to
CLASS_NUMBER	IN	('CP 108','IST 208')	Equal to any member of the list
WORK_PHONE	IS	NULL	Is empty; has missing or no existing data
WORK_PHONE	IS NOT	NULL	Contains data; is not empty
CLASS_NUMBER	LIKE	'IST%' '%208'	The percent sign can match zero or more characters before or after. This will match all classes that have IST in the beginning of the string. It might match values such as IST 208, IST 220, and others. The second value contains 208 at the end of the string. It might match values such as IST 208, ESR 208, and others.
CLASS_NUMBER	LIKE	'IST 20_'	The underscore matches exactly one character. It might match values such as IST 208 and others.

When determining the values that your syntax will produce, remember the following:

- Characters should be surrounded by single quotation marks ('').
- SQL's string values are case sensitive, which means that 'John' and 'JOHN' are different values.
- Dates should be formatted in the dd/mm/yy format, such as '12/31/01'.
- Numbers (such as 10) should not be surrounded by quotation marks.
- Within a table, SQL evaluates the WHERE clause one row at a time. When the WHERE clause results in a true value, SQL copies the row to the results set.

Table 5-5 shows SELECT statements that include WHERE clauses:

Table 5-5   SELECT Statements Containing WHERE Clauses

Code	Function	Description
```SELECT *` `FROM STUDENTS` `WHERE STUDENT_ID > 1;```	greater than	This query displays all rows with STUDENT_ID greater than 1.
```SELECT *` `FROM STUDENTS` `WHERE STUDENT_ID = 1;```	equal to	This query displays a row with STUDENT_ID equal to 1.

Table 5-5 SELECT Statements Containing WHERE Clauses (continued)

Code	Function	Description

`SELECT  *`
`FROM STUDENTS`
`WHERE   STUDENT_ID IN (1,2);`
	IN	This query displays all rows with STUDENT_ID equal to 1 or 2.

`SELECT  *`
`FROM    STUDENTS`
`WHERE   STUDENT_ID = 1`
`OR      STUDENT_ID = 2;`
	Equal to and OR	The IN query could be rewritten to look like this.

5

To include multiple conditions in a WHERE clause, you must use a logical operator between conditions. You can use multiple conditions if the results you want must pass several rules to be included in the result set. Table 5-6 lists the logical operators and provides examples of how to use them.

Table 5-6 WHERE Clause Logical Operators

Operator	Function	Example

NOT	If condition returns TRUE, the NOT condition returns FALSE. If condition returns FALSE, the NOT condition returns TRUE.	`SELECT  *`
		`FROM     STUDENTS`
		`WHERE    WORK_PHONE IS NOT NULL;`

AND	If both conditions are TRUE, returns TRUE. Otherwise, it returns FALSE.	`SELECT  *`
		`FROM   STUDENTS`
		`WHERE   LAST_NAME = 'Smith'`
		`AND FIRST_NAME = 'John';`
		In this instance, the code returns all rows containing "John" in the FIRST_NAME field and "Smith" in the LAST_NAME field.

OR	If either condition is TRUE, returns TRUE. Otherwise, if both are FALSE, then returns FALSE.	`SELECT  *`
		`FROM   STUDENTS`
		`WHERE   LAST_NAME = 'Smith'`
		`OR`
		`FIRST_NAME = 'John';`
		In this instance, code returns any row containing either "John" in the FIRST_NAME field or "Smith" in the LAST_NAME field.

SELECT Statement's ORDER BY Clause

A SELECT query normally returns a results table with rows arranged randomly. To specify the order of the rows in the results table, you must use the ORDER BY clause. The ORDER BY clause sorts rows in a result set according to the contents of the column or groups of columns you specify, in either ascending or descending order.

For example, the following SELECT statement retrieves all rows containing "Smith" in the LAST NAME column, and then sorts these rows first by the contents of the LAST_NAME column and then by the contents of the FIRST_NAME column:

```
SELECT    LAST_NAME,FIRST_NAME
FROM      STUDENTS
WHERE     LAST_NAME = 'Smith'
ORDER BY  LAST_NAME, FIRST_NAME;
```

The preceding example sorted the returned records in ascending order (that is, in alphabetical order from A to Z, or numerically from lowest to highest). To sort records in descending order (from Z to A, or from highest to lowest), you need to use the DESC keyword in the ORDER BY clause. For example:

```
SELECT    LAST_NAME,FIRST_NAME
FROM      STUDENTS
WHERE     LAST_NAME = 'Smith'
ORDER BY  LAST_NAME DESC, FIRST_NAME DESC;
```

This query sorts records in reverse alphabetical order, first by the contents of the LAST_NAME column and then by the FIRST_NAME column.

Using Aggregate Functions in SELECT Statements

An **aggregate** function returns a single row containing the result of mathematical computation. You can incorporate aggregate functions into a SELECT statement in order to analyze data in a results table mathematically. For example, you might use an aggregate function to find the number of students in the STUDENTS table. The most common aggregate functions are listed in Table 5-7.

Table 5-7   Sample Aggregate Functions

Function	Description	Example

AVG(column_name)	Averages the values in a column	`SELECT    AVG(POINTS_EARNED)`
		`FROM      GRADES;`
		Returns the average of all grades in the POINTS_EARNED column of the GRADES table

COUNT(column_name)	Counts the values in a column	`SELECT    COUNT(*)`
		`FROM      STUDENTS;`
		Returns the number of rows in the STUDENTS table

MAX(column_name)	Finds the largest value in a column	`SELECT    MAX(POINTS_EARNED)`
		`FROM      GRADES;`
		Returns the highest grade in the POINTS_EARNED column of the GRADES table

Table 5-7   Sample Aggregate Functions (continued)

Function	Description	Example
MIN(column_name)	Finds the smallest value in a column	`SELECT   MIN(POINTS_EARNED)` `FROM      GRADES;` Returns the lowest grade in the POINTS_EARNED column of the GRADES table
SUM(column_name)	Totals the column	`SELECT   SUM(POINTS_EARNED)` `FROM      GRADES;` Returns the sum of all grades in the POINTS_EARNED column of the GRADES table

5

Note that when you use a function in a query, the columns in the results set are not titled. To make your results set easier to interpret, you can use an **alias**, a special name used in place of a column name when the query returns, to give an explicit name to a column. For example:

```
SELECT   COUNT(*) AS NUM_STUDENTS FROM STUDENTS
```

This query counts the number of rows in the STUDENTS table and displays this number in a results table, in a column named NUM_STUDENTS.

Joining with SELECT Statements

The SELECT statement is limited in that it does not allow you to query more than one table at a time. Thus, alone, it would keep you from finding out which instructor teaches CP 108. Why? Well, to find out this information, you would need to write a query that retrieves the LAST_NAME and FIRST_NAME information from the INSTRUCTORS table, and the CLASS_NUMBER information from the CLASSES table. At the same time, you would need to check the CLASS_SCHEDULES table to see who teaches CP 108. Obviously, this scenario requires you to query more than one table. Fortunately, SQL does provide a solution: you can query, or **connect**, the multiple tables by using a **join** condition.

You add the join condition in the WHERE clause. For instance, if we go back to our database discussion at the beginning of the chapter, you could specify that the primary key (CLASS_ID) in the CLASSES table be equal to the foreign key (CLASS_ID) in the CLASS_SCHEDULES table, and that the foreign key (INSTRUCTOR_ID) in the CLASS_SCHEDULES table be equal to the primary key (INSTRUCTOR_ID) in the INSTRUCTORS table. The following example shows how to write such a query:

Code Example

```
SELECT   CLASS_NUMBER,LAST_NAME,FIRST_NAME
FROM     CLASSES AS CLS,CLASS_SCHEDULES AS CS, INSTRUCTORS INS
WHERE    CLS.CLASS_ID = CS.CLASS_ID
         AND CS.INSTRUCTOR_ID = INS.INSTRUCTOR_ID
         AND CLS.CLASS_NUMBER = 'CP 108';
```

Code Dissection

- The FROM clause should specify all the tables you want to query.

- The WHERE clause must indicate which columns in the tables are identical. The column name to the left of the equal sign should be the primary key of the first table listed in the FROM clause. The column name to the right of the equal sign should be the foreign key of the next table in the FROM clause. The same applies for the second condition after the AND for the next two tables in the FROM clause.

- For a three-table join, you need two join conditions, one for the CLASSES and CLASS_SCHEDULES and the other for the CLASS_SCHEDULES and INSTRUCTORS. The last condition after the second AND requests only CP 108 information. The number of join conditions needed is one less than the number of tables to join.

INSERT Statement

Now that you have reviewed how to use a SELECT statement to display data stored in one or more tables in the form of a results set, you need to learn how to use the INSERT statement in order to add records to a table. The syntax of SQL's INSERT statement is:

Code Example

```
INSERT INTO table-name[(col-list)]

VALUES      (value-list)
```

Code Dissection

- The table-name argument specifies the table into which you want to insert data.

- The column list (col-list) argument specifies the columns into which you want to enter data.

- The value list (value-list) specifies the values you want to insert into the columns listed in the col-list argument.

The following example shows the use of an INSERT statement:

```
INSERT INTO INSTRUCTORS(LAST_NAME,
                        FIRST_NAME,
                        PHONE_NUMBER,
                        E_MAIL,
                        WEB_ADDRESS)
VALUES                  ('Baker',
                         'Vinny',
                         '7033332222',
                         'vbaker@erols.com',
                         'http://www.erols.com/vbaker')
```

You will notice in this example that all columns are listed except the primary key, since the primary key is a counter. The database increments by one any column that is a counter, automatically, by default.

Now it is time to experiment with this code.

To insert data into the INSTRUCTORS table:

1. Start your browser.

2. In the address field, type **http://localhost/Chapter_5/sql.htm**, and then press **Enter**.

3. In the text box, type:

```
INSERT INTO INSTRUCTORS(LAST_NAME,
                        FIRST_NAME,
                        PHONE_NUMBER,
                        E_MAIL,
                        WEB_ADDRESS)
VALUES                  ('Baker',
                         'Vinny',
                         '7033332222',
                         'vbaker@erols.com',
                         'http://www.erols.com/vbaker')
```

4. Click the **Execute** button.

5. Your screen should resemble Figure 5-6, indicating that you inserted one record into the database.

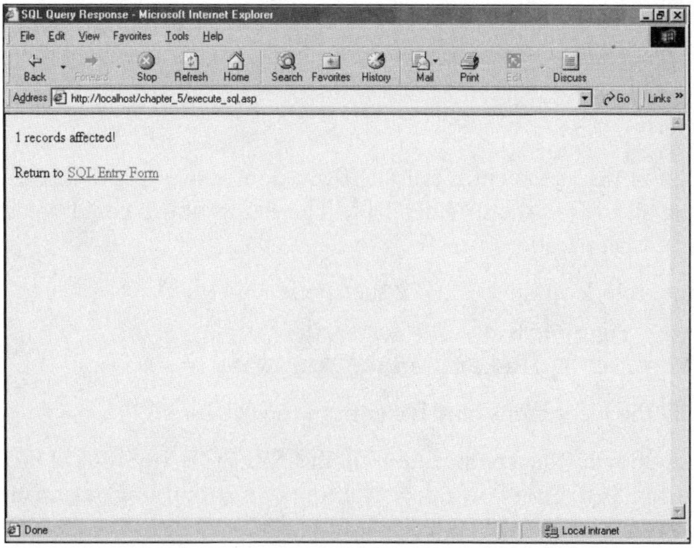

Figure 5-6   Successful insertion of data

6. Close your browser.

UPDATE Statement

In most databases, you need to use the UPDATE SQL statement to modify data already entered into a table. The syntax for the UPDATE statement is:

Code Example

```
UPDATE table-name
SET col-name = new-value, col-name = new-value …
[WHERE condition]
```

Code Dissection

- The column name (col-name) argument allows you to specify the column you want to update.

- The new value (new-value) argument is the new value you want to insert into that column.

The WHERE clause in an UPDATE statement allows you to filter the row or rows you want to update. If you do not supply a WHERE clause, then all rows will be affected. For example, the following code changes the current phone number of instructor 'Vinny Baker' to a new number:

```
UPDATE INSTRUCTORS
SET PHONE_NUMBER = '7033233333'
WHERE LAST_NAME = 'Baker' AND FIRST_NAME = 'Vinny'
```

DELETE Statement

To remove a row from a table in a database you use the DELETE statement, as follows:

```
DELETE FROM table-name
[WHERE condition]
```

The WHERE clause in this statement is crucial. If you do not supply a WHERE clause, the statement will delete all rows in the specified table. The results of this could be drastic, especially in mission-critical applications.

The following is an example of the DELETE statement:

```
DELETE FROM INSTRUCTORS
WHERE LAST_NAME = 'Baker' and FIRST_NAME = 'Vinny'
```

This will delete only the record for Vinny Baker from the database.

As this chapter has shown, the combination of the SELECT, INSERT, UPDATE, and DELETE statements in SQL gives you a powerful way of manipulating data in any database that supports SQL.

CHAPTER SUMMARY

- ◻ Web applications achieve their highest value when they permit you to create, update, delete, and query data in databases. The term "database management system" (DBMS) refers to any database product, including Access, SQL Server, and Oracle. A DBMS provides storage functionality, as well as query, form, and report functionality. When choosing a DBMS, you must consider the volume of data, the number of transactions per time increment, the number of users, the reporting requirements, and the extensibility requirements of the project.

- ◻ A database is a collection of information organized into tables. A table is a two-dimensional structure made up of rows and columns. A primary key is a column that contains information that uniquely identifies each row in a table. Typically, a key contains an identification number, or some other value that is unique for each row. The term "relational database" refers to databases made up of multiple tables, which are linked, or related, to one another by common columns.

- ◻ In a one-to-one relationship, one row in one table has one (and only one) matching row in another table. In a one-to-many relationship, a row in one table has many matching rows in a second table. In a many-to-many relationship, one row in the first table matches many rows in the second table, and one row in the second table matches many rows in the first table.

- ◻ Each column in a database is assigned a particular type of data. Assigning data types is the most important decision you will make when designing database applications. In this book, table and column names are given in all capital letters.

- ◻ To create a database, you must do the following:
  1. In this book, verify that the table and column names are in all capital letters.
  2. Perform the three stages of normalization.
  3. Evaluate your normalization and consider denormalizing.
  4. Create relationships between the tables in the database structure.
  5. Create any constraints needed on the columns in your database structure.

- ◻ SQL consists of commands that allow you to manipulate databases using a predefined syntax, or set of rules. In this chapter, you learned the details of the SELECT, INSERT, UPDATE, and DELETE statements. Each of these statements is a query in SQL.

REVIEW QUESTIONS

1. The _____ supplies the necessary functionality to insert, update, delete, and query information in a database.
   - a. DBMS
   - b. presentation logic
   - c. application logic
   - d. business logic

2. A(n) _____ is an organized collection of information.
   a. object
   b. database
   c. class
   d. service

3. A(n) _____ is a two-dimensional structure made up of rows and columns.
   a. relation
   b. database
   c. attribute
   d. service

4. A(n) _____ is a basic fact such as LAST_NAME, FIRST_NAME, and E_MAIL.
   a. field
   b. relation
   c. attributes
   d. services

5. A(n) _____ uniquely identifies each row in a table.
   a. field
   b. relation
   c. key
   d. entity

6. _____ ensure that each row in a table is unique.
   a. Fields
   b. Primary keys
   c. Foreign keys
   d. Columns

7. A _____ is a column of one table that corresponds to a primary key in another table.
   a. Field
   b. Primary Key
   c. Foreign Key
   d. Column

8. _____ is the process of eliminating redundant information and other problems from a database design.
   a. Normalization
   b. Removal
   c. Normal
   d. None of the above

9. _____ consists of commands that allow you to manipulate databases.

  a. Sequel

  b. MINDATA

  c. SQL

  d. SLL

10. A(n) _____ statement allows you to retrieve data from one or more tables.

  a. SELECT

  b. INSERT

  c. UPDATE

  d. DELETE

11. Which clause in a SELECT statement allows you to filter rows in one or more tables?

  a. WHERE

  b. GROUP BY

  c. ORDER BY

  d. SELECT

12. Which clause in a SELECT statement allows you to sort rows in one or more tables?

  a. WHERE

  b. HAVING

  c. ORDER BY

  d. SELECT

13. In ASP, you can use a SELECT statement to select the columns you want displayed in a results set. True or False?

14. The wildcard character in SQL that allows you to view all columns in a table is _____.

  a. *

  b. &

  c. ^

  d. !

15. 'John' is the same as 'JOHN' in SQL. True or False?

16. What are the valid logical operators in SQL? (Choose all that apply)

  a. AND

  b. OR

  c. NOT

  d. XOR

17. Which of the following are valid aggregate functions? (Choose all that apply.)

    a. ISNULL

    b. AVG

    c. COUNT

    d. UCASE

18. A(n) _____ statement in SQL allows you to add data to a table.

    a. INSERT

    b. UPDATE

    c. DELETE

    d. SELECT

19. A(n) _____ statement in SQL allows you to modify data in a table.

    a. INSERT

    b. UPDATE

    c. DELETE

    d. SELECT

20. A(n) _____ statement in SQL allows you to remove data from a table.

    a. INSERT

    b. UPDATE

    c. DELETE

    d. SELECT

HANDS-ON PROJECTS

Project 5-1

Using the SQL Web application created in this chapter, create and run the following simple queries.

1. A query that returns only the student's name and home phone number:

    a. Open your browser, and navigate to *http://localhost/Chapter_5/sql.htm*.

    b. Enter SELECT LAST_NAME,FIRST_NAME,HOME_PHONE FROM STUDENTS in the Enter the SQL Statement text box, and then click the Execute button. Your screen should resemble Figure 5-7.

    c. Click the SQL Entry Form link to bring you back to the form.

2. A query that returns only the student's name and e-mail address:

    a. Enter SELECT LAST_NAME,FIRST_NAME,E_MAIL FROM STUDENTS in the Enter the SQL Statement text box, and then click the Execute button. Your screen should resemble Figure 5-8.

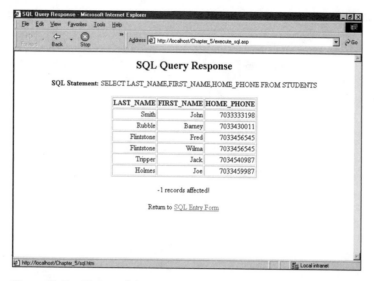

Figure 5-7   Successful query

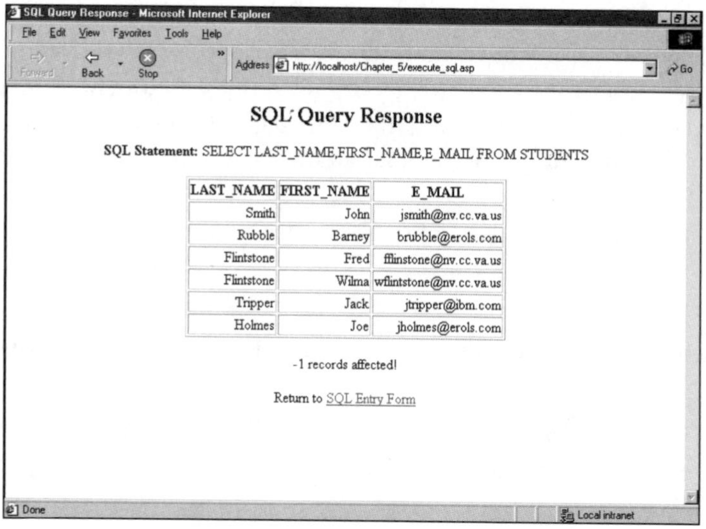

Figure 5-8   Successful query II

    b. Click the SQL Entry Form link to bring you back to the form.

3. A query that returns any student with the last name of Smith:

    a. Enter SELECT * FROM STUDENTS WHERE LAST_NAME = 'Smith' in the text box, and then click the Execute button. Your screen should resemble Figure 5-9.

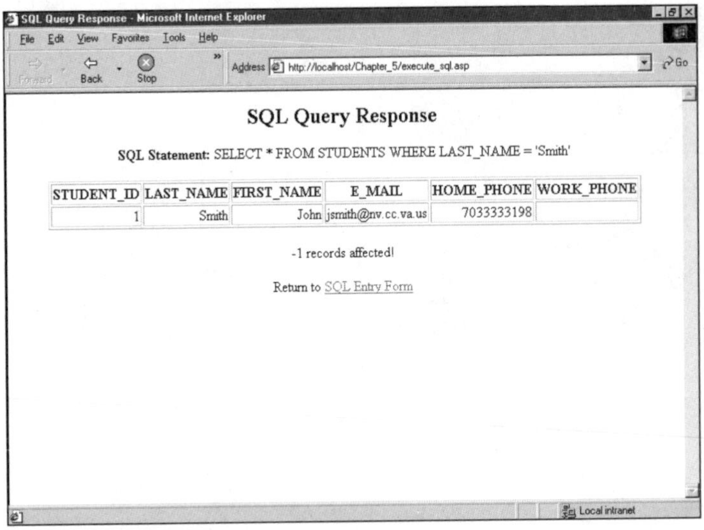

Figure 5-9 Successful query III

  b. Click the SQL Entry Form link to bring you back to the form.

  4. A query that returns anyone with either the first name of John or the last name of Smith:

  a. Enter SELECT * FROM STUDENTS WHERE FIRST_NAME = 'John' AND LAST_NAME = 'Smith' in the Enter the SQL Statement text box and then click the Execute button. Your query will result in the appropriate information being displayed on your browser.

  b. Click the SQL Entry Form link to bring you back to the form.

Project 5-2

Using the SQL Web application created in this chapter, create and run the following complex queries.

  1. A query that returns what each instructor is teaching in the Fall of 1999:

  a. Enter the following in the SQL Statement text box, and then click the Execute button:

```
SELECT    LAST_NAME, FIRST_NAME, CLASS_NUMBER,
          CLASS_NAME
FROM      CLASS_SCHEDULES,
          CLASSES, INSTRUCTORS
WHERE     CLASS_SCHEDULES.CLASS_ID =
          CLASSES.CLASS_ID AND
          CLASS_SCHEDULES.INSTRUCTOR_ID =
          INSTRUCTORS.INSTRUCTOR_ID AND
          TERM = 'Fall' AND YEAR = '1999'
```

  b. Click the SQL Entry Form link to bring you back to the form.

2. A query that returns the classes a student has registered for in Fall of 1999 and shows only the student's name and the class name:

a. Type the following in the Enter the SQL Statement text box, and then click the Execute button:

```
SELECT      LAST_NAME, FIRST_NAME,
            CLASS_NAME
FROM        CLASS_SCHEDULES,
            CLASSES, STUDENT_SCHEDULES, STUDENTS
WHERE       CLASS_SCHEDULES.CLASS_ID =
            CLASSES.CLASS_ID AND
            CLASS_SCHEDULES.CLASS_SCHEDULE_ID =
            STUDENT_SCHEDULES.CLASS_SCHEDULE_ID
            AND STUDENT_SCHEDULES.STUDENT_ID =
            STUDENTS.STUDENT_ID AND
            TERM = 'Fall' AND YEAR = '1999'
```

b. Click the SQL Entry Form link to bring you back to the form.

3. A query that returns all students registered for CP 108 in Fall, 1999. Show only the student name, the class number, and the class name.

a. Type the following in the SQL Statement text box, and then click the Execute button:

```
SELECT      LAST_NAME, FIRST_NAME,
            CLASS_NUMBER, CLASS_NAME
FROM        CLASS_SCHEDULES,
            CLASSES, STUDENT_SCHEDULES, STUDENTS
WHERE       CLASS_SCHEDULES.CLASS_ID =
            CLASSES.CLASS_ID AND
            CLASS_SCHEDULES.CLASS_SCHEDULE_ID =
            STUDENT_SCHEDULES.CLASS_SCHEDULE_ID
            AND STUDENT_SCHEDULES.STUDENT_ID =
            STUDENTS.STUDENT_ID AND
            TERM = 'Fall' AND YEAR = '1999' AND
            CLASS_NUMBER = 'CP 108'
```

b. Click the SQL Entry Form link to bring you back to the form.

4. A query that counts the number of students in each class in Fall, 1999. Show the class number, the class name, and the number of students.

a. Type the following in the SQL Statement text box, and then click the Execute button:

```
SELECT      CLASS_NUMBER, COUNT(*) AS NUM_STUDENTS
FROM        CLASS_SCHEDULES,
            CLASSES, STUDENT_SCHEDULES, STUDENTS
WHERE       CLASS_SCHEDULES.CLASS_ID =
            CLASSES.CLASS_ID AND
            CLASS_SCHEDULES.CLASS_SCHEDULE_ID =
```

```
                STUDENT_SCHEDULES.CLASS_SCHEDULE_ID
                AND STUDENT_SCHEDULES.STUDENT_ID =
                STUDENTS.STUDENT_ID AND
                TERM = 'Fall' AND YEAR = '1999'
        GROUP BY
                CLASS_NUMBER
```

b. Click the SQL Entry Form link to bring you back to the form.

Project 5-3

You are working at Centreville Community College as an intern, and your boss needs to know how many students have the last name of Smith. You decide to write an ASP script to give him an answer.

1. Since you are new to ASP and to databases, you create the following script, called num_of_students.asp. Create this file in the Chapter_5 folder of your Data Disk:

```
<%@ Language=VBScript %>
<% Response.Buffer = True %>
<HTML>
<HEAD>
<TITLE>Number of Students Script</title>
<BODY>
<%
   Dim objRS,objConn
   Set objRS = Server.CreateObject("ADODB.Recordset")
   set objConn = Server.CreateObject("ADODB.Connection")
   objConn.Open "DRIVER={Microsoft Access Driver (*.mdb)};
   DBQ=" & server.mappath("/Chapter_5") & "\" & "course.mdb"
   '"PROVIDER=MSDASQL;DRIVER={SQL Server};SERVER=NOVASMS;
   DATABASE=ctis;UID=kmorneau;PWD=Tpwivetr"
   set objRS = objConn.Execute("SELECT * FROM STUDENTS",
   intRecordsAffected)
    objRS.MoveFirst %>
    <CENTER><H2>Number of Students Response</H2>
    The number of students with last name of 'Smith' is:
     <%
        Dim num_students
        Do while Not objRS.EOF
           If objRS("LAST_NAME") = "Smith" Then
               num_students = num_students + 1
           End If
           objRS.MoveNext
        Loop
        Response.Write(num_students) %>
   <% objRS.close
      set objRS = Nothing
   %>
</CENTER>
</BODY>
</HTML>
```

2. Open your browser, and navigate to *http://localhost/Chapter_5/num_of_students.asp* to observe the changes.

3. When you created the above script, you used VBScript to calculate the number of students with the last name of Smith, using a loop. But your mentor, Jack Chu, tells you that you can use SQL alone to accomplish the same task. He suggests that you change your code in num_of_students.asp to match the following (new code shown in bold):

```
<%@ Language=VBScript %>
<% Response.Buffer = True %>
<html>
<head>
<title>Number of Students Script</title>
<body>
<%
  Dim objRS,objConn
  Set objRS = Server.CreateObject("ADODB.Recordset")
  set objConn = Server.CreateObject("ADODB.Connection")

  objConn.Open "DRIVER={Microsoft Access Driver (*.mdb)};
  DBQ=" & server.mappath("/Chapter_5") & "\" & "course.mdb"
  '"PROVIDER=MSDASQL;DRIVER={SQL Server};SERVER=NOVASMS;
  DATABASE=ctis;UID=kmorneau;PWD=Tpwivetr"
  set objRS = objConn.Execute("SELECT LAST_NAME, COUNT(*) AS
NUM_OF_STUDENTS FROM STUDENTS WHERE LAST_NAME = 'Smith'
GROUP BY LAST_NAME",intRecordsAffected)
  objRS.MoveFirst %>
  <CENTER><H2>Number of Students Response</H2>
  The number of students with last name of 'Smith' is:
    <%
    Dim num_students
    If Not objRS.EOF Then
        num_students = objRS("NUM_OF_STUDENTS")
    else
        num_students = 0
    End If
    Response.Write(num_students) %>

  <% objRS.close
    set objRS = Nothing
  %>
</CENTER>
</body>
</html>
```

4. Open your browser, and navigate to *http://localhost/Chapter_5/num_of_students.asp*. You realize that SQL is a very powerful language and can make your code a lot easier to create; you receive the desired functionality.

5. Save your work.

5

Project 5-4

Using the SQL Web application created in this chapter, create and run the following simple queries to insert or update data in your database.

1. A query that inserts a new instructor, Jack Chu, hired recently by Centreville Community College:

   a. Open your browser, and navigate to *http://localhost/Chapter_5/sql.htm*.

   b. Enter INSERT INTO INSTRUCTORS VALUES(1, 'Chu', 'Jack', '7033333333', 'jchu@centrevillecc.edu', 'http://www.centrevillecc.edu/jchu') in the text box, and then click the Execute button.

   c. Click the SQL Entry Form link to bring you back to the form.

2. A query that updates Vinny Baker's last name to Bakerson:

   a. Enter UPDATE INSTRUCTORS SET LAST_NAME = 'Bakerson' WHERE LAST_NAME = 'Baker' and FIRST_NAME = 'Vinny' in the text box, and then click the Execute button.

   b. Click the SQL Entry Form link to bring you back to the form.

3. A query that removes the instructor Jack Chu from the database:

   a. Enter DELETE FROM INSTRUCTORS WHERE INSTRUCTOR_ID = 1 in the text box, and then click the Execute button.

   b. Click the SQL Entry Form link to bring you back to the form.

Project 5-5

Change the execute_sql.asp script to allow you to use a query string to pass in the SQL statement and bypass the SQL Entry form.

1. Open execute_sql.asp and change the script to match the following (new code shown in bold):

```
<%@ Language=VBScript %>
<% Response.Buffer = True %>
<html>

<head>

<title>SQL Query Response</title>

<body>
<%
   Dim objRS,objConn
   Set objRS = Server.CreateObject("ADODB.Recordset")
   set objConn = Server.CreateObject("ADODB.Connection")

   If cstr(Request.QueryString("txtSQL"))="" Then
     Response.Write("<CENTER><H3>WARNING!</H3>")
     Response.Write("<P>You must enter a query to run!
     </CENTER>")
```

```
            Response.End
        Else
            objConn.Open "DRIVER={Microsoft Access Driver (*.mdb)};
            DBQ=" & server.mappath("/Chapter_5") & "\" & "course.mdb"
            '"PROVIDER=MSDASQL;DRIVER={SQL Server};SERVER=NOVASMS;
            DATABASE=ctis;UID=kmorneau;PWD=Tpwivetr"
            set objRS = objConn.Execute(cstr(Request.QueryString
            ("txtSQL")),intRecordsAffected)
            if intRecordsAffected < 0 Then
            objRS.MoveFirst %>
            <CENTER><H2>SQL Query Response</H2>
            <b>SQL Statement:</b> <%=cstr(Request.QueryString
            ("txtSQL"))%><p>
            <TABLE BORDER=1 COLS=<%=objRS.Fields.Count%>>
              <TR>
                <% For each objField in objRS.Fields %>
                  <TH> <%=objField.Name %> </TH>
                <% Next %>
              </TR>
            <% Do while Not objRS.EOF %>
              <TR>
                <% For Each objField in objRS.Fields %>
                  <TD align=right>
                    <% If IsNull(objField) Then
                          Response.Write(" ")
                       else
                          Response.Write(objField.Value)
                       End If
                    %>
                  </TD>
                <% Next
                   objRS.MoveNext %>
              </TR>
            <%  Loop %>
          </TABLE>

      <% objRS.close
         set objRS = Nothing
         end if
         Response.Write("<p>" & intRecordsAffected & " records
         affected!")
         Response.Write("<p>Return to <a href=sql.htm>SQL Entry
         Form</a>")

      End IF
      %>
    </CENTER>
    </body>
    </html>
```

5

3. Save the file as execute_sql1.asp in the Chapter_5 folder of your Data Disk.

4. Open your browser, and type **http://localhost/Chapter_5/ execute_sql1.asp?txtSQL =SELECT * FROM INSTRUCTORS** and observe the result.

5. Save your work.

CASE PROJECTS

1. John's Software, Inc. has hired you to help develop a gift management information system. This application should track the gifts that are sent out to a person for a given occasion. It should also track what gifts are received, from whom, and the occasion. Using the database design techniques in this chapter, design and implement a database in Microsoft Access.

2. Interstate Bank has hired you to develop an application that tracks a family's income and expenses, to determine whether or not the family is living within its means. The application should track all sources of income. Using the database design techniques in this chapter, design and implement a database in Microsoft Access.

3. Now Interstate Bank wants you to develop a check-balancing application. The application should guide the user through these steps to determine his or her current balance: (1) Sum any deposits not reflected on the statement; (2) Sum any deductions (e.g., outstanding checks) not reflected on the statement; (3) Add the deposits calculated in Step 1 to the balance on the checking statement; and (4) Subtract any deductions (from Step 2) from the balance on the checking statement.

Using the database design techniques in this chapter, design and implement a database in Microsoft Access.

6

AUTOGENERATING SQL

In this chapter, you will:

- Learn what makes a program vulnerable and less commercially viable
- Understand the benefits of HTML forms
- Understand the benefits of script-generated SQL
- Learn about ADO objects
- Learn to handle run-time errors
- Learn the different applications of ODBC and OLE DB

In Chapter 5, the application interface required a sophisticated end user, one who could manually enter SQL and understand the structure of the target database. In Chapter 6, you are going to prepare an application for an end user who is not a programmer. Your preparation will allow the end user to be oblivious to SQL and the structure of the destination database. In other words, instead of the end user manually generating the code, the application will generate the code based on input from the end user.

A PROGRAM INTERFACE THAT INTIMIDATES AN END USER

In an ideal world, the end users of your programs would have the same level of programming sophistication that you have. You could assume enthusiasm on their part for long lines of code and complicated logic structures. Unfortunately, in the real world, your end users will likely be accountants, teachers, businesspeople, and the like—people who are experts in fields other than programming. If being forced to learn about a database does not scare most of your end users away, SQL definitely will.

Just for discussion, let's say one brave soul still sticks around to use your program, the one that requires knowledge of SQL. (You can assume the rest of your company's end users are in the lunchroom complaining about you.) Because this person is willing to use the program, you hand it over, quite positive that if he or she follows the directions, all will be well.

To preview the Student Contact Application as an end user:

1. Go to PWS and prepare a virtual directory named **Chapter_6** that corresponds to the Chapter_6 folder on your Data Disk. Open your browser.

2. Type **http://localhost/Chapter_6/oldRegister/default.htm** in the Address text box, and then press **Enter**. Your screen should resemble Figure 6-1. You will now enter contact information for a new student.

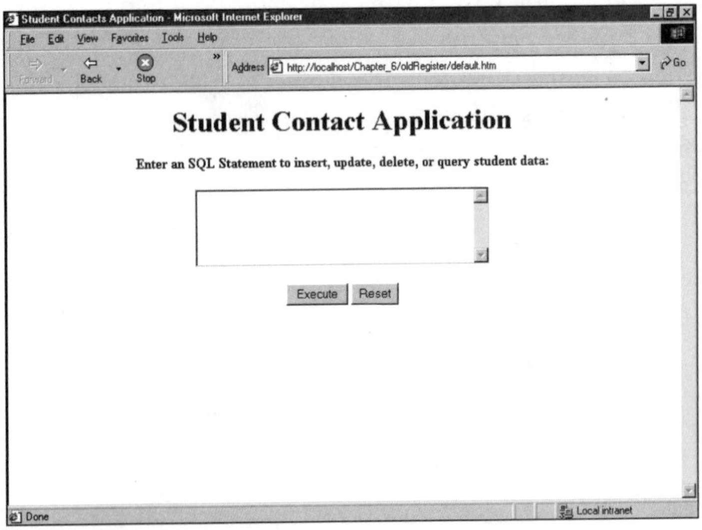

Figure 6-1   Student contact information

3. Type **INSERT INTO STUDENTS VALUES('Morneau','Rebecca', 'rmorneau@erols.com','7033233333','7038303333')** in the text box, and click **Execute**.

Your screen should now resemble Figure 6-2. Note the error message that appears in the browser. This message is cryptic and hard for a programmer to understand—let alone an end user. The problem with the code that you just typed is that it ignored the structure of the database.

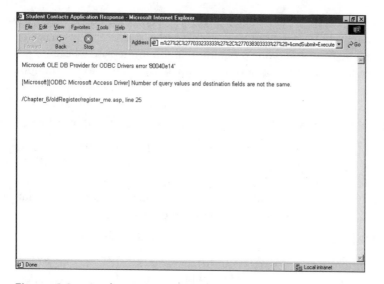

Figure 6-2   Application response

4. Click the **Back** button on your browser.

5. Change the previous insert statement to match the following: **INSERT INTO STUDENTS VALUES(50, 'Morneau', 'Rebecca', 'rmorneau@erols.com', '7033233333', '7038303333').**

6. Click **Execute.** Your screen should now resemble Figure 6-3. Now, thankfully, your code does not ignore the structure of the database.

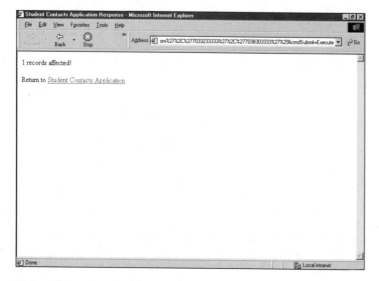

Figure 6-3   Acceptable response

6

The change that we made, which turned incorrect SQL into correct SQL, was minor. Nonetheless, if you wrote a program that assumes the end user can make that "minor change," you would be fired from your programming job immediately because it is your job, as the programmer, to keep the amount of user knowledge needed to a minimum.

A Program Interface That Doesn't Intimidate an End User

Creating an interface, and ultimately a program, that doesn't intimidate the end user requires HTML forms and ASP that generate the SQL on the fly. Since you've already learned how to create HTML forms in previous chapters of this book, we've provided the forms that you will need in this chapter. By the end of this chapter, your ASP scripts will automate the generation of SQL, depending upon what the user needs to be able to do.

To view one HTML form structure that has been created for you:

1. Open your browser and navigate to **http://localhost/Chapter_6/Register/default.htm**. Your screen should resemble Figure 6-4.

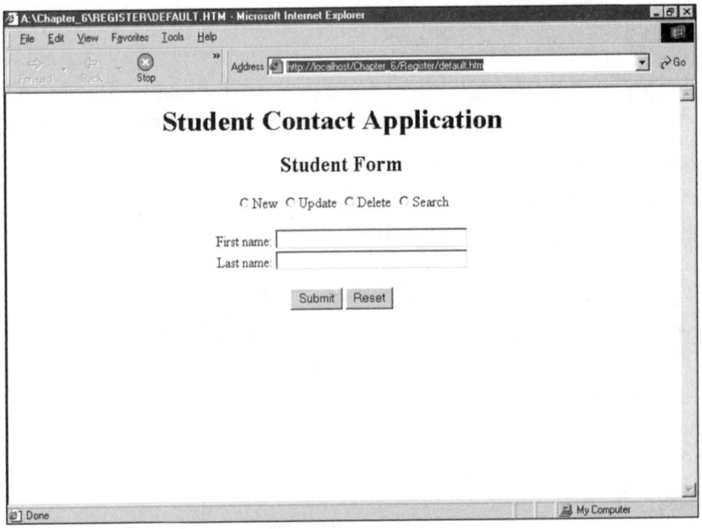

Figure 6-4   Unintimidating interface

2. This form does not completely work because the ASP scripts are incomplete. You will take care of that problem in subsequent sections in this chapter. Close your browser.

Already we've covered one hurdle—protecting the end user from an intimidating interface. Now, we will write the code that creates the ASP that creates the SQL—on the fly and behind the scenes.

UNDERSTANDING ADO

Just as you make life easier for your end user, ADO makes life easier for you by hiding from you the intimate details of interacting with different data sources. In this section, we are going to learn more about the ADO that this chapter's application utilizes. As the discussion evolves, refer to Figure 6-5 for an illustration of the logic flow.

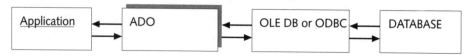

Figure 6-5   Logic flow

ADO's Role

An application accesses a database via a built-in component called ActiveX Data Objects (ADO). ADO contains many objects that allow a programmer's application to communicate with a data source by using OLE DB or ODBC (both are discussed in the next section of this chapter).

ADO provides three main objects to use to interact with databases. The Connection object provides the programmer with interface to connect to a data source. The Recordset object provides an interface that relies on submitting queries using SQL and provides the results of the queries. The Command object also provides an interface to submit queries and obtain results; it also provides an interface for calling procedures and functions stored in a DBMS. These procedures and functions are called **stored procedures**.

The following subsections provide a complete look at the Connection and Recordset objects. You will see the Command object in the next chapter in which we discuss SQL; the Command object is split from the others because programmers use it to call stored procedures in a database. Access does not support stored procedures.

Connection Object

The Connection object allows an application to connect to a database, send queries to the database, receive results from the database, and disconnect from the database. Also, the connection object supplies a transaction interface, which is the ability to make changes to a database permanent or to roll back the changes made to the database. (You will learn more about transactions as you become more proficient in ASP.) Table 6-1 describes the useful properties and methods of the connection object. Additional properties and methods can be found in the online MSDN library at *msdn.microsoft.com.*

Table 6-1   Useful Properties and Methods of the Connection Object

Property/Method	Name	Description
Method	Open	Opens a new connection to the database
Method	Close	Closes a connection to the database
Method	Execute	Runs an SQL query or stored procedure
Method	BeginTrans	Starts a new transaction
Method	CommitTrans	Commits a transaction successfully
Method	RollbackTrans	Cancels a transaction
Property	Attributes	Determines where to begin a new transaction when an old one ends
Property	CommandTimeout	Specifies the number of seconds to wait before terminating a command with an error
Property	ConnectionString	Provides information needed to create a connection to the database such as driver name, database name, username, and password
Property	CursorLocation	Specifies the location of cursor (e.g., adUseClient (on client) or adUseServer (on Server))
Property	DefaultDatabase	Sets or returns the default database to use for a connection
Property	Provider	Sets or returns the provider of the OLE DB driver
Property	State	Returns whether the connection is open (adStateOpen) or closed (adStateClosed)
Property	Version	Returns the version number of ADO

Recordset Object

The Recordset object sends a query to the database and returns a cursor. A **cursor,** which contains the results of a query, allows row-by-row processing of an SQL result set and holds rows of data that contain columns or fields. Table 6-2 describes the useful methods and attributes of the Recordset object. Additional properties and methods can be found in the online documentation.

Table 6-2   Useful Properties and Methods of the Recordset Object

Property/Method	Name	Description
Method	AddNew	Creates a new record in a Recordset
Method	CancelBatch	Cancels a pending batch update of the Recordset
Method	CancelUpdate	Cancels an update to the Recordset
Method	Clone	Creates a duplicate of current Recordset
Method	Close	Closes an open Recordset
Method	Delete	Deletes the current row in a Recordset
Method	MoveFirst	Moves the Recordset pointer (an internal way for ADO to track what row it is on in the cursor) to the first record in the Recordset
Method	MoveNext	Moves the Recordset pointer to the next record in the Recordset
Method	MovePrevious	Moves the Recordset pointer to the previous record in the Recordset
Method	MoveLast	Moves the Recordset pointer to the last record in the Recordset
Method	NextRecordSet	Moves the Recordset pointer to the next Recordset in the query
Method	Open	Opens a new cursor. When you use a file, you must open it first. When in ADO, you must open a cursor to use it.
Method	Requery	Updates the current recordset by rerunning the query
Method	Update	Saves any changes made to the current record
Method	UpdateBatch	Writes all pending batch updates
Property	ActiveConnection	Specifies the connection object to which a recordset belongs
Property	BOF	Indicates whether you are at the beginning of the cursor or not. Has a value of True if the Recordset pointer is at beginning of the recordset
Property	CursorLocation	Provides the location of cursor on the client (adUseClient) or on the server (adUseServer)
Property	CursorType	The type of cursor used in the recordset
Property	EOF	True, if the Recordset pointer is at the end of the recordset
Property	RecordCount	Returns the number of records in the recordset
Property	State	Returns whether the recordset is open or closed

6

Fields Collection

The Fields collection allows you to access the column or field data of the current record of the Recordset. Table 6-3 gives you its useful properties and methods.

Table 6-3   Useful Properties and Methods of the Fields Collection

Property/Method	Name	Description
Method	Refresh	Updates the collection with changes in the fields collection
Property	Count	Returns the number of fields in the collection
Property	Item	Returns the contents of a field or column

Field Object

The field object contains the column name and the value of a column from a result set. Table 6-4 provides properties and methods you should know about.

Table 6-4   Useful Properties and Methods of the Field Object

Property/Method	Name	Description
Method	AppendChunk	Appends data to a large text or binary field such as a memo field or a graphic
Method	GetChunk	Gets data from a large text or binary field
Property	Name	Name of the field
Property	NumericScale	Number of decimal places in a numeric field
Property	OriginalValue	Value of the field before any changes were made
Property	Precision	Number of digits in a numeric field
Property	Type	Data type of the field
Property	Value	The value assigned to the field

Now that you know the logic behind ADO, it's time to see how it is actually implemented. You will do that in the next section.

IMPLEMENTING ADO

An ADO Connection object supplies a straightforward way to connect to a database. When writing the code, your first step is to create an instance of the connection object and open the connection to the database. Below, you'll find sample syntax and code for connecting to a database in JavaScript, which will be the scripting language used in this chapter.

Code Example

```javascript
objConn = new ActiveXObject("ADODB.Connection");
objConn.Open(ConnectionString, User, Password);
objConn.Close();
```

Code Dissection

- For the ConnectionString, you can simply use the System DSN in double quotes, such as "StudentContacts".

- The ConnectionString can be a DSN-less connection. This means that no data source setup in ODBC exists. This is very useful in situations where you do not have access to the ODBC Administrator (a program) to set up the data source in the first place.

- The ConnectionString can be assigned a string such as "File Name=" + Server.MapPath("/Chapter_6/Register") + "\StudentContacts.UDL" which is a JavaScript string that tells JavaScript to use the file StudentContacts.UDL.

- If you need a username and a password to log into a database, then you can supply these in the User and Password arguments.

The following is an example of how to use the syntax discussed above with different connection strings.

```javascript
objConn = new ActiveXObject("ADODB.Connection");
objConn.Open("StudentContacts"); //DSN example
```

or

```javascript
objConn.Open("DRIVER={Microsoft Access Driver (*.mdb)}; DBQ="
 + Server.MapPath("/Chapter_6") + "\\Register\\course.mdb");
//DSN-less example
```

or

```javascript
objConn = new ActiveXObject("ADODB.Connection");
objConn.Open("File Name=" + Server.MapPath("/Chapter_6") +
"\\Register\\StudentContacts.UDL") ; //OLE DB example
```

Changing the Data Source Configuration of the ADO Connection String

This chapter's application uses a DSN-less ODBC data source. The location of that data source was entered by the programmer at the time that ODBC was set up for the application. That information is not accessible by OLE DB; to switch over to using OLE DB, you must overtly enter the location of the database into the application.

To change the database path:

1. In Windows Explorer, navigate to the Register folder of your Chapter_6 Data Disk, and then double-click **StudentContacts.udl**. The Data Link Properties dialog box opens, as shown in Figure 6-6. Note that the pathname shown in your dialog box may differ.

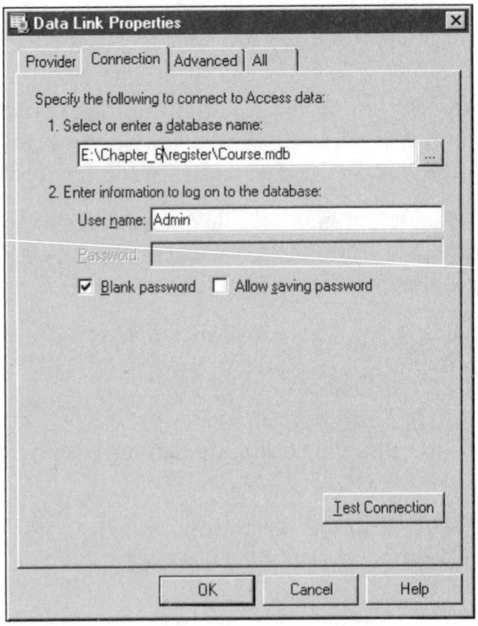

Data Link Properties

Provider | Connection | Advanced | All

Specify the following to connect to Access data:

1. Select or enter a database name:

E:\Chapter_6\register\Course.mdb

2. Enter information to log on to the database:

User name: Admin

Password:

☑ Blank password   ☐ Allow saving password

Test Connection

OK   Cancel   Help

Figure 6-6   Data Link Properties dialog box

2. Enter the path to the database in the Register folder of the Chapter_6 folder on your Data Disk.

3. Click the **Test Connection** button to verify the connection, read the information in the resulting dialog box, click **OK**, and then click **OK** again.

 This change will not affect the functionality of your ODBC-based application because register_me.asp is not programmed to access the information you just manipulated.

How the ADO Recordset Object Queries a Database

Once your code has a connection to the database, the code can query the database. A successful query returns a **result set**, which is a set of rows returned from the database. A query needs an instance of the Recordset object and the use of the Execute method of the Connection object. The Execute method returns a recordset with the results of the query.

Consider the following code, which creates a Recordset object and calls the database with a query that returns all rows and all columns from the Students table:

Code Example

```
1 objRS = new ActiveXObject("ADODB.Recordset");
2 objRS = this.objConn.Execute("select * from students");
```

Code Dissection

- Line 1 creates an instance of the recordset object.

- Line 2 returns a recordset from a SELECT query.

Once the code returns the Recordset object, you can manipulate the rows in the recordset using the EOF property. You can also use the MoveFirst, MoveNext, MovePrevious, and MoveLast methods to move the Recordset pointer around in the recordset. The following illustrates an example of how to maneuver in a recordset:

Code Example

```
1 strEvalString = "(objRS(\"FIRST_NAME\")==\"" +
2                     Request.QueryString("txtFirstName") + "\") && " +
3                     "(objRS(\"LAST_NAME\")==\"" +
4                     Request.QueryString("txtLastName") + "\")";
5 function Search(strEvalString) {
6     var item, e, found;
7     objRS.MoveFirst();
8     while (!objRS.EOF)
9     {
10        found = eval(strEvalString);
11        if (found)
12            return(1);
13        objRS.MoveNext();
14    }
15    return(0);
16 }
```

Code Dissection

- Lines 1 through 4 show the power of the eval function in JavaScript. You can set up the search criteria in a string first and pass this string into the eval function, which will execute the string as a line of code. This allows you to create one Search function that can be used by multiple people.

- Lines 5 through 16 of the "Search function" requires a form using a Get method, which in turn contains a txtLastName and txtFirstName text box. The search criteria allows you to see if a row in the recordset matches the first and last name entered by the user on the form.

- Line 7 of the "Search Function" section moves the recordset pointer to the first row in the recordset.

- Lines 8 through 14 make up the loop that checks the row against the last name and first name. If it finds a match, then it exits the function. Otherwise, the recordset pointer moves to the next row; the loop continues to process until there are no more records in the recordset to process. The EOF property is set to true when all the rows have been processed.

How the ADO Recordset Object Inserts Data

In the following steps, you will enter the last of the code that allows the program to create an SQL query that inserts data (entered by the user in the form) into the database.

To complete the SQL code:

1. Open your text editor and from the Register folder on your Data Disk, open **register_me.asp**.

2. Enter the following code (new code shown in bold):

```
if (Request.Form("Mode") == "New")   {
strSQL = "INSERT INTO STUDENTS" +
    "(FIRST_NAME,LAST_NAME,HOME_PHONE,WORK_PHONE,E_MAIL)" +
        " VALUES(" +
                "'" + Request.Form("FIRST_NAME") + "'," +
                "'" + Request.Form("LAST_NAME") + "'," +
                "'" + Request.Form("HOME_PHONE") + "'," +
                "'" + Request.Form("WORK_PHONE") + "'," +
                "'" + Request.Form("E_MAIL") + "')";
strErr = objForm.Run_SQL(strSQL);
```

3. Save your work and close the file.

How the ADO Fields Collection Allows the Referencing of a Column or Field

The Fields collection is the default property for ADO's Recordset object, which contains the current columns or fields in the recordset. The MoveFirst, MoveNext, MovePrevious, and MoveLast methods cause this collection to change. The fact that Fields is the default allows you to reference a column or a field in the collection directly, such as in this code:

```
objRS("STUDENT_ID")
```

An application can access a field in a recordset using any of the following (note that the default property for all collections is the Item property):

```
objRS.Fields.Item("STUDENT_ID")
objRS.Fields.Item(0)
objRS.Fields("STUDENT_ID")
objRS.Fields(0)
objRS("STUDENT_ID")
objRS(0)
```

This book will use the second to last item in this list, objRS("STUDENT_ID"), but all examples are valid. You will use this format because it is the most concise method of retrieving a column of data.

Handling Run-Time Errors in ASP

This section explains how to handle **run-time errors**, errors that occur in a script while it is executing. Examples of run-time errors in ADO are: trying to access a row of a recordset when you are at the end of the recordset, and trying to access a row of a recordset when you are at the beginning of a recordset.

You can use special syntax to catch and correct any run-time error gracefully. The following examples show how to handle run-time errors in VBScript and in JavaScript. (The application in the Register folder already contains this functionality.) Specifically, these examples are designed to catch a failure to open a connection to the database.

6

Code Example

VBScript

```
On Error Resume Next
  set objConn = CreateObject("ADODB.Connection")
  objConn.Open("StudentContacts")
If Err.Number > 0 Then
    Response.Write("Source: " & Err.Source & "Error Description: "
  & Err.Description)
End If
```

Code Example

JavaScript

```
try {
  objConn = new ActiveXObject("ADODB.Connection");
  objConn.Open("StudentContacts");
}
catch (Err) {
  Response.Write("Error Description: " + Err.Description);
}
```

Code Dissection

- In the VBScript example, the line "On Error Resume Next" tells the VBScript interpreter to continue with the next line if a run-time error occurs.

- VBScript provides a built-in object called Err that you can use to catch errors. VBScript uses Err.Number as an identifier for an error. The Err object includes number, source, and description properties of the run-time error. The example code incorporates these properties. The error description message is very cryptic and hard for a typical user to understand. Usually, this is the error that appears in your browser when a run-time error occurs and there is no code to catch it. Instead of using the built-in messages, you should create your own message—one that is easier for the user to understand. For instance, you could use the message "Unable to create connection to the database. See your System Administrator for help."

- In the JavaScript example, the try…catch syntax is used to catch run-time errors. If a run-time error occurs in JavaScript, then an Err object is created and the error handler is run (inside the catch block; a catch block has a catch keyword followed by { and ends with a }). The Err object contains number and description properties you can use.

Unfortunately, very few software products are free of run-time errors. Thus you need to prepare for them by including run-time error handlers to catch errors before they occur and you can handle them appropriately. This will prevent your application from crashing unexpectedly.

USING ODBC OR OLE DB

The program in this chapter was written to connect to the database via ODBC. ODBC was chosen because it is more likely to be available to the typical Windows 98 user than is OLE DB. With the proper tools installed, however, a programmer could have used OLE DB.

 In this chapter, our target data source is a database; thus, you could use either ODBC or OLE DB to connect to it. If it were not a database but some other type of data source, you would have to use OLE DB.

ODBC provides a programmer with a standard software interface to different DBMS such as Oracle, SQL Server, Access, and others using SQL. This allows a programmer to write software applications that can communicate with different DBMSs using the same software. The ODBC Data Source Administrator is an application that ODBC uses to set up the database driver, which is supplied by the DBMS vendor, and the **data source**, which is the configuration information about the database, such as where the database is located and how to access the database, to be used by ODBC and the programmer.

When setting up an ODBC data source, you have several options available. You can set up a driver using the User DSN, where DSN is the data source name (which applies only to a particular user logged into a computer), a System DSN (which applies to anyone who uses the computer), or a File DSN (which is for file-based data sources such as an Access database). All data sources you set up in ODBC are referenced by a name called the data source name, or DSN. There is one last option you can use to specify a DSN in your code. You can bypass setting up the DSN in the ODBC Data Source Administrator by specifying the driver and the location of the database, which is called DSN-less.

An example of a string that would set up the data source Course.mdb is "DRIVER={Microsoft Access Driver (*.mdb)}; DBQ=" + Server.MapPath("/Chapter_6") + "\\register\\course.mdb". This is a JavaScript string. The DRIVER keyword specifies that you are using the Microsoft Access Driver, and the DBQ keyword specifies the location of the database on the server.

OLE DB provides the programmer with a standard software interface to different types of data sources such as DBMSs, files, and other types. ODBC works specifically with DBMSs, while OLE DB works with any type of data source. Vendors provide OLE DB drivers for their products as they do with ODBC, and they are called **OLE DB providers**. Microsoft provides a special utility, called a **Microsoft Data Link**, with OLE DB that allows you to set up OLE DB data sources. With Microsoft Data Link, you can set up a data source, access that data source in a way similar to ODBC, and save those settings in a file.

Setting Up a Microsoft Data Link (OLE DB Data Source)

If your instructor allows you to use OLE DB, you need do some preparation. Specifically, you need to create a Microsoft Data Link, which is a utility that stores information about your data source in a special file. Unlike a data source name, a Microsoft Data Link is a combination of a utility and a file that stores data source information.

To set up a Microsoft Data Link for the Access 2000 database on your Data Disk, you would right-click your computer's desktop, point to New, and click on Microsoft Data Link. In that data link, in the Provider tab, you would specify information about the data source you wanted to use. If you were making changes to accommodate the database in this chapter, you would select the Microsoft Jet 4.0 OLE DB Provider because you are accessing an Access database.

 If you do not have Microsoft Data Link on your computer, consult with your instructor or technical support person for assistance.

A PROGRAM THAT DOESN'T INTIMIDATE THE END USER

Given the changes that you have made, it is time to preview the new Student Contact Application.

To review the application:

1. Open your browser.

2. Type **http://localhost/Chapter_6/Register/form.asp?LAST_NAME= Padian&FIRST_NAME=Elizabeth&Mode=New** in the Address text box, and then press **Enter**. You have typed the information the "hard way" to demonstrate how to bypass scripts, if necessary. Your screen should resemble Figure 6-7.

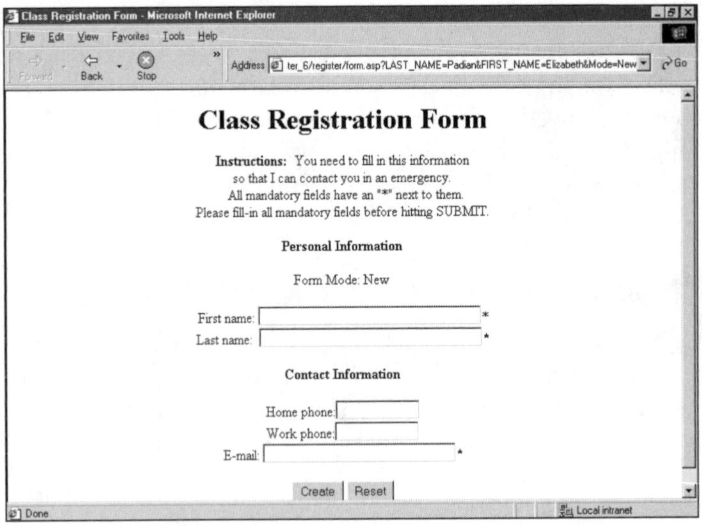

Figure 6-7   Student contact form

3. Now you'll purposely create an error by clicking the **Create** button. Your screen should now resemble Figure 6-8. Note the error message that appears in the browser is much more intuitive to an end user than the error message seen at the beginning of this chapter.

Figure 6-8   Error page

4. Click the Back button on your browser and then type the following into the form:

Last name: **Morneau**
First name: **Deborah**
Home phone: **7033233333**
Work phone: **7038303333**
E-Mail: **dmorneau@erols.com**

5. Click the **Create** button. Your screen should now resemble Figure 6-9.

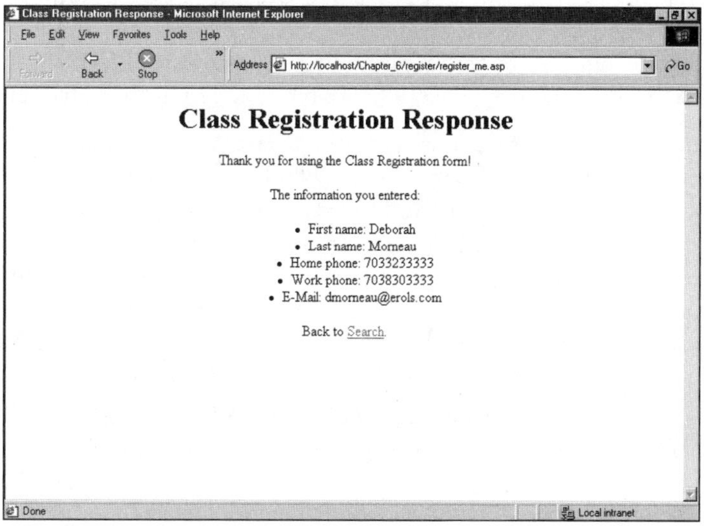

Figure 6-9   Successful data insert

6. Close your browser.

This is a much better designed application because the user needs to know how to use the Web and how to use HTML forms only. The details of the database structure and SQL are hidden from your user, which is by far the most preferred method of designing applications.

TYING TOGETHER WHAT YOU'VE LEARNED IN THE FIRST SIX CHAPTERS

You have created a very dynamic application. Now that it is in the shape that you want, let's examine some particular attributes.

- **default.htm**: This HTML page presents a form that asks the user whether they want to create a new student, update an existing student, delete an existing student, or search for student information. The form asks the user to enter the student's last name and first name.

- **clsForm.cls**: This script file creates a form class that handles the details of interacting with the database and the form.

- **form.asp**: This ASP script page is the form page where the user enters data, updates data, deletes data, or queries data for a particular student.

- **register_me.asp**: This ASP script page takes the student data from the form and then inserts, updates, or deletes it from the database.

Default.htm

The default.htm page is the initial page (entitled "Student Contacts Application") that the user sees when interacting with this application. As you'll recall, **option buttons** allow a user to select only a single item in a group. In this case, the user can select the New, Update, Delete, or Search option buttons. In this application, you will store information indicating whether you are doing a New, Update, Delete, or Search function in a variable called **mode**.

A mode variable causes the application to run certain pieces of code. For example, when the user clicks the New option button, the application will go into New mode, and the "New" string will be stored in a variable called strMode. This allows the programmer to define what to do when you are in a particular mode. This form contains four option buttons that allow the user to specify exactly what he or she would like to do—create a record for a student (using the New button), update a record for an existing student (using the Update button), delete a record for a student (using the Delete button), or search for a record for a particular student (using the Search button). The form requests the user to enter the student's first name and last name. The submit button sends the request to the form.asp page. The reset button clears the page. The HTML for this page is as follows:

Code Example

```
1 <HTML>
2 <HEAD>
3
4 </HEAD>
5 <BODY>
6 <center><h1>Students Contacts Application</h1>
7 <center><h2>Student Form</h2></center>
8 <CENTER>
9
10 <form id="frmStudent" name="frmStudent" action="form.asp"
method="get">
11 <center>
12 <p>
13 <input type="option" name="Mode" value="New">New
14 <input type="option" name="Mode" value="Update">Update
15 <input type="option" name="Mode" value="Delete">Delete
16 <input type="option" name="Mode" value="Browse">Search
17
18 <p>First name: <input type="text" name="txtFirstName"
size="30"><br>
19 Last name: <input type="text" name="txtLastName" size="30">
20 </p>
```

```
21 </center>
22
23 <center>
24 <p><input id="cmdSubmit"  type="submit" value="Submit">
25 <input id="cmdReset"  type="reset" value="Reset"> </p>
26 </center>
27
28 </form>
29
30 </CENTER>
31
32 </BODY>
33 </HTML>
```

6

Code Dissection

- Line 10 indicates that the form.asp file uses a QueryString (Get method). It also indicates that this form calls the form.asp script.

- Lines 13–16 provide the necessary code for the option buttons.

clsForm.cls

This file creates a class called clsForm, which handles the interaction between the form and the database. The clsForm class has the following properties and methods as shown in Table 6-5:

Table 6-5   Properties and Methods of the clsForm Object

Property/Method	Name	Description
Property	strMode	Stores the function that the user requests the form to accomplish, such as creating a record for a student
Property	colFormElements	A collection that stores the data from the form
Property	strServerConnectionString	A DSN-less connection string utilizing ODBC, used to open a connection with the database. You can use either ODBC or OLE DB, as discussed earlier in this chapter.
Property	objConn	An instance of ADO's connection object
Property	objRS	An instance of ADO's recordset object that stores a result set of a query
Method	CreateDict	A function that creates the colFormElements from the Request object

Table 6-5   Properties and Methods of the clsForm Object (continued)

Property/Method	Name	Description
Method	Open_Recordset	A function that opens a recordset, objRS given an SQL SELECT string, search, a function that tries to locate a record in the database given an expression, and run_sql, a function that runs either an insert, update, or delete SQL function
Method	Mode	Returns the mode the HTML form is in; New is the mode when a user is entering new data; Update is the mode when a user is modifying existing data; Delete is the mode when a user is removing data; Browse is the mode when the user is viewing data
Method	Search	Returns true if the record is found in the result set; otherwise, false. If the record is found, a dictionary object is populated with the current record
Method	Run_SQL	Returns a recordset from a query passed into the function

Lets look at the JavaScript code for the clsForm class.

Code Example

```
1 <%
2 function clsForm() {
3    this.strMode = "Browse"
4    this.colFormElements = new ActiveXObject("Scripting.
Dictionary");
5    this.strServerConnectionString = "DRIVER={Microsoft Access
Driver
6 (*.mdb)}; DBQ=" + Server.MapPath("/Chapter_6/register") +
"\\course.mdb";
7    this.objConn = new ActiveXObject("ADODB.Connection");
8    this.objRS = new ActiveXObject("ADODB.Connection");
9    this.CreateDict = CreateDict;
10    this.Open_Recordset = Open_Recordset;
11    this.Search = Search;
12    this.Run_SQL = Run_SQL;
13    this.Mode = Mode;
14 }
15
16 function Mode() {
17    return(this.strMode);
18 }
19
20 function Open_Recordset(strSQL) {
```

```
21  var Err;
22
23  try {
24     this.objConn.Open(this.strServerConnectionString);
25  }
26  catch(Err) {
27     Response.Write(Err.Description);
28     Response.End;
29     return(0);
30  }
31
32  try {
33     this.objRS = this.objConn.Execute(strSQL);
34  }
35  catch(Err) {
36     Response.Write(Err.Description);
37     Response.End;
38     return(0);
39  }
40
41  }
42
43  function Search(strEvalString) {
44     var item, e, found;
45       try {
46     this.objRS.MoveFirst();
47     while (!this.objRS.EOF)
48     {
49       found = eval(strEvalString);
50       if (found)
51          break;
52       this.objRS.MoveNext();
53     }
54
55     if (!this.objRS.EOF) {
56         this.strMode = "Update";
57         this.colFormElements.RemoveAll();
58         e = new Enumerator(this.objRS.Fields);
59         while  (!e.atEnd()) {
60         item = e.item();
61         this.colFormElements.Add(item.name, item.value);
62         e.moveNext();
63         }
64         return(1)
65     }
66     else {
67         this.strMode = "New";
68         this.colFormElements.RemoveAll();
69         e = new Enumerator(Request.Form);
70         while (!e.atEnd()) {
71            item = e.item();
```

```
72              this.colFormElements.Add(item.name, "");
73              e.moveNext();
74          }
75        }
76      }       catch(Err) {
77              }
78      return(0);
79 }
80
81
82 function CreateDict() {
83
84   var item, e;
85
86    e = new Enumerator(Request.Form);
87    for (;!e.atEnd();e.moveNext()) {
88     item = e.item();
89     this.colFormElements.Add(item.name, Request.Form(item.value
));
90   }
91
92 }
93
94 function Run_SQL(strSQL) {
95
96    var Err;
97
98    objConn = new ActiveXObject("ADODB.Connection");
99    objRS = new ActiveXObject("ADODB.Connection");
100    try {
101    objConn.Open(this.strServerConnectionString);
102 }
103   catch(Err) {
104     return(Err.description);
105   }
106
107   try {
108     objRS = objConn.Execute(strSQL);
109   }
110   catch(Err) {
111     return(Err.description);
112   }
113
114   return("");
115
116 }
117
118 %>
```

Code Dissection

- Line 2 shows the constructor clsForm() for this class.

- Lines 5 and 6 illustrate the use of a DSN-less connection string that uses ODBC. You could also have easily used the UDL file here that utilizes OLE DB. The DSN-less connection string was used in this example because it requires the least changes on the different platforms you could be using.

- In line 16, the Mode function returns the contents of strMode.

- Lines 20–41 show the Open_Recordset function. This function opens a connection and runs a query. This example also shows the usage of run-time error handler.

- Lines 43–79 show the Search function, illustrating how to use the move functions of a recordset to maneuver the cursor.

- Lines 94–116 show the Run_SQL function. The Run_SQL function illustrates how to run a query for insert, update, and delete queries. The Open_Recordset function illustrates how to run a select query.

6

Form.asp

This script file contains the student registration form and the scripts that insert, update, delete, and search for data in the STUDENTS table. The ASP script is as follows:

Code Example

JavaScript

```
1 <%@Language=JScript%>
2 <%Response.buffer=true%>
3 <!-- #include file="adojavas.inc" -->
4 <!-- #include file="clsForm.cls" -->
5 <HTML>
6
7 <HEAD>
8 <TITLE>Class Registration Form</TITLE>
9 <!--
10     ************************************************
11     *** Form Name:     frmRegister            ***
12     *** Author:        Keith Morneau          ***
13     *** Date:          8/6/01                 ***
14     *** Description:                          ***
15     ***    This form allows user to enter     ***
16     ***    the student information.           ***
17     ***                                       ***
18     *** Revisions:                            ***
19     ************************************************
20 -->
21 <%
22  var strEval;
23  objForm = new clsForm();
24
```

```
25  objForm.Open_Recordset("select * from students");
26  objForm.strMode = Request.QueryString("Mode");
27
28  if (Request.QueryString("Mode") == "New")
29  {
30
31      strEval = "(this.objRS(\"FIRST_NAME\")==\"" +
32  Request.QueryString("txtFirstName") +
33              "\") && " +
34              "(this.objRS(\"LAST_NAME\")==\"" +
35  Request.QueryString("txtLastName") +
36              "\")";
37
38      if (!objForm.Search(strEval))
39      {
40         objForm.colFormElements.RemoveAll();
41         objForm.colFormElements.Add("FIRST_NAME",
42  Request.QueryString("txtFirstName"));
43         objForm.colFormElements.Add("LAST_NAME",
44  Request.QueryString("txtLastName"));
45         objForm.colFormElements.Add("WORK_PHONE", "");
46         objForm.colFormElements.Add("HOME_PHONE", "");
47         objForm.colFormElements.Add("E_MAIL", "")
48      }
49  }
50  else
51  {
52    if ((objForm.strMode == "Browse") || (objForm.strMode ==
53  "Update") || (objForm.strMode == "Delete"))
54    {
55        strEval = "(this.objRS(\"FIRST_NAME\")==\"" +
56  Request.QueryString("txtFirstName") + "\") && (" +
57              "this.objRS(\"LAST_NAME\")==\"" +
58  Request.QueryString("txtLastName") + "\")";
59
60      if (!objForm.Search(strEval)) {
61        Response.Write("<CENTER><H1>Error Information</H1>");
62        Response.Write("<H3>Student not found!</H3><BR>");
63        Response.Write("Back to <a href=default.htm>Student
Form</a>.</center>");
64        Response.End;
65      }
66      else
67      {
68        if (Request.QueryString("Mode") == "Browse")
69        {
70        objForm.strMode = "Browse";
71        }
72        else
73        {
74           if (Request.QueryString("Mode") == "Delete")
```

```
75                {
76                   objForm.strMode = "Delete";
77                }
78             }
79          }
80       }
81       else
82       {
83             Response.Write("<CENTER><H1>Error Information</H1>");
84             Response.Write("<H3>You did not select a Mode!</H3>
<BR>");
85             Response.Write("Click on the Back button of your
browser to fix!</center>");
86             Response.End;
87       }
88    }
89 %>
90
91 </HEAD>
92
93 <BODY>
94
95 <H1 align="center">Class Registration Form</H1>
96
97 <P align="center"><strong>Instructions:</strong>  You
need to fill in this information so that I can contact you in an
emergency. <br> 
98 All mandatory fields have an &quot;*&quot;
99 next to them. <BR>
100 Please fill in all mandatory fields before
101 hitting SUBMIT.</p>
102
103 <FORM id="frmRegister" name="frmRegister" action="register_me
.asp" method="post">
104
105 <CENTER><P><B>Personal Information</B></P></CENTER>
106
107 <CENTER>Form Mode: <% = objForm.strMode %><INPUT
id="Mode" type="hidden" name="Mode" size="35" value="<% = objForm
.strMode%>" >
108 <INPUT id="STUDENT_ID" type="hidden" name="STUDENT_ID" size=
"35" value="<% = objForm.colFormElements.Item("STUDENT_ID")%>" >
109
110
111 <P>First name: <input id="First_Name" type="text" name="First
_Name" size="35" value="<% = objForm.colFormElements.Item("FIRST_
NAME")%>" >*<BR>
112   Last name: 
113
114 <INPUT id="txtLastName" type = "text" name="Last_Name" size=
"35" value="<% = objForm.colFormElements.Item("LAST_NAME")%>">
<strong>*</strong>  </LABEL></p>
```

6

```
115 </CENTER>
116
117 <CENTER><P><B>Contact Information</B></P>
118 </CENTER>
119
120 <CENTER><P>Home phone:<INPUT type="text" name="Home_Phone"
size="12" value="<% =  objForm.colFormElements.Item("HOME_PHONE")
%>"><BR>
121
122 Work phone:<INPUT type="text" name="Work_Phone" size="12"
value="<% = objForm.colFormElements.Item("WORK_PHONE")%>"><BR>
123
124 E-mail: <INPUT type="text" name="e_mail" size="30" value="
<% = 125 objForm.colFormElements.Item("E_MAIL")%>"><strong>*
</strong>
</P>
126 </CENTER>
127
128 <%if (objForm.strMode == "New") { %>
129 <CENTER><P><INPUT id="cmdSubmit" type="submit" value="Create"
>
130 <INPUT id="cmdReset" type="reset" value="Reset"> </P>
</CENTER>
131 <%}
132 if (objForm.strMode == "Update") { %>
133 <CENTER><P><INPUT id="cmdSubmit" type="submit" value="Update"
>
134 </CENTER>
135 <%}
136  if (objForm.strMode == "Delete") { %>
137 <CENTER><P><INPUT id="cmdSubmit" type="submit" value="Delete"
>
138 </CENTER>
139 <%}
140  if (objForm.strMode == "Browse") {%>
141 <CENTER><P>Back to <A href=default.htm>Search</A>.</CENTER>
142 </CENTER>
143 <%}%>
144 </FORM>
145
146 </BODY>
147 </HTML>
```

Code Dissection

- Line 3, a file, adojavas.inc, is included to supply the ADO constants in JavaScript so that you can refer to the name of the constant instead of the actual numbers.

- Line 25 calls the Open_Recordset function to return a recordset of all students in the STUDENTS table.

- Lines 28–49. In New mode the application must first check to make sure that the database does not already contain a record for the student. If the student does not exist, then the application will prepare a record in the colFormElements collection. Otherwise, the application will switch to Update mode.

- Lines 52–65 look up the student in the database. If a record for the student is found, then the Search function creates a colFormElements collection with the elements of the record stored in it. Each column of a record is stored in the collection as an item. Otherwise, an error message is displayed.

- Lines 82–87 display an error message if the user does not specify a mode by selecting the New, Update, Delete, or Search option button on the default.htm form.

- Line 107 hides the mode from the user. Essentially, this line tells the register_me.asp script what to do. If New is the selected mode, the application inserts a record. If Update is the selected mode, the application updates an existing record. If Delete is the selected mode, the application deletes an existing record. If Browse is the selected mode (the user clicked the Search option button), the application displays an existing record but does not allow any changes to the record.

- Lines 128–143 display the appropriate button for the appropriate mode. For instance, in New mode the application would display the Create and Reset buttons. When the application is in Browse mode, it displays no buttons.

Register_me.asp

The register_me.asp script runs when the form.asp script submits the data to the Web server. Depending on whether the user clicked the New, Update, Delete, or Search option button, the register_me.asp script inserts data, updates data, or deletes data. The necessary code is as follows:

Code Example

```
1 <%@Language=JScript %>
2 <% Response.Buffer = true %>
3 <!-- #include file="clsForm.cls" -->
4 <HTML>
5
6 <HEAD>
7
8 <TITLE>Class Registration Response</TITLE>
9 <%
10 function FormValidation() {
11
12 var blnOK, strSQL;
13
14     blnOK = (Request.Form("First_Name") == "") || (Request.
Form("Last_Name") == "") || (Request.Form("e_mail") == "");
15     if (blnOK) {
16       Response.Write("<CENTER><H1>Error Information</H1>");
```

```
17        Response.Write("<H3>You must enter all the information
that has *'s!</H3><BR>");
18        Response.Write("Click the Back button on your browser to
fix your errors.</CENTER>");
19        Response.End;
20    }
21
22 }
23
24  var objForm,strEval,strErr;
25  FormValidation();
26  objForm = new clsForm();
27    if (Request.Form("Mode") == "New") {
28    strSQL = "INSERT INTO STUDENTS" +
29
30"(FIRST_NAME,LAST_NAME,HOME_PHONE,WORK_PHONE,E_MAIL)" +
31                    " VALUES(" +
32                            "'" + Request.Form("FIRST_NAME") +
33 "'," +
34                             "'" + Request.Form("LAST_NAME") +
35 "'," +
36                             "'" + Request.Form("HOME_PHONE") +
37 "'," +
38                             "'" + Request.Form("WORK_PHONE") +
39 "'," +
40                             "'" + Request.Form("E_MAIL") +   "'
)";
41      strErr = objForm.Run_SQL(strSQL);
42      if (strErr != "") {
43        Response.Write("<CENTER><H1>Error Information</H1>");
44        Response.Write(strErr & "</CENTER>");
45        Response.End;
46      }
47    }
48    else {
49    if (Request.Form("Mode") == "Update") {
50      strSQL = "UPDATE STUDENTS" +
51                    " SET FIRST_NAME = " +
52                            "'" + Request.Form("FIRST_NAME")
+ "'," +
53                        "LAST_NAME = " +
54                            "'" + Request.Form("LAST_NAME") +
  "'," +
55                        "HOME_PHONE = " +
56                            "'" + Request.Form("HOME_PHONE") +
```

```
57 "'," +
58                               "WORK_PHONE = " +
59                                 "'" + Request.Form("WORK_PHONE") +
60 "'," +
61                               "E_MAIL = " +
62                                 "'" + Request.Form("E_MAIL") + "
'" +
63                               " WHERE STUDENT_ID = " +
64                                 Request.Form("STUDENT_ID");
65
66      strErr = objForm.Run_SQL(strSQL);
67
68       if (strErr != "") {
69         Response.Write("<CENTER><H1>Error Information</H1>");
70         Response.Write(strErr & "</CENTER>");
71         Response.End;
72       }
73     }
74     else {
75       strSQL = "DELETE FROM STUDENTS" +
76                         " WHERE STUDENT_ID = " +
77                           Request.Form("STUDENT_ID");
78       strErr = objForm.Run_SQL(strSQL);
79
80       if (strErr != "") {
81         Response.Write("<CENTER><H1>Error Information</H1>");
82         Response.Write(strErr & "</CENTER>");
83         Response.End;
84       }
85     }
86 }
87
88 %>
89 </HEAD>
90 <BODY>
91
92 <CENTER><H1>Class Registration Response</H1></CENTER>
93 <CENTER>
94 <P>Thank you for using the Class Registration form!<P>
95
96 <% if (Request.Form("Mode") != "Delete") { %>
97 <P>The information you entered: <BR>
98 <UL>
99 <LI>First name: <%=Request.Form("First_Name")%></LI>
100 <LI>Last name: <%=Request.Form("Last_Name")%></LI>
101 <LI>Home phone: <%=Request.Form("Home_Phone")%></LI>
102 <LI>Work phone: <%=Request.Form("Work_Phone")%></LI>
103 <LI>E-Mail: <%=Request.Form("e_mail")%></LI>
104 </UL>
105 <% } %>
```

6

```
106 </CENTER>
107 <P>
108 <CENTER>Back to <A href="default.htm">Search</A>.</CENTER>
109 </BODY>
110 </HTML>
```

Code Dissection

- Lines 24–86 show how the mode from the previous form carries over to this ASP script. These lines show how to create the insert, update, and delete queries and how they are run according to whether the user clicked New, Update, Delete, or Search.

CHAPTER SUMMARY

❑ It is unwise to assume that you can create applications or programs that require the end user to enter SQL in an unfriendly HTML form. It is much better to use a friendly HTML form that prompts the end user for information. You can then "hide" the SQL generation behind the forms.

❑ ADO makes life easier for you by hiding the intimate details of interacting with different data sources from you. An application accesses a database via a built-in component called ActiveX Data Objects (ADO). ADO contains many objects that allow a programmer's application to communicate with a data source by using OLE DB or ODBC.

❑ ADO provides three main objects to use to interact with databases: the Connection object, the Recordset object, and the Command object. The Connection object allows an application to connect to a database, send queries to the database, receive results from the database, and disconnect from the database. The Recordset object sends a query to the database and returns a cursor.

REVIEW QUESTIONS

1. What are the two standard database access tools?
   a. ODBC
   b. OLE DB
   c. OLE
   d. OBDC
2. ODBC was designed to access relational data using SQL. True or False?
3. ODBC was designed to access any type of data. True or False?
4. What program do you use to set up an ODBC data source?
   a. OLE DB Administrator
   b. ODBC Administrator
   c. Microsoft Data Link
   d. none of the above

5. What program do you use to setup an OLE DB data source?

   a. OLE DB Administrator

   b. ODBC Administrator

   c. Microsoft Data Link

   d. none of the above

6. What is ActiveX Data Objects (ADO)?

   a. another name for ODBC

   b. a built-in component used to communicate through the ODBC or OLE DB driver to a database

   c. another name for OLE DB

   d. none of the above

7. What ADO object allows you to set up communication to a database?

   a. Connection

   b. Recordset

   c. Command

   d. none of the above

8. What ADO object returns a cursor from the database?

   a. Connection

   b. Recordset

   c. Command

   d. none of the above

9. What method of the Connection object allows you to run an SQL query?

   a. Open

   b. Close

   c. Execute

   d. none of the above

10. What method of the Connection object allows you to set up a connection to the database?

   a. Open

   b. Close

   c. Execute

   d. none of the above

6

11. What method of the Recordset object allows you to move the pointer to the first record in the result set?

    a. MoveLast

    b. MovePrevious

    c. MoveFirst

    d. MoveNext

12. What method of the Recordset object allows you to know whether the recordset pointer is before the first record in the recordset?

    a. EOF

    b. BOF

    c. MoveNext

    d. MovePrevious

13. What method of the Recordset object allows you to know whether the recordset pointer is after the last record in the recordset?

    a. EOF

    b. BOF

    c. MoveNext

    d. MovePrevious

14. What method of the Recordset object allows you to move the recordset pointer to the next record in the recordset?

    a. EOF

    b. BOF

    c. MoveNext

    d. MovePrevious

15. What method of the Recordset object allows you to move the recordset pointer to the previous record in the recordset?

    a. EOF

    b. BOF

    c. MoveNext

    d. MovePrevious

16. What is the syntax for catching run-time errors in VBScript?

    a. An On Error Resume Next statement and using the Err's object number, source, and destination properties

    b. try…catch statement

    c. You cannot catch run-time errors in VBScript.

    d. none of the above

17. What is the syntax for catching run-time errors in JavaScript?

    a. An On Error Resume Next statement and using the Err's object number, source, and destination properties

    b. try…catch statement

    c. You cannot catch run-time errors in JavaScript.

    d. none of the above

18. The Execute method of the Recordset object can return a cursor. True or False?

19. The Connection and Recordset objects are part of ADO. True or False?

20. Microsoft recommends that you use ODBC over OLE DB. True or False?

6

HANDS-ON PROJECTS

Project 6-1

Create the necessary script to create a recordset from the CLASSES table and display the contents of the recordset in a table. Make sure to create a database connection first.

1. With the following code, create project_6_1.asp in the Chapter_6 folder of your Data Disk:

```
<%@ Language=JavaScript %>
<% Response.Buffer = true %>
<html>

<head>

<title>Hands-on Project 6.1</title>

<body>
<%

  //Create the connection and a recordset
  var objRS,objConn,intRecordsAffected,e;
  objRS = new ActiveXObject("ADODB.Recordset");
  objConn = new ActiveXObject("ADODB.Connection");

  //Use a DSN-less connection string
  objConn.Open("DRIVER={Microsoft Access Driver (*.mdb)};
DBQ=" + Server.MapPath("/Chapter_6") + "\\register\\" +
"course.mdb");
  objRS = objConn.Execute("select * from classes",intRecords
Affected);

  if (intRecordsAffected < 0)
  {
    objRS.MoveFirst();
  }
  %>
```

```
<CENTER><H2>Class Query Response</H2>
<TABLE BORDER=1 COLS=<%=objRS.Fields.Count%>>
  <TR>
    <% e = new Enumerator(objRS.Fields);
    while  (!e.atEnd()) {
    item = e.item();
    %>
    <TH> <%=item.name %> </TH>
    <%
    e.moveNext();
    }
    %>
  </TR>

  <% while (!objRS.EOF) { %>
    <TR>
    <% e = new Enumerator(objRS.Fields);
    while  (!e.atEnd()) {
    item = e.item();
    %>
        <TD align=right>
          <% if (item.value==null) {
              }
              else
              {
                  Response.Write(item.value);
              }
          %>
        </TD>
      <%   e.moveNext();
          }
          objRS.MoveNext(); %>
      </TR>
  <%  } %>
</TABLE>

  <% objRS.close();
  %>
</CENTER>
</body>
</html>
```

2. The code that you just wrote is missing one critical line of code. Insert the missing code, and then save the file.

3. Open your browser, and navigate to *http://localhost/Chapter_6/project_6_1.asp* and view the results of the script.

4. Save your work and close all files.

Project 6-2

Create the necessary script for creating a recordset from the INSTRUCTORS table. Make sure to create a database connection first.

1. With the following code, create project_6_2.asp in the Chapter_6 folder of your Data Disk:

```
<%@ Language=JavaScript %>
<% Response.Buffer = true %>
<html>

<head>

<title>Hands-on Project 6.2</title>

<body>
<%

  //Create the connection and a recordset
  var objRS,objConn,intRecordsAffected,e;
  objRS = new ActiveXObject("ADODB.Recordset");
  objConn = new ActiveXObject("ADODB.Connection");

  //Use a DSN-less connection string
  objConn.Open("DRIVER= ...(*.mdb)};"
  + "DBQ= ..." + "\\register\\"
  + "course.mdb");
  objRS = objConn.Execute("select * from instructors",
  intRecordsAffected);

  if (intRecordsAffected < 0)
  {
    objRS.MoveFirst();
  }
   %>

    <CENTER><H2>Instructor Query Response</H2>
    <TABLE BORDER=1 COLS=<%=objRS.Fields.Count%>>
      <TR>
        <% e = new Enumerator(objRS.Fields);
        while  (!e.atEnd()) {
        item = e.item();
        %>
        <TH> <%=item.name %> </TH>
        <%
        e.moveNext();
        }
        %>
      </TR>
```

6

```
<% while (!objRS.EOF) { %>
  <TR>
   <% e = new Enumerator(objRS.Fields);
   while  (!e.atEnd()) {
   item = e.item();
   %>
     <TD align=right>
       <% if (item.value==null) {
             Response.Write(" ");
         }
         else
         {
             Response.Write(item.value);
         }
       %>
     </TD>
     <%   e.moveNext();
       }
         objRS.MoveNext(); %>
   </TR>
  <%  } %>
 </TABLE>

   %>
 </CENTER>
 </body>
 </html>
```

2. The code that you just wrote is missing one critical line of code. Insert that line of code, and then save the file.

3. Open your browser, and navigate to *http://localhost/Chapter_6/project_6_2.asp* and view the results of the script.

4. Save your work and close all files.

Project 6-3

Create the necessary script to insert, update, and delete data from the CLASSES table using a query string. The query string will contain the insert, update, or delete statement.

1. With the following code, create project_6_3.asp in the Chapter_6 folder of your Data Disk:

```
<%@ Language=JavaScript %>
<% Response.Buffer = true %>
<html>
<head>
<title>Hands-on Project 6.3</title>
<body>
<%
 //Create the connection and a recordset
  var objRS,objConn,intRecordsAffected,e;
```

```
objRS = new ActiveXObject("ADODB.Recordset");
objConn = new ActiveXObject("ADODB.Connection");
//Use a DSN-less connection string
objConn.Open("DRIVER={Microsoft Access Driver (*.mdb)};"
+ "DBQ=" + Server.MapPath ("/Chapter_6") + "\\register\\"
+ "course.mdb");
objRS = objConn.Execute(Request.QueryString(txtSQL),
intRecordsAffected);
%
   <CENTER><H2>Classes Query Response</H2>
   <% Response.Write("Success!")%>
   </CENTER>
</body>
</html>
```

2. Open your browser, and navigate to *http://localhost/Chapter_6/project_6_3.asp? txtSQL=insert into classes values('9000', 'IST 100', 'Intro to Info Systems')* and view the results of the script. Close your browser and all files.

Project 6-4

Using the techniques learned in this chapter, create a Web application, using JavaScript, based on the CLASSES table, using the techniques learned in the Student Contact Application. Make sure to handle run-time errors.

1. Create a file called clsForm.cls in the Chapter_6\classes folder of your Data Disk:

```
<%
  this.strMode = "Browse"
  this.colFormElements = new ActiveXObject("Scripting.
Dictionary");
  this.strServerConnectionString = "DRIVER={Microsoft Access
 Driver (*.mdb)}; DBQ=" + Server.MapPath("/Chapter_6/
register") + "\\course.mdb";
  this.objConn = new ActiveXObject("ADODB.Connection");
  this.objRS = new ActiveXObject("ADODB.Connection");
  this.CreateDict = CreateDict;
  this.Open_Recordset = Open_Recordset;
  this.Search = Search;
  this.Run_SQL = Run_SQL;
  this.Mode = Mode;
}

function Mode() {
  return(this.strMode);
}

function Open_Recordset(strSQL) {
  var Err;

  try {
    this.objConn.Open(this.strServerConnectionString);
  }
```

6

```
      catch(Err) {
        Response.Write(Err.Description);
        Response.End;
        return(0);
      }

      try {
        this.objRS = this.objConn.Execute(strSQL);
      }
      catch(Err) {
        Response.Write(Err.Description);
        Response.End;
        return(0);
      }

  }

  function Search(strEvalString) {
      var item, e, found;
      try{this.objRS.MoveFirst();
      while (!this.objRS.EOF)
      {
        found = eval(strEvalString);
        if (found)
           break;
        this.objRS.MoveNext();
      }

      if (!this.objRS.EOF) {
          this.strMode = "Update";
          this.colFormElements.RemoveAll();
          e = new Enumerator(this.objRS.Fields);
          while  (!e.atEnd()) {
          item = e.item();
          this.colFormElements.Add(item.name, item.value);
          e.moveNext();
          }
          return(1)
      }
     else {
          this.strMode = "New";
          this.colFormElements.RemoveAll();
          e = new Enumerator(Request.Form);
          while (!e.atEnd()) {
            item = e.item();
            this.colFormElements.Add(item.name, "");
            e.moveNext();
          }
        }
```

```
        }catch(Err){}
     return(0);
   }


   function CreateDict() {

     var item, e;

     e = new Enumerator(Request.Form);
     for (;!e.atEnd();e.moveNext()) {
      item = e.item();
       this.colFormElements.Add(item.name, Request.Form(item.
   value));
       }


   }

   function Run_SQL(strSQL) {

     var Err;

     objConn = new ActiveXObject("ADODB.Connection");
     objRS = new ActiveXObject("ADODB.Connection");
     try {
       objConn.Open(this.strServerConnectionString);
     }
     catch(Err) {
       return(Err.description);
     }

     try {
       objRS = objConn.Execute(strSQL);
     }
     catch(Err) {
       return(Err.description);
     }
     return("");
   }
   %>
```

2. The code that you just typed is missing one critical line. Insert the missing line of code, and then save your work.

3. Open your browser and navigate to *http://localhost/Chapter_6/classes/default.htm.*

4. On the Search form, click the **New** option button.

5. In the Class number text box, enter **IST 200**.

6. Click the **Submit** button. The Class Form page appears.

7. In the Class name text box, enter **Local Area Networks.**

8. Click the **Create** button. The Class Response page appears.

9. Click on the **Search** link to return to the search page.

10. On the Search form, click the **Update** option button.

11. In the Class number text box, enter **IST 200**.

12. Click the **Submit** button. The Class Form page appears.

13. In the Class name text box, enter **Introduction to Telecommunications.**

14. Click the **Update** button. The Class Response page appears.

15. Click on the **Search** link to return to the search page.

16. On the Search form, click the **Delete** option button.

17. In the Class number text box, enter **IST 200**.

18. Click the **Submit** button. The Class Form page appears.

19. Click the **Delete** button. The Class Response page appears. Close your browser and all files.

Project 6-5

Using the techniques learned in this chapter, create a Web application, using JavaScript, based on the INSTRUCTORS table, using the techniques learned in the Student Contact Application. Make sure to handle run-time errors.

1. Create a file called clsForm.cls in the Chapter_6\instructors folder of your Data Disk:

```
<%
function clsForm() {
   this.strMode = "Browse"
   this.colFormElements = new ActiveXObject("Scripting.
   Dictionary");
   this.strServerConnectionString = "DRIVER="
   + "{Microsoft Access Driver (*.mdb)};"
   + "DBQ="
   + Server.MapPath("/Chapter_6/Register")
   + "\\course.mdb";
   this.objConn = new ActiveXObject("ADODB.Connection");
   this.objRS = new ActiveXObject("ADODB.Connection");
   this.CreateDict = CreateDict;
   this.Open_Recordset = Open_Recordset;
   this.Search = Search;
   this.Run_SQL = Run_SQL;
   this.Mode = Mode;
}

function Mode() {
   return(this.strMode);
}

function Open_Recordset(strSQL) {
   var Err;
```

```
    try {
      this.objConn.Open(this.strServerConnectionString);
    }
    catch(Err) {
      Response.Write(Err.Description);
      Response.End;
      return(0);
    }

    try {
      this.objRS = this.objConn.Execute(strSQL);
    }
    catch(Err) {
      Response.Write(Err.Description);
      Response.End;
      return(0);
    }

}

function Search(strEvalString) {
    var item, e, found;
try {
    this.objRS.MoveFirst();
    while (!this.objRS.EOF)
    {
      found = eval(strEvalString);
      if (found)
         break;
      this.objRS.MoveNext();
    }

    if (!this.objRS.EOF) {
        this.strMode = "Update";
        this.colFormElements.RemoveAll();
        e = new Enumerator(this.objRS.Fields);
        while  (!e.atEnd()) {
        item = e.item();
        this.colFormElements.Add(item.name, item.value);
        e.moveNext();
        }
        }catch(Err){}
        return(1)
    }
    else {
        this.strMode = "New";
        this.colFormElements.RemoveAll();
        e = new Enumerator(Request.Form);
        while (!e.atEnd()) {
          item = e.item();
```

```
                    this.colFormElements.Add(item.name, "");
                    e.moveNext();
                }
            }
        }catch(Err){}
    return(0);
}


function CreateDict() {

  var item, e;

  e = new Enumerator(Request.Form);
  for (;!e.atEnd();e.moveNext()) {
   item = e.item();
   this.colFormElements.Add(item.name, Request.Form(item.
value));
  }


}

function Run_SQL(strSQL) {

  var Err;

  objConn = new ActiveXObject("ADODB.Connection");
  objRS = new ActiveXObject("ADODB.Connection");
  try {
    objConn.Open(this.strServerConnectionString);
  }
  catch(Err) {
    return(Err.description);
  }

  try {
    objRS = objConn.Execute(strSQL);
  }
  catch(Err) {
    return(Err.description);
  }
  return("");
}
%>
```

2. Open your browser, and navigate to *http://localhost/Chapter_6/instructors/default.htm*.

3. On the Search form, click the **New** option button.

4. In the First name text box, enter **Jack**.

5. In the Last name text box, enter **Chu**.

6. Click the **Submit** button. The Instructor Form page appears.

7. In the text boxes, enter the following:

   Phone number: 7033333333
   E_Mail: jchu@erols.com
   Web address: http://www.erols.com/jchu

8. Click the **Create** button. The Instructor Response page appears.

9. Click on the **Search** link to return to the search page.

10. On the Search form, click the **Update** option button.

11. In the First name and Last name text boxes, enter **Jack** and **Chu**.

12. Click the **Submit** button. The Instructor Form page appears.

13. In the Phone number text box, enter 7031231234.

14. Click the **Update** button. The Instructor Response page appears.

15. Click on the **Search** link to return to the search page.

16. On the Search form, click the **Delete** option button.

17. In the First name and Last name text boxes, enter **Jack** and **Chu**.

18. Click the **Submit** button. The Instructor Form page appears.

19. Click the **Delete** button. The Instructor Response page appears.

6

CASE PROJECTS

1. Recall from Chapter 5 that John's Software, Inc. has hired you as a systems analyst to help develop a gift management information system. Begin with the database you created in Chapter 5. Create an application for one table; your application need not manipulate foreign keys.

2. Recall from Chapter 5 that Interstate Bank recently hired you as a system analyst to help develop a Web application. Begin with the database you created in Chapter 5. Create an application for one table; your application need not manipulate foreign keys.

3. Recall from Chapter 5 that Interstate bank recently hired you to develop a check balancing information system. Begin with the database you created in Chapter 5.

   Create an application for one table; your application need not manipulate foreign keys.

7

WHEN IT'S TIME TO MOVE YOUR DATABASE FROM ACCESS TO SQL SERVER

In this chapter, you will:

♦ Understand the logic flow from an application to an Access database

♦ Learn when a migration from Access to SQL Server 7.0 might be necessary

♦ Understand the logic flow from an application to an SQL Server 7.0 database

♦ Learn how to convert the contents of Access database to SQL Server 7.0

♦ Understand the role of the SQL Server Enterprise Manager

♦ Learn the structure of stored procedures

♦ Understand how to call a stored procedure

In Chapters 4 and 5, you learned about forms and using SQL to interact with Access databases. In Chapter 6, you learned how to separate the end user from the task of writing SQL code; the code was produced by your scripts in response to the end user's input. In this chapter, you will learn how to determine when Access no longer serves your organization's needs and how you can migrate that database to SQL Server 7.0.

A TYPICAL SCENARIO WITH ACCESS

Suppose you were just hired by Tien Phen, an IT manager for Centreville Community College, to work on the college's Web application. This application makes it possible for instructors to make test grades available to students online. Currently, the application runs on top of Access, and the application worked fine when it was used by only a few instructors. The logic flow of the application is represented in Figure 7-1.

Figure 7-1   Logic flow under Access

Now, however, the application supports well over 200 instructors, with a total student population of over 5000 students. Mr. Phen is noticing a substantial increase in complaints from students and faculty, indicating that the application is slow and sluggish.

The performance degradation is the result of two independent issues. The first is the sheer number of activities that must occur each time a student or professor accesses the database, as detailed in Figure 7-2. It is between Steps 2 and 3 that the most performance degradation occurs because the SQL must be interpreted each time the database is accessed. The second reason is that Access is not a server-based DBMS, but a file-based DBMS. Because it is a file-based DBMS, Access is, by definition, not designed to handle high-speed access.

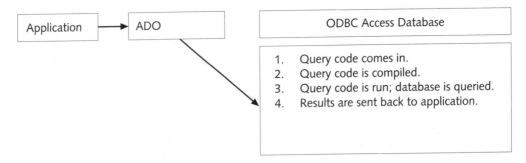

Figure 7-2   Activities that occur when an Access database is accessed

To solve these problems, you decide to move the contents of the Access database to a new home: SQL Server 7.0. SQL Server 7.0 is made for high-volume 24/7 access and will give your school the access power it needs. It has the logic flow shown in Figure 7-3.

Figure 7-3   SQL Server 7.0 logic flow

While the logic flow is, of course, very similar, it is what happens within SQL Server 7.0 (hereafter called "SQL Server") that produces the performance improvement, as shown in Figure 7–4.

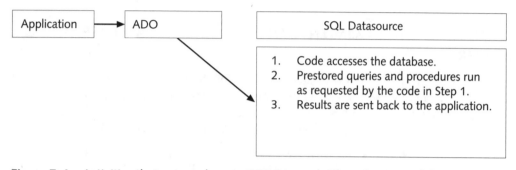

Figure 7-4   Activities that occur when an SQL Server database is accessed

It is in Step 2 that performance is enhanced. Because SQL Server uses an internal procedural language, the procedures are already in the native language of the database. In other words, SQL Server can skip the second step that Access has to take and, thus, perform faster.

I KNOW WHERE I WANT TO GO, BUT HOW DO I GET THERE?

Actually, simply realizing that you need to switch over from Access to SQL Server is more than half the battle. The switching over simply requires that you follow a well-defined path, as outlined in Figure 7-5.

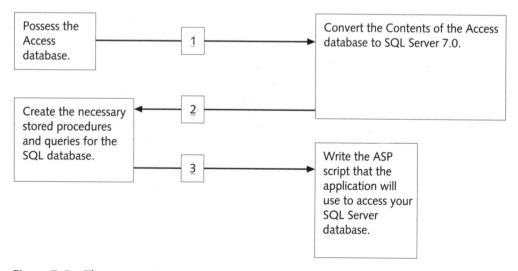

Figure 7-5   The conversion process

Conveniently enough, this figure, while showing the process for accomplishing your goal, also provides the outline for this chapter. So, since we already possess the Access database, we will move to the next stage: converting its contents to SQL Server.

CONVERTING THE CONTENTS OF THE ACCESS DATABASE TO SQL SERVER 7.0

Converting an Access database to an SQL Server database is easy; you simply run the Migration Wizard, following the prompts as you do so. Because you are pressed for time, Tien Phen's database administrator has graciously run the database through that conversion wizard for you and has e-mailed you the result, which is on your Data Disk.

Figure 7-6 shows you what has already been accomplished (the first and second boxes) and what you will do to finish the process (the third and fourth boxes). So, based on this figure, your next step is to prepare the SQL shell and then restore the database into that shell. Both steps are accomplished with the SQL Server Enterprise Manager, which we will discuss next.

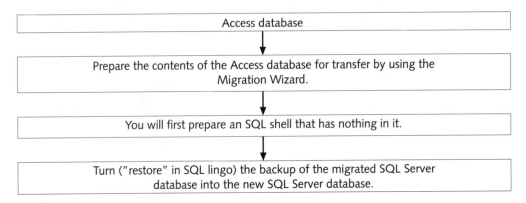

Figure 7-6   Actions necessary to complete the conversion

SQL Server Enterprise Manager

SQL Server Enterprise Manager is a graphical tool you can use to configure, manage, and maintain SQL Server databases. Figure 7-7 illustrates the SQL Server Enterprise Manager environment.

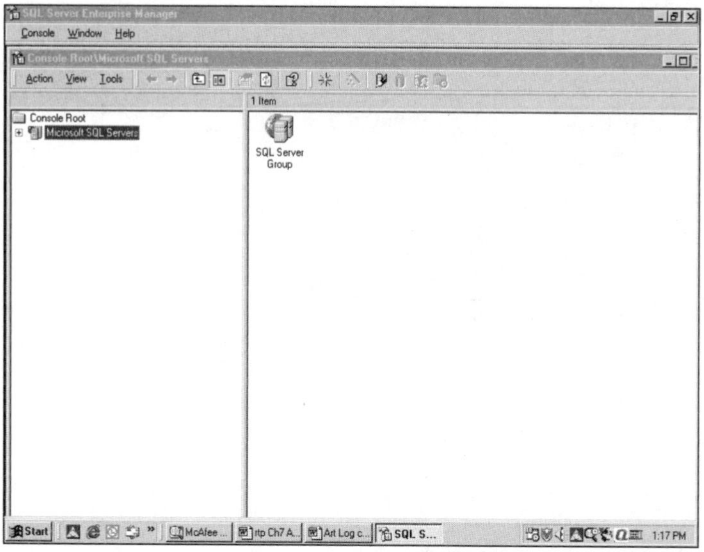

Figure 7-7   SQL Server Enterprise Manager environment

The SQL Server Enterprise Manager is part of **Microsoft's Management Console (MMC)**, an administrative tool used to manage hardware, software, and network components of different Windows operating systems. MMC simplifies many administrative tasks by providing a common interface for all administrative tools and integrating all administrative tools under a single application environment. You can use it to configure different components, and save configurations for use on other computers. The left pane in the SQL Server Enterprise Manager is the MMC console tree, which provides a hierarchical view of the different components in the SQL Server environment.

Preparing the SQL Shell

Now that you are familiar with the SQL Server Enterprise Manager, you can use it to prepare the SQL shell:

To prepare the shell:

1. Click **Start**, point to **Programs**, point to **Microsoft SQL Server 7.0**, and then click **Enterprise Manager**.

2. In the left pane, double-click **Microsoft SQL Servers**, if necessary. A list of SQL Server components is displayed.

3. Double-click **SQL Server Group**. The name of your server appears.

4. Double-click the **name** of your server.

5. Right-click **Databases** to open a shortcut menu, and then click **New Database**. The Database Properties dialog box opens, as shown in Figure 7-8.

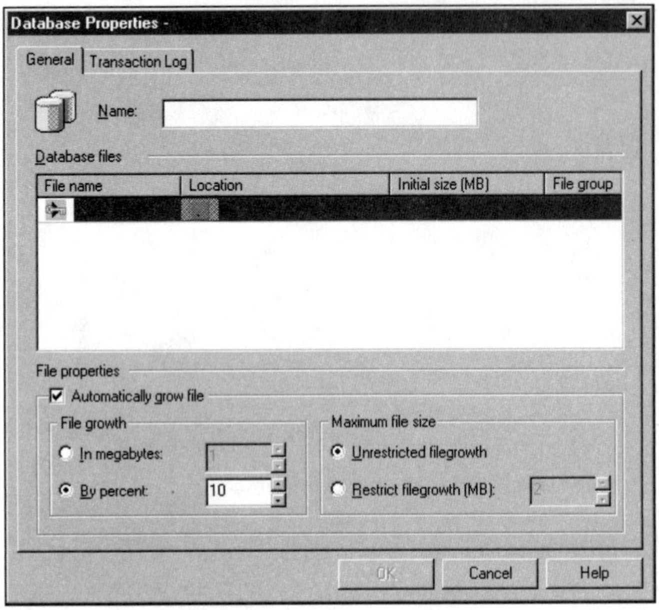

Figure 7-8   Database Properties dialog box

6. In the Name Textbox, type **Course**, and then click **OK**. You return to the SQL Server Enterprise Manager window.

7. Double-click the **Databases** folder in the right pane. The Course database is included in the resulting list of databases. Leave this SQL Server Enterprise Manager window open; you will use it again in the next section.

You have just prepared the database shell. Now it is time to restore the database itself.

Restoring the Database

To restore the Course database:

1. Open Windows Explorer, and copy **Course.dmp** from the Chapter_7 folder on your Data Disk to c:\Mssql7\Backup.

2. Return to the Server Enterprise Manager window and verify that the Database folder is still expanded.

3. Right-click **Course** in the right pane, point to **All Tasks**, and click **Restore Database**. The Restore database dialog box opens, as shown in Figure 7-9. It is in this dialog box that you will specify the database to restore.

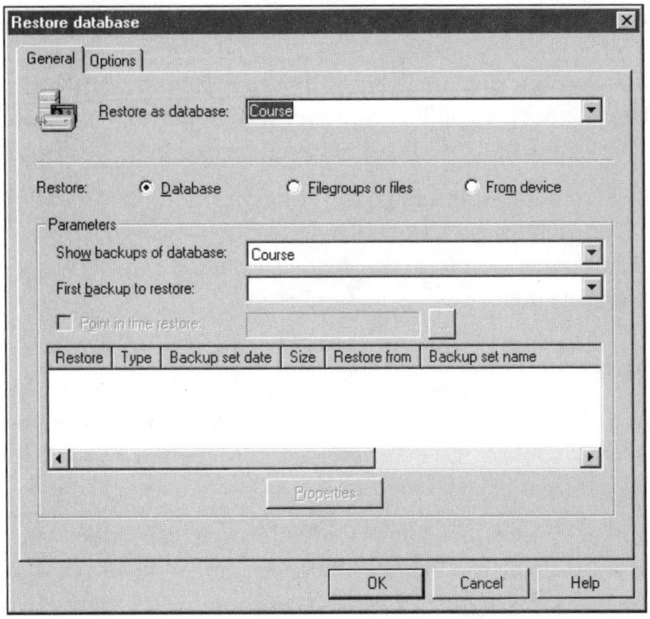

Figure 7-9   Restore database dialog box

4. In the Restore Option Group, click the **From device** option button.

5. In the Parameters section, click the **Select Devices** button.

6. In the Restore from section, click the **Add** button.

7. In the File name text box, type **c:\Mssql7\Backup\Course.dmp**.

8. Click **OK** to close the Choose Restore Destination dialog box, and then click **OK** again.

9. Click the **Options** tab, and then check the **Force restore over existing database** check box. This option overwrites the current database (Course) with the copy of the SQL Server database on your Data Disk.

10. Now you need to define the database files you need to restore to. If necessary, change the entries in the Move to physical file name column to the following:

    c:\mssql7\data\Course_data.mdf
    c:\mssql7\data\Course_log.ldf

11. Click the **General** tab.

12. Change, if necessary, the Restore as database text box to read **Course**.

13. Click **OK** to restore the database. A dialog box will tell you when the restoration is complete.

14. Click **OK**. You return to the SQL Server Enterprise Manager window.

STORED PROCEDURES

OK, you've realized the limitations of Access, and you've migrated the database from Access to SQL Server. What you have now, if you'll excuse the analogy, is a very nice ball of unleavened dough. Your next step is to add the yeast—the stored procedures.

We've broken this "adding" step into substeps; in the following sections, you will learn about procedural language, the capabilities of Transact-SQL, and the use of variables. Only then will we add stored procedure functionality to this chapter's application. Note that for brevity, only VBScript is used in this chapter.

What Is a Procedural Language?

A procedural language is a language that allows you to write code logic (as opposed to logical code, pun intended), and then save it. The saved logic is known as a **stored procedure**. Visual Basic is an example of a procedural language.

SQL, on the other hand, is an example of a nonprocedural language; it works with sets of data but does not work well with a single row of data. Thus, to write procedures for SQL Server, you need to use an adaptation of SQL known as the **Transact-SQL** procedural extension.

The syntax of Transact-SQL is very similar to Visual Basic, and it provides the following procedural capabilities:

- Assignment statements
- If/Else logic
- Case logic
- Loops
- Error handling
- Transaction handling
- Targeted processing of records rather than entire data sets

A Procedural Language and Its Variables

In Transact-SQL, you store values in variables. **Variables** store results for calculations or the processing of data within a program. As the stored procedure executes, the values stored in the variables can change.

Variables can be declared as global or as local. When they are global, it means all stored procedures have access to the data. When they are local, they are only seen by the procedure declaring them. In this chapter's application, your variables will be declared as local because it is good programming practice to keep your variables as close to the procedure as possible, because such a practice will ease code maintenance in the future.

The syntax for declaring local variables in SQL Server is as follows; Table 7-1 shows valid data types in SQL Server.

Syntax Example

DECLARE @v_varname datatype, @v_varname1 datatype

Code Example

```
DECLARE @v_age int
DECLARE @v_date datetime, num_of_months int
DECLARE @v_lastname varchar(35), @v_firstname varchar(35)
```

VBScript

Table 7-1 Data Types in SQL Server

Data Type	Uses	Size
Int	Whole numbers from −2,147,483,648 to 2,147,483,647	4 bytes
Smallint	Whole numbers from −32,768 to 32,767	2 bytes
Tinyint	Whole numbers from 0 to 255	1 byte
numeric(*p,s*)	Whole or fractional numbers from −10^38 to 10^38. *p* is the precision (number of digits), and *s* is the size (the number of decimal points).	2–17 bytes
decimal(*p,s*)	Same as numeric	Same as numeric
Float(*n*)	Whole or fractional numbers from −1.79E308 to 1.79E308	8 bytes
Real	Whole or fractional numbers from −3.40E38 to 3.40E38	4 bytes
Char(*n*)	Characters (up to 255); *n* specifies the number of chars	1 byte/char
varchar(*n*)	Variable length characters (up to 255); *n* specifies the number of characters stored	1 byte/char
Money	Currency values with accuracy to four decimal places	8 bytes
Smallmoney	Currency values with accuracy to four decimal places	4 bytes
Datetime	Date and time Date format: 01-JAN-1753–31-DEC-9999 Time format: Number of miliseconds since midnight of a given date	8 bytes
smalldatetime	Date and time Date format: 01-JAN-1753–6-JUNE-2079 Time format: Number of minutes since midnight of given date	4 bytes
binary(*n*)	Binary representation (up to 255 bytes)	*n* bytes
varbinary(*n*)	Variable binary representation (up to 255 bytes)	number of bytes actually stored
text and image	Text: character data up to 2 GB Image: binary data up to 2 GB	number of bytes stored
Bit	Boolean values (0 or 1)	1 bit

7

Assigning Values to Variables

Once you have defined your variables, you can assign values to those variables. The syntax for assigning a value to a variable is:

Syntax Example

SELECT @v_varname = 0

Code Example

```
SELECT @v_age = 13
SELECT @v_counter = @v_counter + 1
SELECT @v_lastname = 'Morneau'
```

Flow Control

Once you know how to declare a variable and then assign a value to it, you are ready to control the sequence in which your programming logic is executed. This is done by mastering flow control by learning the syntax of flow control statements. Table 7-2 defines some of the different flow control statements supported in Transact-SQL.

Table 7-2 Flow Control in Transact-SQL

Construct	Description	Example

BEGIN...END	Defines a block of statements. Usually used with IF, ELSE, or WHILE in SQL Server and defines the start and end of a procedure in PL/SQL	```IF @v_age < 20```
		```BEGIN```
		```SELECT @v_message =```
		``` 'You are young'```
		```SELECT @v_type = 'Youth'```
		```END```

IF...THEN...ELSE	Defines a conditional statement that executes code after "then if true", or optionally executes code after "else if false"	```IF @v_age < 20```
		```BEGIN```
		```SELECT @v_message =```
		```'You are young'```
		```SELECT @v_type = 'Youth'```
		```END```
		```ELSE```
		```BEGIN```
		```SELECT @v_message =```
		```'You are old'```
		```SELECT @v_type = 'Adult'```
		```END```

GOTO label	Unconditionally branches to the line following the label	```GOTO Goodbye```
		```...```
		```Goodbye:```
		```SELECT @v_message =```
		```'Goodbye'```

Table 7-2   Flow Control in Transact-SQL (continued)

Construct	Description	Example
RETURN (*n*)	Exits unconditionally with a return code of *n*	RETURN (0) or RETURN(1) Returns 0 for successful operation and 1 for unsuccessful operation

WHILE	The looping construct that executes a block of statements until the while condition is false	```SELECT @v_counter = 0```
		```WHILE @v_counter <> 20```
		```BEGIN```
		``` PRINT @v_counter```
		``` SELECT @v_counter =```
		```@v_counter + 1```
		```END```

... BREAK
(SQL Server)
	Exits the innermost WHILE loop unconditionally	```SELECT @v_counter = 0```
		```WHILE @v_counter <> 20```
		```BEGIN```
		``` PRINT @v_counter```
		``` SELECT @v_counter =```
		```@v_counter + 1```
		``` IF @v_counter = 10```
		``` BEGIN```
		``` BREAK```
		``` END```
		```END```

Error Handling

Though SQL Server has built-in error handling capabilities, it is difficult to read and understand the messages. Thus, to translate those messages, you should map each potential SQL Server error message to an error message that you yourself have written (and conveniently stored within the database for easy maintenance). An example of code that contains error-handling capabilities is as follows:

```
INSERT INTO TEST(TEST_ID,TEST)
VALUES(1,'Exam #1')
If @@ERROR <> 0
    Goto INSERT_ERROR
 .  .  .
    Return (0)
INSERT_ERROR:
[Error handler]
Return (1)
```

The Syntax of Stored Procedures

You now have enough information to understand the syntax of stored procedures. The following shows the code for creating a stored procedure in SQL Server.

```
CREATE PROCEDURE proc_name
@p_argument1 datatype,
@p_argument2 datatype
AS

. . .
RETURN(0)
```

> Note that code for modifying a stored procedure in SQL Server is identical to the proceeding code, except that you need to change "CREATE" (in the first line) to "ALTER."

Creating a Stored Procedure in SQL Server

To finish setting up the SQL Server database for this chapter, you need to insert a stored procedure.

To create a stored procedure in SQL Server:

1. In the left pane of the SQL Server Enterprise Manager window, expand **Databases**, and then expand **Course**, if necessary.

2. Right-click **Stored Procedures** under the Course database, and then click **New Stored Procedure**. The Stored Procedure Properties - New Stored Procedure dialog box opens, as shown in Figure 7-10.

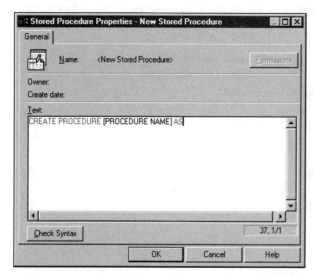

Figure 7-10   Stored Procedure Properties - New Stored Procedure dialog box

3. Replace the contents of the text box with the following code:

```
CREATE PROCEDURE proc_class_schedule
@p_ClassScheduleID int, @p_mode varchar(10), @p_section
varchar(10),
@p_year varchar(4), @p_term varchar(6), @p_classID int,
@p_instructorID int,
@p_error_message varchar(200) OUTPUT
AS

If ((@p_section = '') or (@p_year = '') or (@p_term = ''))
Goto ClsError

IF @p_mode = 'New'
BEGIN

INSERT INTO CLASS_SCHEDULES (SECTION, YEAR, TERM, CLASS_ID,

INSTRUCTOR_ID)
VALUES (@p_section, @p_year, @p_term, @p_classID,
@p_instructorID)

END
ELSE
BEGIN
  IF @p_mode = 'Update'
  BEGIN

    UPDATE CLASS_SCHEDULES
    SET SECTION = @p_section,
    YEAR = @p_year,
    TERM =  @p_term,
    CLASS_ID = @p_classID,
    INSTRUCTOR_ID = @p_instructorID
    WHERE CLASS_SCHEDULE_ID = @p_ClassScheduleID

  END
  ELSE
  BEGIN
    IF @p_mode = 'Delete'
    BEGIN

      DELETE FROM  CLASS_SCHEDULES
      WHERE CLASS_SCHEDULE_ID = @p_ClassScheduleID

    END
  END
END

SELECT @p_error_message = ''
RETURN (0)
```

7

```
ClsError:

SELECT @p_error_message = 'Mandatory fields cannot be blank
!'
Return (1)
```

4. Click **OK** to save the stored procedure.

CALLING A STORED PROCEDURE WITH THE ADO COMMAND OBJECT

Once you migrate your database from Access to SQL Server and then stock that database with the requisite procedures and queries, it is time to write the code that allows your application to access those procedures and queries. You do this by using the Command object in ADO.

Table 7-3 describes the methods and properties of the Command object.

Table 7-3   Useful Properties and Methods of the Command Object

Property/Method	Name	Description
Method	CreateParameter	Creates a parameter object in the Parameters collection. The parameter object supplies argument information for a stored procedure.
Method	Execute	Runs the SQL statement or stored procedure specified in the CommandText property.
Property	ActiveConnection	Sets the Connection to use with this Command object. Must be set to send SQL statements or stored procedures to the database and retrieve them from it.
Property	CommandText	The text of the SQL statement or stored procedure name to execute.
Property	CommandTimeout	The number of seconds to wait when executing a command before an error is returned.
Property	CommandType	Type of query **adcmdUnknown** 0 Unknown type of query **adCmdText** 1 SQL statement **adCmdTable** 2 Name of the table **adCmdStoredProc** 4 Stored procedure or query that is stored in the data source
Property	Name	Allows a name to be assigned to the command object.
Property	State	Returns whether the command is open (adStateOpen) or closed (adStateClosed).

A Parameters collection holds one or more parameter objects, which are the arguments that your code will use to pass information to the procedures. The collection grows and shrinks as necessary, depending on the number of items in the collection. Tables 7-4 and 7-5 describe the methods and properties of the Parameters collection and the Parameter object.

Table 7-4   Useful Properties and Methods of the Parameters Collection

Property/Method	Name	Description
Method	Append	Adds a Parameter object to the collection
Method	Delete	Removes a parameter from the collection
Method	Refresh	Updates the collection with changes to the parameters
Property	Count	Returns the number of Parameter objects in the collection
Property	Item	Returns the contents of a Parameter object in the collection

Table 7-5   Useful Properties and Methods of the Parameter Object

Property/Method	Name	Description
Property	Attributes	Type of data that the parameter accepts
Property	Direction	Determines whether the Parameter object is for input, output, or both
Property	Name	Name of the parameter
Property	NumericScale	Number of decimal places in a numeric parameter
Property	Precision	Number of digits in a numeric parameter
Property	Size	Maximum size in bytes of the parameter
Property	Type	Data type of the parameter. Examples: adInteger, adVarChar, and adNumeric. Refer to the online documentation for more data types.
Property	Value	Value assigned to a parameter

7

In your chapter's application, the clsForm.cls script handles the functions of a form. To call a stored procedure, you need to add a new function to the application. This function will call the stored procedure on the server; the results of the function are then returned to the client.

To add the Run_SP function to the clsForm.cls:

1. In your text editor, open **clsForm.cls** from the Chapter_7\schedulingSP folder of your Data Disk.

2. Add the following code before the existing Public Property Get Mode code:

```
Public Function Run_SP(objCom)

    Dim objConn

    set objConn = CreateObject("ADODB.Connection")

    On Error Resume Next
    objConn.Open strServerConnectionString

    If Err.Number <> 0 Then
      Run_SP = Err.Description
      Exit Function
```

```
          End If


     set objCom.ActiveConnection = objConn
     objCom.CommandType = adCmdStoredProc
     objCom.Execute

     If Err.Number <> 0 Then
       Run_SP = Err.Description
       Exit Function
     End If

     Run_SP = trim(objCom(7))
     set objConn = nothing

   End Function
```

3. Save the file.

Updating the SERVER Name

You must change the SERVER attribute in SQL.htm and the schedulingSP\clsForm.cls in the Chapter_7 folder of your student disk to your server's name for the SQL Server's DSN-less connection for this to work properly.

To determine your server name:

1. On your desktop, right-click **Network Neighborhood**, and then click **Properties**.

2. Click the Identification tab, note the computer name, and then close the dialog box.

3. In a text editor, open the **sql.htm** file from the Chapter_7 folder on your Data Disk.

4. Change the bolded name below to the name of your own computer.

   ```
   <INPUT type="radio" id="ConnectTo" name="optConnect" value=
   "PROVIDER=MSDASQL;DRIVER={SQL Server};SERVER=CRT_SERVER;
   DATABASE=course;UID=sa;PWD=;">SQL Server
   ```

5. Save the change and then close the file. Open **clsForm.cls** from the Chapter_7\schedulingSP folder of your Data Disk, if necessary.

6. Change the bolded text below to your computer name.

   ```
   strServerConnectionString = "PROVIDER=MSDASQL;DRIVER={SQL
   Server};SERVER=CRT_SERVER;DATABASE=Course;UID=sa;PWD=;"
   ```

7. Save the file, close the file, and then exit your text editor.

EXAMINING THE FINAL PRODUCT

To view the Class Scheduling Application:

1. Prepare a virtual directory within PWS named Chapter_7 that points to your Data Disk for Chapter 7. Start Internet Explorer.

   Type **http://localhost/Chapter_7/schedulingSP/default.asp** in the Address text box, and then press **Enter**. The Class Scheduling Application form appears.

2. To search for schedules for a particular class, type **IST 212** in the Class number text box.

3. Click the **Search** option button, and then click the **Submit** button. A list of schedules is displayed.

4. Click the **Back** button on your browser to go back to the previous form.

5. To add a new schedule to the database, click the **New** option button, and then click the **Submit** button. Because the schedule number is already in the database, some of the registration information is already filled in for you.

6. In the Term text box, type **Fall**, in the Year text box, type **2001**, and in the Section text box, type **01**.

7. Click the **Create** button to save this new schedule. The Class Registration Response page appears.

8. Click the **Search** link to go back to the Class Scheduling Application form.

9. Next, you will try updating an existing class schedule. Click the **Update** option button, type **IST 212** in the Class number text box, and then click the **Submit** button. Multiple rows are displayed for your use, which will include the new schedule you inserted; this is the result of a complex query that will be explained in the next section of this chapter.

10. Click the **Select** link for the first item.

11. Change Section to **ELI**.

12. Click the **Update** button. When the schedule is successfully updated, the Class Registration Response page appears.

13. Click the **Search** link to go back to the Class Scheduling Application form.

14. Now you will try deleting an existing class schedule. Click the **Delete** radio button, type **IST 212** into the Class number text box.

15. Click the **Submit** button.

16. Click the **Select** link for the first item.

17. A form with the information appears. Click the **Delete** button to delete the class schedule.

7

18. Click the **Search** link to go back to the Class Schedule Application form. Conduct a search on IST 212 to make sure the schedule item was deleted. Close your browser.

19. Close SQL Enterprise Manager.

KEY POINTS IN THE CODE

You are now ready to explore key parts of the code from the application in this chapter. In the first file, we will point out where and how the application retrieved multiple rows during a search. (*Hint*: It was through the use of a complex query.) In the second file, we will show additional changes worthy of note.

The following is the code for the default.asp file, which you will find in the schedulingSP folder of your Chapter_7 folder on your Data Disk.

Code Example

```
1 <%@ Language=VBScript %>
2 <% Response.Buffer = True %>
3 <!-- #include file="clsForm.cls" -->
4 <HTML>
5 <HEAD>
6
7 </HEAD>
8 <BODY>
9 <center><H1>Class Scheduling Application</H1>
10
11 <% Dim blnOK,strQuery
12
13     blnOK = Request.QueryString("txtClassNumber")<> "" AND
(Request.QueryString("txtSection") <> "" AND Request.QueryString
("txtTerm") <> "" AND Request.QueryString("txtYear") <> "")
14
15    if blnOK Then
16       strQuery = ""
17       strQuery = strQuery & _
18         "Mode=" & replace(Request.QueryString("Mode")," ","+") &
 "&" & _
19         "CLASS_NUMBER=" &  replace(Request.QueryString("txtClass
Number")," ","+") & "&" & _
20         "TERM=" & replace(Request.QueryString("txtTerm")," ","+"
) & "&" & _
21         "YEAR=" & replace(Request.QueryString("txtYear")," ","+"
) & "&" & _
22         "SECTION=" & replace(Request.QueryString("txtSection"),"
 ","+")
23
24      Response.Redirect("form.asp?" & strQuery)
```

```
25      Response.End
26    End If
27
28    blnOK = Request.QueryString("txtClassNumber")= "" AND
(Request.QueryString("txtSection") = "" OR Request.QueryString
("txtTerm") = "" OR Request.QueryString("txtYear") = "")
29
30 If Request.QueryString("Mode") = "New" Then
31   Response.Redirect("form.asp?Mode=New&CLASS_NUMBER=" &
replace(Request.QueryString("txtClassNumber")," ","+"))
32   Response.End
33 End If
34
35   If blnOK Then
36 %>
37
38 <CENTER>
39
40 <form id="frmSchedule" name="frmSchedule" action="default.asp"
method="get">
41 <center>
42 <p>
43 <input type="radio" name="Mode" value="New">New
44 <input type="radio" name="Mode" value="Update">Update
45 <input type="radio" name="Mode" value="Delete">Delete
46 <input type="radio" name="Mode" value="Browse">Search
47
48 <p>Class number: <input type="text" name="txtClassNumber" size
="30"><br>
49 Term: <input type="text" name="txtTerm" size="10">
50 Year: <input type="text" name="txtYear" size="5">
51 Section: <input type="text" name="txtSection" size="30">
52
53 </p>
54 </center>
55
56 <center>
57 <p><input id="cmdSubmit"  type="submit" value="Submit">
58 <input id="cmdReset"  type="reset" value="Reset"> </p>
59 </center>
60
61 </form>
62
63 </CENTER>
64
65 <%
66 Else %>
67
68 <CENTER>
69
```

7

```
70 <center>
71 <p>
72 INSTRUCTIONS: You must select schedule information <BR> for
the
73 form to process.
74 <p>
75   <%
76   Dim objForm,objField
77   set objForm = new clsForm
78
79   objForm.Open_Recordset(""& _
80   "select  CLASSES.CLASS_NUMBER,CLASSES.CLASS_NAME,CLASS_
SCHEDULES.TERM,CLASS_SCHEDULES.YEAR,CLASS_SCHEDULES.SECTION " &_
81   "from classes, class_schedules " & _
82   "where CLASSES.class_id = CLASS_SCHEDULES.class_id AND " & _
83   "CLASSES.CLASS_NUMBER = '" &  Request.QueryString("txtClass
Number") & "' " &_
84   "ORDER BY CLASS_SCHEDULES.TERM, CLASS_SCHEDULES.YEAR,  CLASS
_SCHEDULES.SECTION")
85
86
87 %>
88
89 <TABLE BORDER=1 COLS=<%=objForm.objRS.Fields.Count%>>
90       <TR>
91          <TH></TH>
92       <% For each objField in objForm.objRS.Fields %>
93         <TH> <%=objField.Name %> </TH>
94       <% Next %>
95      </TR>
96     <% Do while Not objForm.objRS.EOF %>
97      <TR>
98         <TD align=right>
99        <% if Request.QueryString("Mode") <> "Browse" Then
100         strQuery = ""
101         For Each objField in objForm.objRS.Fields
102           strQuery = strQuery & objField.Name & "=" &
replace(objField.Value," ","+") & "&amp;"
103         Next
104         strQuery = strQuery & "Mode=" & Request.QueryString
("Mode")
105         %>
106         <a href=form.asp?<% = strQuery %>>Select</a>
107        <%End If%>
108        </TD>
109      <% For Each objField in objForm.objRS.Fields %>
110        <TD align=right>
111          <% If IsNull(objField) Then
112               Response.Write(" ")
113             else
114               Response.Write(objField.Value)
```

```
115                    End If
116             %>
117                </TD>
118          <% Next
119             objForm.objRS.MoveNext %>
120          </TR>
121     <% Loop %>
122    </TABLE>
123
124 </CENTER>
125
126 <%End If %>
127 </BODY>
128 </HTML>
```

Code Dissection

- Lines 13–26 check to see if the class number, section, term, and year fields are filled in. If these text boxes are empty, a form with search criteria appears. (This form begins on line 35.) If some of the fields are filled in, then the application builds a search string that is used to query the CLASS_SCHEDULES table for all schedules based on the CLASS_NUMBER. This form will be called again with a search string. The replace function is used to replace spaces with + as needed by the query string.

- Lines 28–29 check to see if the CLASS_NUMBER, the SECTION, the TERM, and the YEAR are filled in.

- Lines 30–33: If you select New, then the code looks to see this and redirects you to the main form.

- Lines 35–64 run if none of the fields is filled in; then the search form displays, requesting the search form.

- Lines 65–126: If a query string exists, then a complex query is run. (This query contains a join between CLASS_SCHEDULES and CLASSES.) The results of the query are then displayed to the user. If the user initially selected the Update or Delete option buttons on the form, then the user can select a record within the query results to update or delete. If the user initially selected the Search option button, then the user can only view the data

The structure of the form.asp code differs from that in Chapter 7. With it, the application now has the ability to view the CLASS_NUMBER and the INSTRUCTOR name on the form instead of the respective foreign key numbers. Let's review the changes to the form.asp code.

Code Example

```
1 <%@ Language=VBScript%>
2 <%Option Explicit%>
3 <%Response.buffer=true%>
4 <!-- #include file="clsForm.cls" -->
5 <!-- #include file="adovbs.inc" -->
6 <HTML>
7 <HEAD>
8 <TITLE>Class Registration Form</TITLE>
9 <!--
10     **************************************************
11     *** Form Name:       frmSchedule             ***
12     *** Author:          Keith Morneau           ***
13     *** Date:            8/6/00                   ***
14     *** Description:                              ***
15     ***    This form allows user to enter         ***
16     ***    the class schedule information.        ***
17     ***                                          ***
18     *** Revisions:                               ***
19     **************************************************
20 -->
21 <%
22   Dim objForm,strEval,blnOK
23   set objForm = new clsForm
24
25   objForm.Open_Recordset(""& _
26   "select CLASS_SCHEDULES.CLASS_SCHEDULE_ID,CLASSES.CLASS_ID,
CLASSES.CLASS_NUMBER,CLASSES.CLASS_NAME,CLASS_SCHEDULES.TERM,
CLASS_SCHEDULES.YEAR,CLASS_SCHEDULES.SECTION " &_
27   "from classes, class_schedules " & _
28   "where CLASSES.class_id = CLASS_SCHEDULES.class_id AND " & _
     "CLASSES.CLASS_NUMBER = '" & Request.QueryString("CLASS_
NUMBER") & "' ")
'   "ORDER BY CLASS_SCHEDULES.TERM, CLASS_SCHEDULES.YEAR, CLASS_
SCHEDULES.SECTION")
29   objForm.Mode = Request.QueryString("Mode")
30
31   If objForm.Mode = "New" Then
32
33        strEval = "objRS(" & CHR(34) & "CLASS_NUMBER" & CHR(34)
&
34 ")=" & CHR(34) & Request.QueryString("CLASS_NUMBER") & CHR(34)
 &
35 " AND " & _
36                      "objRS(" & CHR(34) & "TERM" & CHR(34) & ")="
 &
37 CHR(34) & Request.QueryString("TERM") & CHR(34) & " AND " & _
38                      "objRS(" & CHR(34) & "YEAR" & CHR(34) & ")="
&
```

```
39 CHR(34) & Request.QueryString("YEAR") & CHR(34) & " AND " & _
40                   "objRS(" & CHR(34) & "SECTION" & CHR(34) & " _
)="
41 & CHR(34) & Request.QueryString("SECTION") & CHR(34)
42
43
44       If Not objForm.Search(strEval)Then
45           objForm.Open_Recordset("select  CLASS_ID,CLASS_ _
NUMBER,CLASS_NAME from classes where class_number =
46 '" & Request.QueryString("CLASS_NUMBER") & "'")
47           if Not objForm.objRS.EOF Then
48              objForm.colFormElements.RemoveAll
49              objForm.colFormElements.Add "CLASS_SCHEDULE_ID",0
50              objForm.colFormElements.Add "CLASS_NAME",objForm.
objRS("CLASS_NAME")
51              objForm.colFormElements.Add "CLASS_NUMBER",
Request.QueryString("CLASS_NUMBER")
52              objForm.colFormElements.Add "TERM", ""
53              objForm.colFormElements.Add "YEAR", ""
54              objForm.colFormElements.Add "SECTION", ""
55              objForm.colFormElements.Add "CLASS_ID",objForm.
objRS("CLASS_ID")
56              objForm.colFormElements.Add "INSTRUCTOR_ID",0
57          Else
58              Response.Write("<CENTER><H1>Error Information
</H1>")
59              Response.Write("<H3>No class information found!</H3
><BR>")
60              Response.Write("Back to <a href=default.asp>Class
Form</a>.</center>")
61              Response.End
62          End If
63       End If
64    Else
65
66    If objForm.Mode = "Browse" or objForm.Mode = "Update" or obj
Form.Mode = "Delete" Then
67
68          strEval = "objRS(" & CHR(34) & "CLASS_NUMBER" & CHR(34)
&
69 ")=" & CHR(34) & Request.QueryString("CLASS_NUMBER") & CHR(34)
 &
70 " AND " & _
71                   "objRS(" & CHR(34) & "TERM" & CHR(34) & ")="
&
72 CHR(34) & Request.QueryString("TERM") & CHR(34) & " AND " & _
73                   "objRS(" & CHR(34) & "YEAR" & CHR(34) & ")=" _
&
74 CHR(34) & Request.QueryString("YEAR") & CHR(34) & " AND " & _
75                   "objRS(" & CHR(34) & "SECTION" & CHR(34) & " _
)="
```

```
76 & CHR(34) & Request.QueryString("SECTION") & CHR(34)
77
78          If Not objForm.Search(strEval)Then
79             Response.Write("<CENTER><H1>Error Information</H1>")
80             Response.Write("<H3>Scheduling information not  found
!</H3><BR>")
81              Response.Write("Back to <a href=default.asp>Class
Form</a>.</center>")
82             Response.End
83          Else
84            If Request.QueryString("Mode") = "Browse" Then
85             objForm.Mode = "Browse"
86            Else
87            if Request.QueryString("Mode") = "Delete" Then
88             objForm.Mode = "Delete"
89           End If
90          End If
91     End If
92     Else
93             Response.Write("<CENTER><H1>Error Information</H1>")
94             Response.Write("<H3>You did not select a mode!</H3>
<BR>")
95             Response.Write("Click the Back button of your
browser to fix!</center>")
96             Response.End
97   End If
98 End If
99
100 %>
101
102 </HEAD>
103
104 </BODY>
105
106 <H1 align="center">Class Scheduling Form</H1>
107
108 <p align="center"><strong>Instructions:</strong>  All
mandatory fields have an &quot;*&quot; next to them. <br> Please
fill in all mandatory fields before hitting SUBMIT.</p>
109
110 <form id="frmSchedule" name="frmSchedule" action="save_
schedule.asp" method="post">
111
112 <center><p><b>Class Information</b></p></center>
113
114 <center>Form Mode: <% = objForm.Mode %><input id="Mode"
type="hidden" name="Mode" size="35" value="<% = objForm.Mode%>" >
115 <input id="CLASS_SCHEDULE_ID" type="hidden" name="CLASS_
SCHEDULE_ID" size="35" value="<% = objForm.colFormElements.Item
("CLASS_SCHEDULE_ID")%>" >
116 <input id="CLASS_NUMBER" type="hidden" name="CLASS_NUMBER"
```

```
117 size="35" value="<% = objForm.colFormElements.Item("CLASS_
NUMBER")%>" >
118 <input id="CLASS_NAME" type="hidden" name="CLASS_NAME" size=
"35" value="<% = objForm.colFormElements.Item("CLASS_NAME")%>" >
119
120 <p>Class number: <% = objForm.colFormElements.Item("CLASS
_NUMBER")%><br>
121  Class name: <% = objForm.colFormElements.Item("CLASS_
NAME")%></p>
122
123 <input id="CLASS_ID" type="hidden" name="CLASS_ID" value="<%
= objForm.colFormElements.Item("CLASS_ID")%>">
124
125 </center>
126
127 <center><p><b>Schedule Information</b></p>
128 </center>
129
130 <center><p>Term:<input type="text" name="TERM" size="12"
value="<% = objForm.colFormElements.Item("TERM")%>"><strong>*</
strong><br>
131
132 Year:<input type="text" name="YEAR" size="12" value="<% = obj
Form.colFormElements.Item("YEAR")%>"><strong>*</strong><br>
133
134 Section: <input type="text" name="SECTION" size="30" value="<
% = objForm.colFormElements.Item("SECTION")%>"><strong>*</strong>
</p>
135 Instructor: <SELECT NAME="INSTRUCTOR_ID">
136 <% Dim objOtherForm
137    Dim OtherFormItem
138   set objOtherForm = new clsForm
139   objOtherForm.Open_Recordset("select INSTRUCTOR_ID, LAST_
NAME, FIRST_NAME from INSTRUCTORS")
140
141   If Not objOtherForm.objRS.EOF Then
142   objOtherForm.objRS.MoveFirst
143   do while Not objOtherForm.objRS.EOF %>
144
145    <OPTION VALUE="<%=objOtherForm.objRS("INSTRUCTOR_ID")%>">
<% = objOtherForm.objRS("LAST_NAME") & ", " & objOtherForm.objRS
("FIRST_NAME") %>
146
147 <%
148   objOtherForm.objRS.MoveNext
149   Loop
150   End If
151 %>
152 </SELECT>
153 </center>
154
```

```
155 <%Select Case objForm.Mode %>
156 <% Case "New"%>
157 <center><p><input id="cmdSubmit" type="submit" value="Create">
158 <input id="cmdReset" type="reset" value="Reset"> </p>
</center>
159 <%Case "Update" %>
160 <center><p><input id="cmdSubmit" type="submit" value="Update">
161 </center>
162 <%Case "Delete" %>
163 <center><p><input id="cmdSubmit" type="submit" value="Delete">
164 </center>
165 <%Case "Browse"%>
166 <center><p>Back to <a href=default.asp>Search</a>.</center>
167 </center>
168 <% End Select %>
169 </FORM>
170
171 </BODY>
172 </HTML>
```

Code Dissection

- Lines 25–29 illustrate the complex query that must be run against the database.

- Lines 135–152 illustrate how to create a drop-down list box from a query against the INSTRUCTOR's table. The user will see the last name and first name of the instructor but the code will return the INSTRUCTOR_ID to be used in processing, since the CLASS_SCHEDULES table needs an INSTRUCTOR_ID.

CHAPTER SUMMARY

❑ Access databases work well under low-volume access conditions. When high-volume access conditions occur, it is best to use a product such as SQL Server 7.0. Converting an Access database to an SQL Server database is simple; you simply run the Migration Wizard, following the prompts as you do so. If you are restoring a database that has already been run through the Migration Wizard, you can restore the database using the SQL Server Enterprise Manager. SQL Server Enterprise Manager is a graphical tool you can use to configure, manage, and maintain SQL Server databases.

❑ A procedural language is a language that allows you to write code logic, and then save it. The saved logic is known as a stored procedure. To write procedures for SQL Server, you need to use an adaptation of SQL known as the Transact-SQL procedural extension.

❑ In Transact-SQL, you store values in variables. Variables store results for calculations or processing of data within a program. Once you have defined your variables, you can assign values to those variables. After you declare a variable and then assign a value to it, you are ready to control the sequence in which your programming logic is executed. This is done by mastering flow control by mastering the syntax of flow control statements.

❑ Once you migrate your database from Access to SQL Server and then stock that database with the requisite procedures and queries, you can then write the code that allows your application to access those procedures and queries. You do this by using the Command object in ADO.

REVIEW QUESTIONS

1. _____ is good for small applications, while _____ is good for medium to large applications.

   a. Access/SQL Server

   b. Access/Access

   c. File System/Access

   d. none of the above

2. Microsoft supplies a Migration Wizard that you can use to convert a database from Access to SQL Server. True or False?

3. _____ is a graphical tool that allows you to configure, manage, and maintain SQL Server databases.

   a. SQL Plus

   b. Enterprise Manager

   c. Visual Basic

   d. ASP

4: To determine a server name, you use the _____ name in Windows 98/NT.

   a. Group

   b. Computer

   c. Server

   d. Client

5. SQL is a procedural language. True or False?

6. SQL Server uses a language called _____ to create stored procedures.

   a. PL/SQL

   b. TRANSACT-SQL

   c. SQL

   d. none of the above

7

7. SQL is excellent for working with ———————— of data.

   a. rows

   b. columns

   c. sets

   d. none of the above

8. Which of the following is a valid declaration in TRANSACT-SQL?

   a. `v_name varchar2(40);`

   b. `DECLARE @v_name varchar(40)`

   c. `v_name varchar2(40)`

   d. none of the above

9. Which of the following is a valid assignment statement in TRANSACT-SQL?

   a. `SELECT @v_name = 'Morneau'`

   b. `v_name = 'Morneau';`

   c. `v_name := 'Morneau';`

   d. none of the above

10. Which of the following are valid flow control statements in TRANSACT-SQL?

    a. IF

    b. WHILE

    c. DO

    d. none of the above

11. SQL Server provides a method of handling run-time errors. True or False?

12. Which property of the Command object allows you to set a connection to a Connection object?

    a. CommandText

    b. CommandTimeout

    c. ActiveConnection

    d. none of the above

13. Which method of the Command object allows you to run a query or stored procedure?

    a. CommandText

    b. Execute

    c. CreateParameter

    d. none of the above

14. Which of the following is the proper syntax for creating a Command object in VBScript?

    a. `objCom = CreateObject("ADODB.Connection:")`

    b. `objCom = CreateObject("ADODB.Command")`

   c. `set objCom = CreateObject("ADODB.Command")`

   d. none of the above

15. The _____ is an administrative tool used to manage hardware, software, and network components of different Windows operating systems.

   a. MMC

   b. ADO

   c. Command object

   d. Console

16. A procedural language is a language that allows you to write code _____.

17. SQL is a procedural language. True or False?

18. Variables can be declared as global or as local; when they are declared as global, all stored procedures have access to the data. True or False?

19. The _____ method of the Command object runs the SQL statement or stored procedure specified in the CommandText property.

   a. Execute

   b. ActiveConnection

   c. CommandText

   d. CommandTimeExpired

20. In the Command object, the CommandTimeout property tells the number of seconds to wait when executing a command before a(n) _____ is returned.

HANDS-ON PROJECTS

Project 7-1

Use the sql.htm application in the Chapter_7 folder of your Data Disk to create and run the following simple queries.

1. A query that displays the student's last name, first name, and class schedule. The class schedule should include the term, year, section, and class name for each class the student is taking.

   a. Open your browser, and navigate to *http://localhost/Chapter_7/sql.htm*.

   b. Enter

      SELECT LAST_NAME,FIRST_NAME,TERM,YEAR,SECTION, CLASS_NAME FROM STUDENTS, STUDENT_SCHEDULES, CLASS_SCHEDULES, CLASSES WHERE STUDENTS.STUDENT_ID= STUDENT_SCHEDULES.STUDENT_ID AND STUDENT_SCHEDULES.CLASS_SCHEDULE_ID = CLASS_ SCHEDULES.CLASS_SCHEDULE_ID AND CLASS_SCHEDULES.CLASS_ID = CLASSES.CLASS_ID

7

in the Enter the SQL Statement text box. Select the SQL Server option button and then click the Execute button.

c. Click the SQL Entry Form link to bring you back to the SQL Entry form.

d. Close your browser.

Project 7-2

Use the sql.htm application in the Chapter_7 folder of your Data Disk to run a query that requests an instructor's last name, first name, and classes taught. The list of classes taught should include the class name, term, year, and section.

1. Open your browser, and navigate to *http://localhost/Chapter_7 /sql.htm.*

2. Enter

SELECT LAST_NAME,FIRST_NAME,TERM,YEAR,SECTION,
CLASS_NAME FROM INSTRUCTORS, CLASS_SCHEDULES, CLASSES
WHERE INSTRUCTORS.INSTRUCTOR_ID =
CLASS_SCHEDULES.INSTRUCTOR_ID AND
CLASS_SCHEDULES.CLASS_ID = CLASSES.CLASS_ID

in the Enter the SQL Statement text box. Select the SQL Server option button and then click the Execute button.

3. Click the SQL Entry Form link to bring you back to the SQL Entry form.

4. Close your browser.

Project 7-3

Using the techniques learned in this chapter, create a stored procedure in SQL Server for the STUDENTS table that inserts, updates, and deletes data.

1. Open SQL Server Enterprise Manager.

2. Expand Microsoft SQL Servers, SQL Server Group, your server name, Databases, and Course.

3. Right-click Stored Procedures, and then click New Stored Procedure.

4. Type the following code into the text box:

```
CREATE PROCEDURE proc_students
@p_StudentID int, @p_mode varchar(10), @p_FirstName
varchar(35), @p_LastName varchar(35), @p_HomePhone
varchar(10), @p_WorkPhone varchar(10), @p_email
varchar(100),
@p_error_message varchar(200) OUTPUT
AS

If ((@p_FirstName = '') or (@p_LastName = '') or (@p_email =
'')) Goto ClsError

IF @p_mode = 'New'
BEGIN
```

```
INSERT INTO STUDENTS (LAST_NAME,FIRST_NAME,HOME_PHONE,WORK_
PHONE,E_MAIL) VALUES (@p_LastName, @p_FirstName,
@p_HomePhone, @p_WorkPhone, @p_email)

END
ELSE
BEGIN
  IF @p_mode = 'Update'
  BEGIN

    UPDATE STUDENTS
    SET LAST_NAME = @p_LastName,
    FIRST_NAME = @p_FirstName,
    HOME_PHONE =  @p_HomePhone,
    WORK_PHONE = @p_WorkPhone,
    E_MAIL = @p_email
    WHERE STUDENT_ID = @p_StudentID

  END
  ELSE
  BEGIN
    IF @p_mode = 'Delete'
    BEGIN

      DELETE FROM  STUDENTS
      WHERE STUDENT_ID = @p_StudentID

    END
  END
END

SELECT @p_error_message = ''
RETURN (0)

ClsError:

SELECT @p_error_message = 'Mandatory fields cannot be
blank!'
Return (1)
```

5. Click OK to save the stored procedure.

6. Close SQL Server Enterprise Manager.

Project 7-4

Using the techniques learned in this chapter, create a stored procedure in SQL Server for the STUDENTS SCHEDULES table that inserts, updates, and deletes student schedules.

1. Open SQL Server Enterprise Manager.

2. Expand Microsoft SQL Servers, SQL Server Group, your server name, Databases, and Course.

3. Right-click Stored Procedures, and then click New Stored Procedure.

4. Type the following code into the text box:

```
CREATE PROCEDURE proc_student_schedule
@p_StudentScheduleID int, @p_mode varchar(10), @p_StudentID
int,
@p_ClassScheduleID int,
@p_error_message varchar(200) OUTPUT
AS

IF @p_mode = 'New'
BEGIN

INSERT INTO STUDENT_SCHEDULES (STUDENT_ID,CLASS_SCHEDULE_ID)
VALUES (@p_StudentID, @p_ClassScheduleID)

END
ELSE
BEGIN
  IF @p_mode = 'Update'
  BEGIN

    UPDATE STUDENT_SCHEDULES
    SET STUDENT_ID = @p_StudentID,
    CLASS_SCHEDULE_ID = @p_ClassScheduleID
    WHERE STUDENT_SCHEDULE_ID = @p_StudentScheduleID

  END
  ELSE
  BEGIN
    IF @p_mode = 'Delete'
    BEGIN

      DELETE FROM  STUDENT_SCHEDULES
      WHERE STUDENT_SCHEDULE_ID = @p_StudentScheduleID

    END
  END
END

SELECT @p_error_message = ''
RETURN (0)

ClsError:

SELECT @p_error_message = 'Mandatory fields cannot be
blank!'
Return (1)
```

5. Click OK to save the stored procedure.

Project 7-5

Using the techniques learned in this chapter, create a Web application for the Students Schedules table; have the application call the SQL Server stored procedure.

1. Create a folder called studentscheduling.

2. Create an ASP script called default.asp in the studentscheduling folder with the following code:

```
<%@ Language=VBScript %>
<% Response.Buffer = True %>
<!-- #include file="clsForm.cls" -->
<HTML>
<HEAD>

</HEAD>
<BODY>
<center><H1>Student Scheduling</H1>

<% Dim blnOK,strQuery

 If Request.QueryString("Mode") = "New" Then
  Response.Redirect("form.asp?Mode=New&LAST_NAME=" &_
replace(Request.QueryString("txtLastName")," ","+")&_
"&FIRST_NAME="&_
replace(Request.QueryString("txtFirstName")," ","+"))
  Response.End
 End If


   blnOK = (Request.QueryString("OK")= "Y")

   if blnOK Then
     strQuery = ""
     strQuery = strQuery &_
       "Mode=" &_
replace(Request.QueryString("Mode")," ","+") & "&" &_
       "LAST_NAME=" &_
replace(Request.QueryString("txtLastName")," ","+") & "&" &_
       "FIRST_NAME=" &_
replace(Request.QueryString("txtFirstName")," ","+")

     Response.Redirect("form.asp?" & strQuery)
     Response.End
   End If

  blnOK = (Request.QueryString("txtLastName")="")

  If blnOK Then
%>
```

```
<CENTER>

<form id="frmSchedule" name="frmSchedule" action="default.
asp" method="get">
<center>
<p>
<input type="radio" name="Mode" value="New">New
<input type="radio" name="Mode" value="Update">Update
<input type="radio" name="Mode" value="Delete">Delete
<input type="radio" name="Mode" value="Browse">Search

<p>Last name: <input type="text" name="txtLastName" size=
"30"><br>
First name: <input type="text" name="txtFirstName" size=
"10">
</p>
</center>

<center>
<p><input id="cmdSubmit"  type="submit" value="Submit">
<input id="cmdReset"  type="reset" value="Reset"> </p>
</center>

</form>

</CENTER>

<%
Else %>

<CENTER>

<center>
<p>
INSTRUCTIONS: You must select schedule information <BR> for
the form to process.
<p>
<%
   Dim objForm,objField
   set objForm = new clsForm

   objForm.Open_Recordset(""& _
"select STUDENTS.LAST_NAME,STUDENTS.FIRST_NAME," &_
"CLASSES.CLASS_NUMBER,STUDENTS.STUDENT_ID," &_
"CLASSES.CLASS_NAME," &_
"CLASS_SCHEDULES.TERM," &_
"CLASS_SCHEDULES.CLASS_SCHEDULE_ID" &_
"CLASS_SCHEDULES.YEAR,CLASS_SCHEDULES.SECTION," &_
"STUDENT_SCHEDULES.STUDENT_SCHEDULE_ID " &_
"from STUDENTS,STUDENT_SCHEDULES,CLASSES," &_
"CLASS_SCHEDULES " & _
```

```
"where CLASSES.CLASS_ID = CLASS_SCHEDULES.CLASS_ID " &_
" AND " &_
"STUDENT_SCHEDULES.CLASS_SCHEDULE_ID = " &_
"CLASS_SCHEDULES.CLASS_SCHEDULE_ID AND " &_
"STUDENTS.STUDENT_ID = STUDENT_SCHEDULES.STUDENT_ID" &_
" AND " &_
"STUDENTS.LAST_NAME = '" &
Request.QueryString("txtLastName") &_
"' AND " &_
"STUDENTS.FIRST_NAME = '" &
Request.QueryString("txtFirstName") &_
"'" & " ORDER BY CLASS_SCHEDULES.TERM," &_
"CLASS_SCHEDULES.YEAR," &_
"CLASS_SCHEDULES.SECTION"
%>

<TABLE BORDER=1 COLS=<%=objForm.objRS.Fields.Count%>>
      <TR>
            <TH></TH>
          <% For each objField in objForm.objRS.Fields %>
            <TH> <%=objField.Name %> </TH>
          <% Next %>
      </TR>
     <% Do while Not objForm.objRS.EOF %>
       <TR>
          <TD align=right>
         <% if Request.QueryString("Mode") <> "Browse" Then
          strQuery = ""
          For Each objField in objForm.objRS.Fields
            strQuery = strQuery & objField.Name & "=" &_
replace(objField.Value," ","+") & "&amp;"
          Next
          strQuery = strQuery & "Mode=" &_
Request.QueryString("Mode") & "&OK=Y"
          %>
          <a href=form.asp?<% = strQuery %>>Select</a>
         <%End If%>
          </TD>
        <% For Each objField in objForm.objRS.Fields %>
          <TD align=right>
            <% If IsNull(objField) Then
                  Response.Write(" ")
               else
                  Response.Write(objField.Value)
               End If
            %>
              </TD>
         <% Next
            objForm.objRS.MoveNext %>
          </TR>
      <%  Loop %>
    </TABLE>
```

7

```
</CENTER>

<%End If %>
</BODY>
</HTML>
```

3. Create an ASP script called save_schedule.asp in the studentscheduling folder with the following code:

```
<%@ Language=VBScript %>
<% Response.Buffer = True %>
<!-- #include file="adovbs.inc" -->
<!-- #include file="clsForm.cls" -->
<HTML>

<HEAD>

<TITLE>Class Registration Response</TITLE>
<%
  Dim objForm,strEval,strErr,objCom, ID
  set objForm = new clsForm
  set objCom = CreateObject("ADODB.Command")

    if Request.Form("Mode") = "New" or Request.Form("Mode")
= "Update" or Request.Form("Mode") = "Delete" Then

    objCom.CommandText = "proc_student_schedule"

objCom.Parameters.Append objCom.CreateParameter("" &_
,adInteger,adParamInput,4, &_
cint(Request.Form("STUDENT_SCHEDULE_ID")))

objCom.Parameters.Append objCom.CreateParameter("" &_
,adVarChar,adParamInput,10,cstr(Request.Form("Mode")))

objCom.Parameters.Append objCom.CreateParameter("" &_
,adInteger,adParamInput,4, &_
cint(Request.Form("STUDENT_ID")))

objCom.Parameters.Append objCom.CreateParameter("" &_
,adInteger,adParamInput,4, &_
cint(Request.Form("CLASS_SCHEDULE_ID")))

objCom.Parameters.Append objCom.CreateParameter( &_
"strErrorMessage",adVarChar,adParamOutput,200)
      strErr = objForm.Run_SP(objCom)
      If strErr <> "" Then
        Response.Write("<CENTER><H1>Error Information</H1>")
        Response.Write(strErr & "</CENTER>")
        Response.End
      End If
```

```
    End If

%>
</HEAD>
<BODY>

<center><H1>Class Registration Response</H1></center>
<center>
<p>Thank you for using the Class Scheduling form!<p>

</center>
<center>Back to <a href="default.asp">Search</a>.</center>
</BODY>
</HTML>
```

7

4. The code you just typed is missing four critical lines. Restore those lines, and then save the file.

5. Copy Adovbs.inc and Global.asa into the new directory.

6. Test the new application in your browser by browsing to
   http://localhost/Chapter_7/studentscheduling/default.asp

CASE PROJECTS

1. John's Software, Inc. has hired you as a systems analyst to help develop a gift management information system as described in Chapter 5. Use the database design you created in Chapter 5 to create a Web application in SQL Server. (*Note*: Use the gifts SQL Server database backup on your Data Disk. The solution requires only the PERSONS table and the OCCASION table.)

2. Interstate bank recently hired you as a systems analyst to help develop a Web application as described in Chapter 5. Use the database you created in Chapter 5 to create a Web application in SQL Server. (*Note*: Use the budget SQL Server database backup on your Data Disk. The solution requires only the PERSONS and FAMILY tables.)

3. Interstate bank recently hired you as a consultant to help develop a check balancing information system as described in Chapter 5. Use the database you created in Chapter 5 to create a Web application in SQL Server. (*Note*: Use the checkbook SQL Server database backup on your Data Disk. The solution requires only the TRANSACTIONS BALANCE_STATEMENTS tables.)

8

ASP AND E-COMMERCE

In this chapter, you will:

♦ Understand how multiple browsers in the market complicate ASP programming

♦ Learn the uses of the Browscap.ini file

♦ Learn how to check whether a browser supports frames

♦ Understand the role of cookies in ASP programming

♦ Understand the role of the Response object in cookies

♦ Understand the role of the Request object in cookies

♦ Prepare a shopping cart

Up to this point, you have created Web applications using generic HTML that is supported by the majority of browsers. You should keep in mind, however, that each browser on the market provides its own additional features. How do you support these nongeneric features? In ASP, the Browser Capabilities component allows you to determine which features are supported by a particular browser and provides a foundation for taking advantage of these specific browser features. In this chapter you will investigate how to determine a browser's capabilities and use them in your Web applications. This chapter also covers another topic related to browsers—storing small amounts of information on the client in ASCII text files called cookies. This chapter explains how cookies work, how to use them in your applications, and the role that ASP plays in the cookie arena.

THE ROLE OF THE BROWSER CAPABILITIES COMPONENT

One of the problems you face when designing Web applications is determining which of the many browser features to support in your applications. Each browser has its own set of features, which you must master before you can incorporate them into your Web application. The Browser Capabilities component simplifies the situation enormously, because it helps you to identify and take advantage of browser features in your Web applications. This section provides a framework you can follow when incorporating browser features.

Because of the huge number of browser features available, this book cannot discuss the details of each and every one. For more specific information, refer to the online documentation for the browsers you want to support in your Web applications.

Understanding the Browser Capabilities Component

So how does the Browser Capabilities component work? When requesting a Web page, a browser tells the Web server its type and version number. The server then checks the type and version of the browser in a special file in the Browser Capabilities component, called Browscap.ini. The **Browscap.ini** file contains feature information specific to each browser listed in this special file. Let's look at part of this file:

```
 1 ;;;;;;;;;;;;;;;;;;;;;;;;;;;;;;;;;;;;;;;;;;;;;; IE 5.0
 2 [IE 5.0]
 3 browser=IE
 4 Version=5.0
 5 majorver=#5
 6 minorver=#0
 7 frames=True
 8 tables=True
 9 cookies=True
10 backgroundsounds=True
11 vbscript=True
12 javaapplets=True
13 javascript=True
14 ActiveXControls=True
15 Win16=False
16 beta=True
17 AK=False
18 SK=False
19 AOL=False
20 Update=False
21
22 [Mozilla/4.0 (compatible; MSIE 5.*; Windows 95*)]
23 parent=IE 5.0
24 platform=Win95
25 beta=True
26
27 [Mozilla/4.0 (compatible; MSIE 5.*; Windows 98*)]
28 parent=IE 5.0
```

```
29 platform=Win98
30 beta=True
31
32 [Mozilla/4.0 (compatible; MSIE 5.*; Windows NT*)]
33 parent=IE 5.0
34 platform=WinNT
35 beta=True
```

You will notice a string that reads Mozilla/4.0 (compatible; MSIE 5.*; Windows 95*). The browser passes this string in the header of an HTTP request (which is called the HTTP_USER_AGENT). You can access this string using the ServerVariables collection of the Request object. An example of how to access the contents of the HTTP_USER_AGENT is shown below:

```
<%=Request.ServerVariables("HTTP_USER_AGENT")%>
```

The Browser Capabilities component takes this string and finds the location in the Browscap.ini file that matches this string, which is line 22. On lines 23 and 24, you see two important properties: parent and platform. The Parent property tells the Browser Capabilities component to use the settings for IE 5.0, and the Platform property tells the Browser Capabilities component that this browser runs in Windows 95. Table 8-1 explains each property for IE 5.0 as it is listed in the Browscap.ini file.

Table 8-1   Key properties of IE 5.0

Property	Question This Property Answers
browser=IE	What browser is sending the request?
Version=5.0 majorver=#5 minorver=#0	What version of the browser is sending the request?
frames=True	Does the browser support frames?
tables=True	Does the browser support tables?
cookies=True	Does the browser support cookies?
backgroundsounds=True	Does the browser support background sounds?
vbscript=True	Does the browser support VBScript?
javaapplets=True	Does the browser support Java Applets?
javascript=True	Does the browser support JavaScript?
ActiveXControls=True	Does the browser support ActiveX controls?
Win16=False	Does the browser support Win16 API?
beta=True	Is the browser in beta?
AOL=False	Does the browser support AOL?
Update=False	Does the browser have an update?

The Browser Capabilities component makes it possible for an application to check any one of the properties described above. You can find a listing of the major browsers in this file. If the browser sending a request is not listed in the Browscap.ini file, the Browser Capabilities component uses the default section of code, which is the last section of the file. The next section shows you how to use this component.

Using the Browser Capabilities Component

In the previous section, you reviewed the properties available in the Browscap.ini file. Next, you will look at code that checks whether the browser supports cookies.

```vbscript
Dim objBrowsCap, blnOK
set objBrowsCap = Server.CreateObject("MSWC.BrowserType")
blnOK = objBrowsCap.cookies
if blnOK then
. . .
End If
```

```javascript
var objBrowsCap, blnOK;
objBrowsCap = Server.CreateObject("MSWC.BrowserType");
blnOK = objBrowsCap.cookies;
if (blnOK) {
. . .
};
```

Of course, you can check other properties in addition to the cookies property. Table 8-2 shows some properties that you might want to check and the code that you would use to do so.

Table 8-2   Commonly Checked Properties

Property to Check	VBScript Code Used to Check It	JavaScript Code Used to Check It

browser	if (objbrowscap.browser) then
	...
	end if
		if (objbrowscap.browser) {
		...
		};

Version
majorver
minorver
	if (objbrowscap.Version) then
	...
	end if
		if (objbrowscap.Version) {
		...
		};

frame	if (objbrowscap.frame) then
	...
	end if
		if (objbrowscap.frame) {
		...
		};

tables	if (objbrowscap.tables) then
	...
	end if
		if (objbrowscap.tables) {
		...
		};

cookies	if (objbrowscap.cookies) then
	...
	end if
		if (objbrowscap.cookies) {
		...
		};

backgroundsounds	if (objbrowscap.background
	sounds) then
	...
	end if
		if (objbrowscap.background
		sounds) {
		...
		};

Table 8-2   Commonly Checked Properties (continued)

Property to Check	VBScript Code Used to Check It	JavaScript Code Used to Check It

vbscript	```if (objbrowscap.vbscript) then```
	```...```
	```end if```
		```if (objbrowscap.vbscript) {```
		```...```
		```};```

javaapplets	```if (objbrowscap.javaapplets) then```
	```...```
	```end if```
		```if (objbrowscap.javaapplets)```
		```{```
		```...```
		```};```

javascript	```if (objbrowscap.javascript) then```
	```...```
	```end if```
		```if (objbrowscap.javascript){```
		```...```
		```};```

ActiveXControls	```if (objbrowscap.ActiveXControls)```
	```then```
	```...```
	```end if```
		```if (objbrowscap.ActiveX```
		``` Controls) {```
		```...```
		```};```

Win16	```if (objbrowscap.Win16) then```
	```...```
	```end if```
		```if (objbrowscap.Win16) {```
		```...```
		```};```

beta	```if (objbrowscap.beta) then```
	```...```
	```end if```
		```if (objbrowscap.beta) {```
		```...```
		```};```

AOL	```if (objbrowscap.AOL) then```
	```...```
	```end if```
		```if (objbrowscap.AOL) {```
		```...```
		```};```

Update	```if (objbrowscap.Update) then```
	```...```
	```end if```
		```if (objbrowscap.Update) {```
		```...```
		```};```

8

Now that you are familiar with the theory behind the Browser Capabilities component, let's look at a real-world example. It is very common in Web applications to have a frames page for browsers that support frames and a nonframes page for browsers that do not support frames.

On your Chapter_8 Data Disk, you will see a frames.htm page and a banner.htm page. Even though the files exist, the default.asp page does not yet know to check with the browser for the browser's ability to use a frames page. How do you change the current default.asp page to check if your user's browser supports frames? You make the changes as detailed in the following set of steps.

To change the default.asp page so that it checks whether the browser supports frames:

1. Open the **default.asp** page from the Chapter_8\Register folder of your Data Disk.

2. Add the following code that is in bold:

```
<%@Language=JScript%>
<%Response.buffer=true%>
<% if (Request.Cookies("LOGININFO") == "") {
%>
<!-- #include file="login.asp" -->
<%
Response.End;
}

var objbrowscap, blnFrames;
objbrowscap = Server.CreateObject("MSWC.BrowserType");
blnFrames = objbrowscap.frames;

if (blnFrames) {
 Response.Redirect("frames.htm");
 Response.End;
}
else
{
 Response.Redirect("contents.asp");
 Response.End;
} %>
```

The ASP script checks the Frames property of objBrowsCap and redirects the output to the frames.htm page or the nonframes page of contents.asp.

3. Save the file.

4. Prepare a virtual directory named Chapter_8 in PWS for the Chapter_8 folder on your Data Disk. Open your browser and browse to *http://localhost/ Chapter_8/Register/default.asp* to test the results. Your screen will match Figure 8-1. After you log in, you will go to the frames page. If your browser did not support frames, you would see the image in Figure 8-2. Note the spacing issue after the word "Welcome," indicating the noninsertion of login data.

5. Close the browser.

Maintaining the Browscap.ini File

You need to keep the browscap.ini file current since new browsers and new features are added to browsers every day. One way to keep this file up to date is to download the browscap.ini file from cyScape, Inc. (*www.cyscape.com/browscap*). You can add yourself to the company's mailing list and receive updates periodically.

 You can also acquire new versions of the browscap.ini file at Microsoft's Web site.

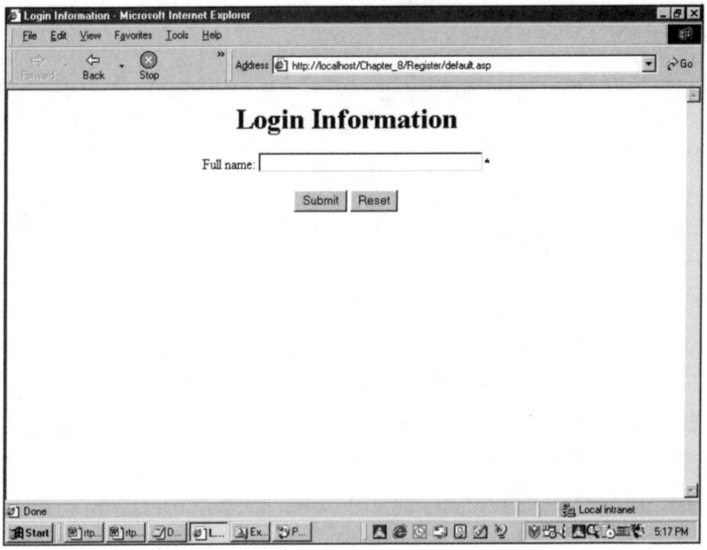

Figure 8-1 Login page

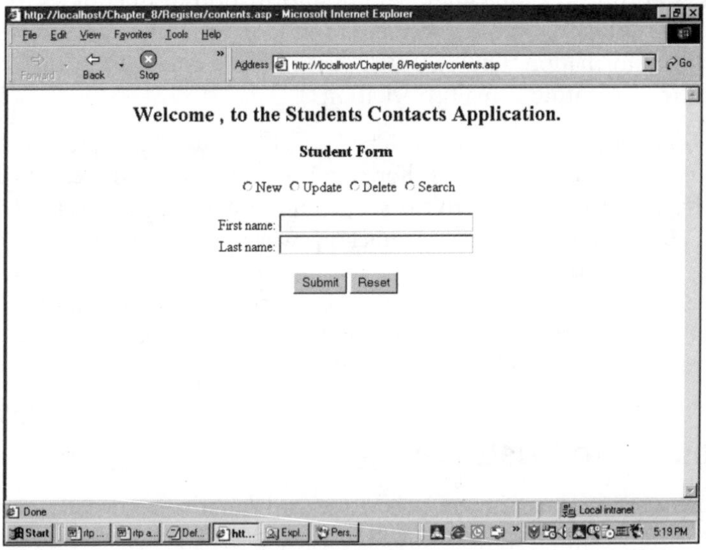

Figure 8-2 Nonframes page

COOKIES IN APPLICATIONS

A cookie is a simple text file that stores a small amount of information (up to 255 characters) on the client computer. Cookies are commonly used to store small pieces of information such as usernames, passwords, and e-mail addresses.

When a user visits a Web site, a script on the Web page tells the browser to store information in a cookie on the client computer's hard drive. If the user returns to the Web site at a later time, the Web page reads the cookie and uses it to personalize the user's visit to the site. Cookies have many uses in Web applications. These include:

- **User identity**: Some sites require the user to log in. The site could store login information in a cookie and automatically log in the user at successive visits.

- **Personal touches**: On some sites, the user can change the background color or add a background image. The Web site stores these settings in a cookie for future use.

- **Web site tracking**: Web sites can track the user's every move on a site, recording information such as which links the user clicked and who referred the user to the site. This feature is useful for developers who want to evaluate the layout of their sites. Some users object to this as an invasion of privacy.

- **Targeted marketing**: Companies can use information from cookies to determine what the user likes and dislikes and then target the user for advertising based on this information. Thus, a quick visit to a site could mean that a user is targeted to receive future e-mail solicitations.

- **Online ordering**: Cookies are used to keep track of a user's past purchases, as well as the current contents of the user's shopping basket. The latter is useful in case the user loses his or her connection to the site; with the shopping basket information stored in a cookie, the user can simply pick up where he or she left off.

 On Internet Explorer, there is a Cookies directory within the Windows folder or in the profiles\user_name\Cookies folder, where user_name is the user logged in to the computer.

How Cookies Come into Existence

Now that you know what a cookie is, you need to learn how they come into existence.

Note that cookies can be multivalued or single-valued. A multivalued cookie gives you the ability to store more than one piece of data in the cookie. A single-valued cookie, on the other hand, allows you to store one value only.

The central figure in the cookie's life is the Web application. It is this application that directs the creation of the cookie; it is also this application that reads the cookie once it has been created; and ultimately, it will be this application that determines the life span of the cookie itself. Figure 8-3 illustrates this life cycle.

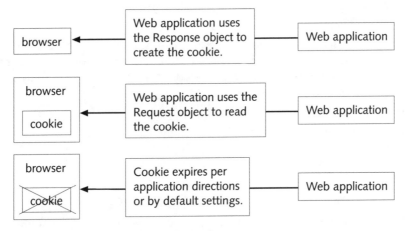

Figure 8-3   The life of a cookie

8

Response Object

You use the Cookies collection of the Response object to have the application create a cookie. The Response object provides access to several properties, as explained in Table 8-3. These properties allow you to specify when a cookie expires, the domain where the cookie can be used, where to store the cookie, and whether to use a secure connection to retrieve the cookie.

Table 8-3   Response Object Properties

Property/Method	Name	Description
Property	Cookies	Contents of the cookie collection to be sent to the browser
Property	buffer	A property that indicates whether to buffer the contents of the response until complete
Property	status	The status of the HTTP request, as returned by the server

Consider the following code:

Code Example

JavaScript

```
1 ExpireDate = new Date();
2 ExpireDate.setMonth(ExpireDate.getMonth()+3); //Expires in 3
months from today
3 Response.Cookies("LOGININFO").expires = ExpireDate.toLocale
String();
4 Response.Cookies("LOGININFO") = Request.Form("FullName");
```

Code Dissection

- The first line of the script shows how to create a date variable that you can use to increase the expiration date, which is set for an additional three months in the second line. You could also use setDay or setYear methods of the Date object if you wanted the cookie to expire at other times.

- The third line shows you how to set the Expires property of the cookie to expire at a certain date. The toLocaleString method converts the date into a string.

Request Object

You use the Cookies collection of the Request object to allow the application to view the contents of a cookie. The following code shows how to access a cookie using the Request object.

```
Request.Cookies("LOGININFO");
```

Incorporating Cookies into Applications

When you visit an e-commerce Web site such as Amazon.com, the site keeps track of items you want to purchase by using an electronic "shopping cart". A shopping cart is a wonderful example of the way cookies can be used with your Web application. The application keeps track of items your customer wants to purchase, and even if he or she leaves the site and comes back, the items are still in the cart.

We will now finish developing a simple shopping cart example in ASP. The shopping cart example needs an HTML form and an ASP script that handles the details of storing the items in a shopping cart. You will use a cookie called ShoppingCart to store a collection of items being purchased.

To create the HTML form for the shopping cart:

1. Open your text editor, and then with the following code, create a file called **ShoppingCart.htm** in the Chapter_8/Register folder of your Data Disk:

```
<HTML>
<HEAD>
    <TITLE>Simple shopping cart Example</TITLE>
</HEAD>

<BODY>

<CENTER><H1>Student's Book Shop</H1></CENTER>

<HR>
```

```
<FORM ACTION="http://localhost/Chapter_8/Register/Shopping
Cart.asp"

METHOD="post">
<TABLE CELLSPACING="5" CELLPADDING="5">
<TR>
    <TD ALIGN="LEFT"><B>Add to Cart</B></TD>
    <TD ALIGN="center"></TD>
</TR>
<TR>

    <TD ALIGN="right"><SELECT MULTIPLE SIZE="2" NAME="item">
    <OPTION>Introduction to TCP/IP
    <OPTION>Visual Basic I
    </SELECT>
    <TD></TD>

</TR>

</TABLE>
<HR>
<INPUT TYPE="Submit" VALUE="Add to Cart">
</FORM>

</BODY>
</HTML>
```

2. Using the following code, create a file called **ShoppingCart.asp** in the Chapter_8\Register folder of your Data Disk:

```
<%@Language=JavaScript%>
<%Response.buffer=true%>
<HTML>
<HEAD>
    <TITLE>Simple shopping cart Example</TITLE>
</HEAD>

<BODY>

<CENTER><H1>Student's Book Shop</H1></CENTER>

<H2>Books currently in your cart</H2>
<HR>
<%
  var i,j,itemcount,item,items;

  if (Request.Cookies("ShoppingCart") == "") {
    Response.Cookies("ShoppingCart")("itemcount") = 0;
    itemcount = 0;
    j = 0;
  }
  else
```

```
    {
      itemcount = Request.Cookies("ShoppingCart")
("itemcount");
      j = 0;
    }


for (i=0; i<itemcount; i++) {

   Response.Cookies("ShoppingCart")("item"+i) =
   Request.Cookies("ShoppingCart")("item"+i);

   Response.Write(Request.Cookies("ShoppingCart")("item"+i)+"
   <BR>");
      j = j + 1;
   }


items = new Enumerator(Request.Form("item"));
while (!items.atEnd())
{
   item = items.item();
   Response.Cookies("ShoppingCart")("item"+j) = item;
   Response.Write(item+"<BR>");
   j = j + 1;
   items.moveNext();
}

ExpireDate = new Date();
   ExpireDate.setMonth(ExpireDate.getMonth()+3);

//Expires in 3 months from today
Response.Cookies("ShoppingCart").expires =

ExpireDate.toLocaleString();

Response.Cookies("ShoppingCart")("itemcount") = j;
%>

<HR>
</BODY>
</HTML>
```

3. Save the files. Open your browser and navigate to *http://localhost/Chapter_8/ Register/ShoppingCart.htm.* Your screen should resemble Figure 8-4.

4. Select **Visual Basic 1**, and then click the **Add to Cart** button. Your screen should resemble Figure 8-5.

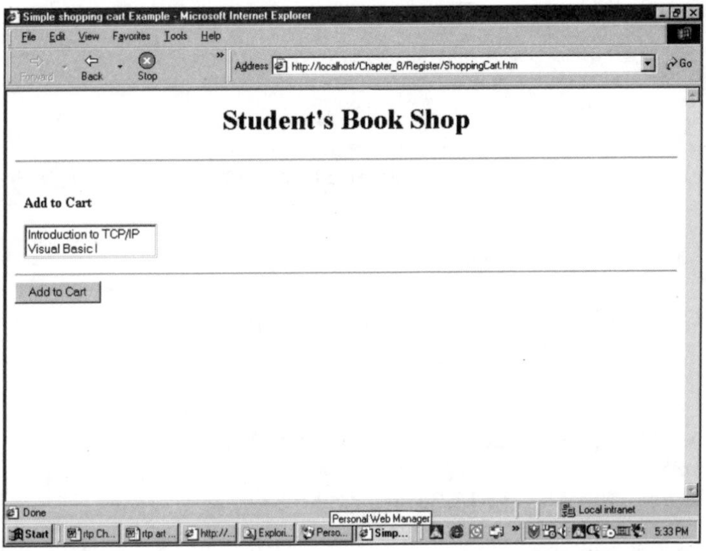

Figure 8-4   Shopping screen

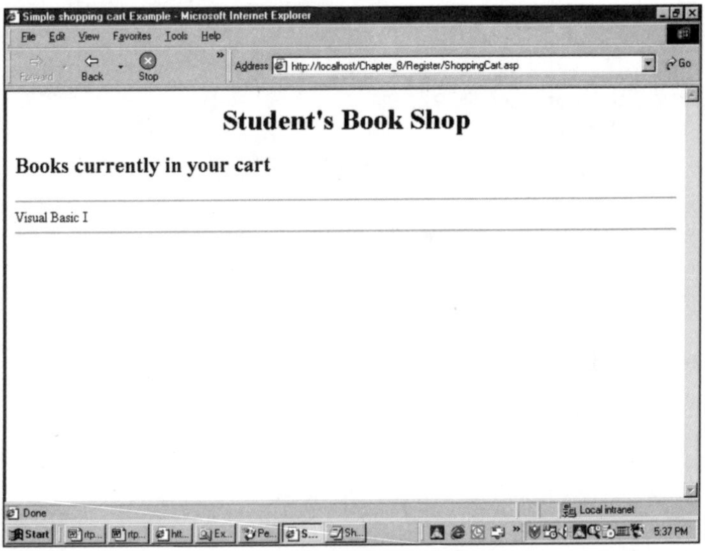

Figure 8-5   Item in shopping cart

5. Close your browser, open your browser, and then navigate to *http://localhost/ Chapter_8/Register/ShoppingCart.htm*. Click the **Add to Cart** button. Your Visual Basic book is still contained in your shopping cart.

6. Exit your browser.

Now that you have seen the code in action, let's review the ShoppingCart.htm file.

Code Example

```
1  <HTML>
2  <HEAD>
3     <TITLE>Simple shopping cart Example</TITLE>
4  </HEAD>
5
6  <BODY>
7
8  <CENTER><H1>Student's Book Shop</H1></CENTER>
9
10 <HR>
11
12 <FORM ACTION="http://localhost/Chapter_8/register/ShoppingCart
.asp" METHOD="post">
13 <TABLE CELLSPACING="5" CELLPADDING="5">
14 <TR>
15    <TD ALIGN="LEFT"><B>Add to Cart</B></TD>
16    <TD ALIGN="center"></TD>
17 </TR>
18 <TR>
19
20   <TD ALIGN="right"><SELECT MULTIPLE SIZE="2" NAME="item">
21   <OPTION>Introduction to TCP/IP
22   <OPTION>Visual Basic I
23   </SELECT>
24   <TD></TD>
25
26 </TR>
27
28 </TABLE>
29 <HR>
30 <INPUT TYPE="Submit" VALUE="Add to Cart">
31 </FORM>
32
33</BODY>
34 </HTML>
```

Code Dissection

- Lines 20–23 show that you have to use a list box that allows you to select multiple items at a time. The name of the list box is item. Therefore, item will be a collection when you select multiple items in the list. You will end up with a name/value pair for each item selected.

Let's look at ShoppingCart.asp next.

Code Example

```
1 <%@Language=JavaScript%>
2 <%Response.buffer=true%>
3 <HTML>
4 <HEAD>
5   <TITLE>Simple shopping cart Example</TITLE>
6 </HEAD>
7
8 <BODY>
9
10 <CENTER><H1>Student's Book Shop</H1></CENTER>
11
12 <H2>Books currently in your cart</H2>
13 <HR>
14 <%
15   var i,j,itemcount,item,items;
16
17   if (Request.Cookies("ShoppingCart") == "") {
18     Response.Cookies("ShoppingCart")("itemcount") = 0;
19     itemcount = 0;
20     j = 0;
21   }
22   else
23   {
24     itemcount = Request.Cookies("ShoppingCart")("itemcount");
25     j = 0;
26   }
27
28
29 for (i=0; i<itemcount; i++) {
30
31   Response.Cookies("ShoppingCart")("item"+i) =
32
33 Request.Cookies("ShoppingCart")("item"+i);
34
35
36 Response.Write(Request.Cookies("ShoppingCart")("item"+i)+"<BR>
");
37   j = j + 1;
38 }
39
40
41 items = new Enumerator(Request.Form("item"));
42 while (!items.atEnd())
43 {
44   item = items.item();
45   Response.Cookies("ShoppingCart")("item"+j) = item;
46   Response.Write(item+"<BR>");
47   j = j + 1;
```

8

```
48  items.moveNext();
49 }
50
51 ExpireDate = new Date();
52   ExpireDate.setMonth(ExpireDate.getMonth()+3);
//Expires in 3months from today
53   Response.Cookies("ShoppingCart").expires =
54 ExpireDate.toLocaleString();
55
56 Response.Cookies("ShoppingCart")("itemcount") = j;
57 %>
58
59 <HR>
60 </BODY>
61 </HTML>
```

Code Dissection

- Lines 17–26 check to see if a cookie called ShoppingCart exists in the Request object. If it does, then they extract the number of items in the list. If it does not, then they initialize the number of items to zero. The variable j is keeping track of the current number of items in the shopping cart.

- Lines 29–38 loop through the ShoppingCart collection and initializes the ShoppingCart cookies with the current contents of the cookie. You need to do this so that you do not lose your current shopping cart entries.

- Lines 41–50 loop through the item collection, which is the items the user selected off the ShoppingCart form. As they loop, they put the new items in the cart and track the number of items currently in the cart.

- Lines 51–54 set up the cookie to expire in three months.

- Line 56 updates the cookie's number of items to the current number of items in the cart.

You have created a very simple shopping cart that uses cookies to save information about what the user wants to buy.

KEY REVIEW POINTS

This chapter's version of the Student Contact application uses the Browser Capabilities component and cookies to personalize the application for the user. In this section, you will review the login.asp file and the save_login.asp file to see exactly how the application incorporates these features. The scripts in the following files are in JavaScript.

Login.asp

The default.asp file includes the login.asp script that determines whether to create a cookie. If a cookie does not exist, then a login form with last name and first name is displayed.

The following code shows the contents of the login.asp script.

Code Example

```
1 <HTML>
2 <HEAD>
3 <TITLE>Login Information</TITLE>
4 </head>
5 <BODY>
6 <form id="frmLogin" name="frmLogin" action="save_login.asp"
method="post">
7
8 <CENTER><H1><b>Login Information</b></H1></CENTER>
9
10 <CENTER>
11 <p>Full name:
12 <input id="FullName" type="text" name="FullName" size="35"
value="" ><strong>*</strong><br>
13
14 </CENTER>
15
16 <CENTER>
17 <p><input id="cmdSubmit"  type="submit" value="Submit">
18 <input id="cmdReset"  type="reset" value="Reset"> </p>
19 </CENTER>
20
21</FORM>
22
23 </BODY>
24
25 </HTML>
```

Code Dissection

- This form will request the user's name, if a cookie does not exist.

Save_login.asp

The save_login.asp script runs when the login.asp form is submitted. The contents of this page are as follows:

Code Example

```
1 <%@Language=JavaScript%>
2 <%Response.buffer=true%>
3 <% if (Request.Form("FullName") == "") {
4 %>
5 <HTML>
6 <HEAD>
7 <TITLE>Error Information</TITLE>
```

8

```
8  </HEAD>
9  <BODY>
10 <CENTER><H1><b>Error Information</b></H1></CENTER>
11 <CENTER>You must fill in all mandatory fields such as First
name and Last name.<BR>
12 Click back on your browser to fix your mistakes! </CENTER>
13
14 </BODY>
15
16 </HTML>
17 <% }
18 else
19 {
20    ExpireDate = new Date();
21    ExpireDate.setMonth(ExpireDate.getMonth()+3);
//Expires in 3months from today
22    Response.Cookies("LOGININFO").expires =  ExpireDate.toLocale
String();
23    Response.Cookies("LOGININFO") = Request.Form("FullName");
24
25    Response.Redirect("default.asp");
26    Response.End;
27 }
28 %>
```

Code Dissection

- Lines 20–24 show how to specify an expiration date, which is required for a cookie to be saved to the user's hard drive.

CHAPTER SUMMARY

- When requesting a Web page, a browser tells the Web server its type and version number. The server then checks the type and version of the browser in a special file in the Browser Capabilities component called Browscap.ini.

- You need to keep the Browscap.ini file current, since new browsers and new browser features are added every day. One way to keep this file up to date is to download the Browscap.ini file from cyScape, Inc.

- A cookie is a simple text file that stores a small amount of information (up to 255 characters) on the client computer. Cookies are commonly used to store small pieces of information such as usernames, passwords, and e-mail addresses.

- The central figure in the cookie's life is the Web application. It is this application that directs the creation of the cookie; it is also this application that reads the cookie once it has been created; and ultimately, it will be this application that determines the life span of the cookie itself.

- You use the Cookies collection of the Response object to have the application create a cookie. You use the Cookies collection of the Request object to allow the application to view the contents of a cookie.

- A shopping cart is a wonderful example of the way cookies can be used with your Web application. The application keeps track of items your customer wants to purchase, and even if he or she leaves the site and comes back, the items are still in the cart.

REVIEW QUESTIONS

1. An application can create a cookie to determine a browser's type and version. True or False?

2. An application can use the Browser Capabilities component to determine the features supported by a particular browser. True or False?

3. A _____ is a simple text file stored on the client computer that contains information such as the user's name, password, and e-mail address.

   a. Browser Capabilities component

   b. cookie

   c. text file

   d. none of the above

4. What is the name of the file used in conjunction with the Browser Capabilities component?

   a. MSWC.BrowserType

   b. BrowserType

   c. Browser

   d. MWSC.BrowserType

5. What is the name of the collection that supplies the HTTP_USER_AGENT property?

   a. Request

   b. Response

   c. ServerVariables

   d. none of the above

6. IE 5.0 supports frames. True or False?

7. If the browser is not found in the Browscap.ini file, then the Browser Capabilities component uses the _____.

   a. default section

   b. IE 5.0 section

   c. Netscape 4.0 section

   d. none of the above

8

8. Cookies have many uses, such as _____. [Choose all that apply.]

   a. tracking the user's identity

   b. tracking a user's progress through a Web site

   c. compiling marketing information

   d. none of the above

9. Cookies can be single-valued or multivalued. True or False?

10. Browsers all have identical features. True or False?

11. When requesting a Web page, a browser tells the Web server its type and _____.

   a. version number

   b. capabilities

   c. Browscap.ini

   d. component

12. The Parent property tells the Browser Capabilities component to use the settings for a particular browser, and the Platform property tells the Browser Capabilities component that this browser runs in a particular operating system. True or False?

13. The following line of JavaScript code is a correctly written line of code:

```
objbrowscap = Server.CreateObject("MSWC.BrowserType");.
```

   True or False?

14. One way to keep the Browscap.ini file up to date is to download it from _____.

   a. *www.msdn.com*

   b. *www.cyscape.com/browscap*

   c. *www.yardstick.com*

   d. *www.course.com*

15. You can acquire new versions of the Browscap.ini file at Microsoft's Web site. True or False?

16. A multivalued cookie gives you the ability to store more than one piece of data in the cookie. True or False?

17. You use the Cookies collection of the Response object to allow the application to view the contents of a cookie. True or False?

18. When you visit an e-commerce Web site such as Amazon.com, the site keeps track of items you want to purchase by using a(n) _____.

   a. e-commerce protocol

   b. server

   c. shopping cart

   d. HTML script

19. A shopping cart application should have both a form and a script. True or False?

20. On Internet Explorer, there is a Cookies directory within the Windows folder. True or False?

HANDS-ON PROJECTS

Project 8-1

Write an ASP script in JavaScript that displays information about the browser requesting a page. Test the script using either Internet Explorer or Netscape.

1. Create a file called browser.asp in the Chapter_8 folder of your Data Disk, and type the following script into this file:

```
<%@Language=JScript%>
<%Response.buffer=true%>
<HTML>
<HEAD>

</HEAD>
<BODY>
<%
objbrowscap = Server.CreateObject("MSWC.BrowserType");
%>
<CENTER><H2>Your browser information</H2>
<%
Response.Write("browser=" + objbrowscap.browser + "<BR>");
Response.Write("Version=" + objbrowscap.Version + "<BR>");
Response.Write("majorver=" + objbrowscap.majorver + "<BR>");
Response.Write("minorver=" + objbrowscap.minorver + "<BR>");
Response.Write("frames=" + objbrowscap.frames + "<BR>");
Response.Write("tables=" + objbrowscap.tables + "<BR>");
Response.Write("cookies=" + objbrowscap.cookies + "<BR>");
Response.Write("backgroundsounds=" +
objbrowscap.backgroundsounds +

"<BR>");
Response.Write("vbscript=" + objbrowscap.vbscript + "<BR>");
Response.Write("javaapplets=" + objbrowscap.javaapplets +
"<BR>");
Response.Write("javascript=" + objbrowscap.javascript + "
<BR>");
Response.Write("ActiveXControls=" + objbrowscap.Active
XControls +

"<BR>");
Response.Write("Win16=" + objbrowscap.Win16 + "<BR>");
Response.Write("beta=" + objbrowscap.beta + "<BR>");
Response.Write("AOL=" + objbrowscap.AOL + "<BR>");
```

8

```
Response.Write("Update=" + objbrowscap.Update + "<BR>");
%>
</CENTER>
</BODY>
</HTML>
```

2. Save the document.

3. Exit your text editor.

4. Open your browser and navigate to *http://localhost/Chapter_8/browser.asp.*

5. Close your browser.

Project 8-2

Write an ASP script in JavaScript that prompts the user for a username and password and stores this information in a cookie that expires on the current day and month, in 2001.

1. Create a file called auth.htm in the Chapter_8 folder of your Data Disk, and type the following HTML into this file:

```
<HTML>
<HEAD>
<TITLE>Login Information</TITLE>
</HEAD>
<BODY>
<form id="frmLogin" name="frmLogin" action="auth.asp"
method="post">

<CENTER><H1><b>Login Information</b></H1></CENTER>

<CENTER>
<p>Username:
<input id="UserName" type="text" name="UserName" size="35"
value="" ><strong>*</strong><br>
Password:<input id="Password" type="password" name="Password
" size="35" value="" ><strong>*</strong><br>

</CENTER>

<CENTER>
<p><input id="cmdSubmit"  type="submit" value="Submit">
<input id="cmdReset"  type="reset" value="Reset"> </p>
</CENTER>

</FORM>

</BODY>

</HTML>
```

2. Save the document.

3. Create a file called auth.asp in the Chapter_8 folder of your Data Disk, and type the following script into this file:

```
<%@Language=JavaScript%>
<%Response.buffer=true%>
<% if (Request.Form("UserName") == "" || (Request.Form("Pass
word") == "")) {
%>
<HTML>
<HEAD>
<TITLE>Error Information</TITLE>
</HEAD>
<BODY>
<CENTER><H1><b>Error Information</b></H1></CENTER>
<CENTER>You must fillin all mandatory fields such as First
name and Last name.<BR>
Click back on your browser to fix your mistakes! </CENTER>

</BODY>

</HTML>
<% }
else
{
    ExpireDate = new Date();
    ExpireDate.setYear(ExpireDate.getYear()+1); //Expires in
1 year from today
    Response.Cookies("User").expires = ExpireDate.toLocale
String();
    Response.Cookies("User")("Username") =

    Response.Write("Username and password saved in cookie!");
    Response.End;
}
%>
```

4. Three critical lines of code are missing from the file that you just created. Find the spot where they would reside, re-create these lines, insert them where appropriate, and then save the file.

5. Open your browser and navigate to *http://localhost/Chapter_8/auth.htm.*

6. Test the new application.

8

Project 8-3

Create a shopping cart similar to the example in this chapter, except that you are going to sell school supplies instead of books.

1. Create a file called SupplyCart.htm in the Chapter_8 folder of your Data Disk, and type the following HTML into this file:

```
<HTML>
<HEAD>
   <TITLE>Simple shopping cart Example</TITLE>
</HEAD>

<BODY>

<CENTER><H1>Student's Supply Shop</H1></CENTER>

<HR>


<TABLE CELLSPACING="5" CELLPADDING="5">
<TR>
   <TD ALIGN="LEFT"><B>Add to Cart</B></TD>
   <TD ALIGN="center"></TD>
</TR>
<TR>

  <TD ALIGN="right"><SELECT MULTIPLE SIZE="2" NAME="item">
  <OPTION>Pencils
  <OPTION>Pens
  <OPTION>Notebook Paper
  <OPTION>Notebooks
  </SELECT>
  <TD></TD>

</TR>

</TABLE>
<HR>
<INPUT TYPE="Submit" VALUE="Add to Cart">
</FORM>

</BODY>
</HTML>
```

2. One critical line of code is missing from the file that you just created. Find the spot where the code would reside, re-create the line, insert it where appropriate, and then save the file.

3. Create a file called SupplyCart.asp in the Chapter_8 folder of your Data Disk, and type the following script into this file:

```
<%@Language=JavaScript%>
<%Response.buffer=true%>
<HTML>
<HEAD>
    <TITLE>Simple shopping cart Example</TITLE>
</HEAD>

<BODY>

<CENTER><H1>Student's Supply Shop</H1></CENTER>

<H2>Items currently in your cart</H2>
<HR>
<%
  var i,j,itemcount,item,items;

  if (Request.Cookies("SupplyCart") == "") {
    Response.Cookies("SupplyCart")("itemcount") = 0;
    itemcount = 0;
    j = 0;
  }
  else
  {
    itemcount = Request.Cookies("SupplyCart")
("itemcount");
    j = 0;
  }


  for (i=0; i<itemcount; i++) {

    Response.Cookies("SupplyCart")("item"+i) =
Request.Cookies("SupplyCart")("item"+i);

    Response.Write(Request.Cookies("SupplyCart")("item"+i)+"<BR>
");
    j = j + 1;
  }


  items = new Enumerator(Request.Form("item"));
  while (!items.atEnd())
  {
    item = items.item();
    Response.Cookies("SupplyCart")("item"+j) = item;
    Response.Write(item+"<BR>");
    j = j + 1;
    items.moveNext();
```

```
}

ExpireDate = new Date();
   ExpireDate.setMonth(ExpireDate.getMonth()+3); //Expires
in 3 months from today
   Response.Cookies("SupplyCart").expires =
ExpireDate.toLocaleString();

Response.Cookies("SupplyCart")("itemcount") = j;
%>

<HR>
</BODY>
</HTML>
```

4. Save the document.

5. Open your browser and navigate to *http://localhost/Chapter_8/SupplyCart.htm*.

6. Test the new application.

Project 8-4

Write a script that determines whether a browser supports VBScript or JavaScript. Display the results in the browser.

1. Create a file called script.asp in the Chapter_8 folder of your Data Disk, and type the following script into this file:

```
<%@Language=JavaScript%>
<%Response.buffer=true%>
<HTML>
<HEAD>

</HEAD>
<BODY>
<%
%>
<center><H2>Script information</H2>
<%

if (objbrowscap.vbscript) {
Response.Write("This browser supports VBScript!" + "<BR>");
}

if (objbrowscap.javascript) {
Response.Write("This browser supports JavaScript!" + "<BR>")
}

%>
</CENTER>
</BODY>
</HTML>
```

2. The code that you just created contains an error. Find the error, correct the error, and then save the file.

3. Exit your text editor.

4. Open your browser and navigate to *http://localhost/Chapter_8/script.asp*.

5. Exit the browser.

CASE PROJECTS

1. Lee Marketing has hired you to help determine what browser is most commonly used to access the company's Web site. The company's Web developers need this information to determine whether they should tailor their Web application to a specific browser. Your job is to write a Web application that discretely tracks each user's request and counts the number of IE browsers, Netscape browsers, or other browsers accessing the site. You can use an Application variable to track this information for simplicity.

2. Webman's Software, Inc. is a thriving business selling software over the Web. The company's Web developers have hired you to help track the site's users. Specifically, the developers would like to know the number of times each user accesses the site. You decide to store all information in a cookie. Your job is to create a skeleton Web application that provides all the information requested by the developers at Webman's Software. In the future, Webman's Software will advertise specials to loyal customers based on the number of times they use the site.

3. Lee and Lee Consulting is a premier Web development company specializing in e-commerce solutions using ASP. Centreville Community College has recently hired this consulting company to provide a shopping cart to give students the ability to register for multiple classes at one time. Using the Student Contact Application in the Register folder, create a shopping cart for classes being offered. Name your .mdb file "Course for EOC.mdb".

8

CHAPTER

9

MANAGING ADS AND TABLES OF CONTENTS IN YOUR WEB APPLICATION

In this chapter, you will:

- ◆ Learn how to use the Ad Rotator component
- ◆ Learn about the Ad Rotator Component Schedule File
- ◆ Learn about the Ad Rotator Component Redirection File
- ◆ Work with the Content Linking component and the corresponding List File
- ◆ Learn to differentiate between the PageCounter Object and the Counters Object

The key to a successful Web site is managing the content of that site. In this chapter, you will learn the role ASP plays in managing the insertion and timing of Web advertisements. In the process, you will become quite familiar with the Ad Rotator component and the Schedule and Redirection Files. Then, we'll take a look at the Content Link component and List File, which will help you present dynamically generated tables of contents to your Web visitors. Last, we'll explore the PageCounter and Counters objects, both of which permit you to enumerate the frequency of specified events.

USING THE AD ROTATOR COMPONENT

We are all familiar with flashy, rotating ads on Web sites. If the site is a search engine site, the ad may be for an online book company that is trying to sell you a book about the keyword that you just typed into the search engine. If the site has a specialty, such as politics or sports, the ads are related to that specialized topic. These rotating ads—so called because they are swapped in and out of circulation on a predetermined schedule—are made possible by the Ad Rotator component. In this section, you will investigate how to use the Ad Rotator component.

The application for this chapter uses the Ad Rotator component. The application, Course Tracking Information System, has a start page, default.asp, that the browser accesses. The default.asp file reads its scripts and begins generating the HTML to send to the browser. One of the lines of script will tell default.asp to request an ad from the Ad Rotator component.

When the Ad Rotator component receives the request from default.asp, it returns (to default.asp) the ad that the schedule file, which is named ad.txt, dictates should be sent. The schedule file determines the number of ads and the configuration of each ad.

Once the Ad Rotator component returns (or sends) the ad to default.asp, default.asp accepts the ad and continues processing the ASP script. Eventually, the entire contents are sent to the browser. Once the page is on the browser, the user can click the ad; at that point, the browser will be redirected to the advertiser's Web site, per the instructions received from the Ad Rotator's Redirection File.

To use the Ad Rotator component, you need to do the following:

- Create the Ad Rotator Object
- Create the Ad Rotator Schedule File
- Create the Ad Rotator Redirection File

Conveniently enough, these three bulleted items create the outline for our continued discussion.

Creating the Ad Rotator Component

To use the Ad Rotator component in your applications, you must first create an instance of the Ad Rotator Component Object. The following code shows an example of how to do this in VBScript and JavaScript:

Code Example

```vbscript
Dim objRotator
set objRotator = Server.CreateObject("MSWC.AdRotator")
```

```javascript
var objRotator;
objRotator = Server.CreateObject("MSWC.AdRotator");
```

Code Dissection

- The MSWC component contains the AdRotator Object.

- The first line of code declares the object variable.

- The second line of code creates an instance of the AdRotator Object.

Once the Web application creates an instance to the AdRotator Object, the Web application has access to the AdRotator's properties and methods. Table 9-1 shows the properties and methods of the AdRotator Object.

Table 9-1   Useful Properties and Methods of the AdRotator Object

Property/Method	Name	Description
Method	GetAdvertisement	Gets the details of the next advertisement and formulates them as HTML
Property	Border	Sets the border size around the advertisement
Property	Clickable	Determines whether the advertisement is a hyperlink
Property	TargetFrame	Determines the name of the frame where the advertisement will reside; frame names can be one of the following: _top, _new, _child, _self, _parent, or _blank

The following code shows, in both VBScript and JavaScript, how to create the AdRotator Object and use the properties and methods of that object:

Code Example

```
Dim strHTML,objRotator
set objRotator = Server.CreateObject("MSWC.AdRotator")
objRotator.Border = 1
objRotator.Clickable = True
strHTML =
objRotator.GetAdvertisement("/Chapter_9/Advertisements/ad.txt")
```

or

```
var strHTML,objRotator;
objRotator = Server.CreateObject("MSWC.AdRotator");
objRotator.Border = 1;
objRotator.Clickable = True;
strHTML =
objRotator.GetAdvertisement("/Chapter_9/Advertisements/ad.txt");
```

Code Dissection

- The first line in each example declares the object variable.

- The second line in each example creates an instance of the AdRotator Object.

- The third and fourth lines in each example set the advertisement to have a border of width 1 and to be a hyperlink.

- The fifth line in each example shows an example of how to get an ad from the ad.txt file using GetAdvertisement.

Now that you have seen the Ad Rotator Object in action, you need to learn how to create the Ad Rotator Schedule File.

Creating the Ad Rotator Component's Schedule File

The Ad Rotator component uses a schedule file, called ad.txt, to determine which advertisements will be sent back to default.asp and ultimately displayed in the browser for the viewing pleasure of the end user. The following shows the syntax for creating a schedule file in VBScript.

Syntax Example

REDIRECT *URL*
WIDTH *width*
HEIGHT *height*
BORDER *border*
*
adURL
adHomeURL
text
impressions

Syntax Dissection

- REDIRECT *URL* is the ASP script that handles the redirection to an advertiser's site.

- *width* is the width of the advertisement.

- *height* is the height of the advertisement.

- *border* is the width of the border around the advertisement.

- *adURL* is the graphic file in which the advertisement is stored.

- *adHomeURL* is the advertiser's Web site URL.

- *text* is a textual message of the Advertisement, used if the browser does not support graphics.

- *impressions* is a number that indicates the relative display time of the advertisement.

Now that you have the syntax, it's time to apply what you know to the application in this chapter. In the following sequence of steps, you will add a schedule file.

To add the schedule file:

1. Create a file called **ad.txt** in the Advertisements folder of your Chapter_9 Data Disk.

2. Add the following code:

```
REDIRECT /Chapter_9/Advertisements/ad.asp
WIDTH 440
HEIGHT 90
BORDER 1
*
/Chapter_9/Advertisements/course.gif
http://www.course.com
Course Technology -- Teaching without fear!
10
/Chapter_9/Advertisements/Solutions_Architecture.gif
http://www.amazon.com/exec/obidos/ASIN/0760011788/
keithamorne
MCSD Guide to Solutions Architecture by Keith A. Morneau
10
```

3. Save your work and close the text editor.

Let's examine the code that you just wrote:

- Line 1 tells the Ad Rotator Object which ASP script (ad.asp, in this example) redirects the application to the advertiser's site.

- Lines 2 and 3 initialize the ad's width and height to 440 and 90.

- Line 4 sets the width of the border at 1.

- Lines 6–9 describe one of the advertisements.

- Lines 10–13 describe a second advertisement.

Creating the Ad Rotator's Redirection File

So, you have your ad and your ad schedule. Exactly what happens when the user clicks that ad? The redirection file, which contains the ad.asp script, provides the necessary code to redirect the browser to the advertiser's site.

Let's look at the contents of ad.asp for our chapter's sample application. This script contains a query string. The query string will accept the URL associated with the ad that was just clicked and redirect the browser to that URL.

Code Example

```
1 <%@ Language=VBScript%>
2 <%Option Explicit%>
3 <%Response.buffer=true
4 Response.redirect(Request.QueryString("url"))
5 Response.End
6 %>
```

Code Dissection

- The code in line 4 redirects the browser to the site related to the advertisement clicked by the end user.

THE AD ROTATOR COMPONENT IN ACTION

You are now ready to review the Ad Rotator component in action.

To review the application:

1. Copy **counters.dll** from the Chapter_9 folder of your Data Disk to the Windows\System\inetsrv folder on your computer. Then, go to your MS-DOS prompt and type regsur32 **c:\windows\system\inetsrv\counters.dll**. Then, restart PWS. Create a virtual directory to the Chapter_9 folder on your Data Disk. Start Internet Explorer.

2. Type **http://localhost/Chapter_9/default.asp** in the Address field, and then press **Enter**. Your screen will resemble Figure 9-1. Note that due to the use of cookies in this application, the Login page appears only the first time you use the application.

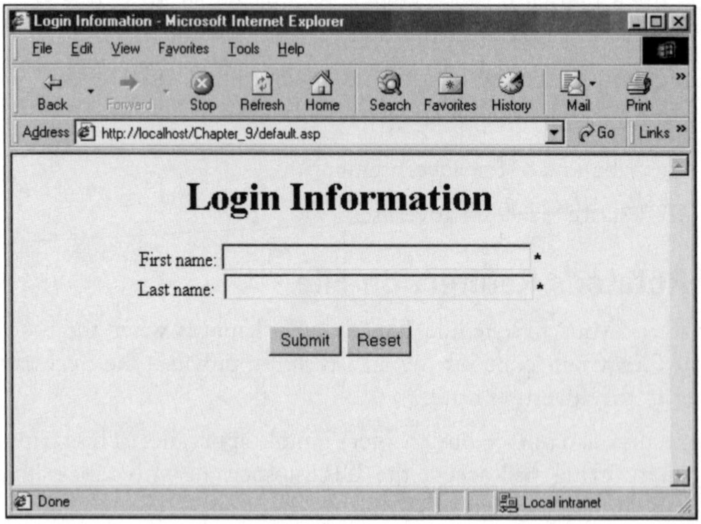

Figure 9-1   Login page

3. Enter your **first name** and **last name**, and then click **Submit**. The Course Tracking Information System start page loads, as shown in Figure 9-2.

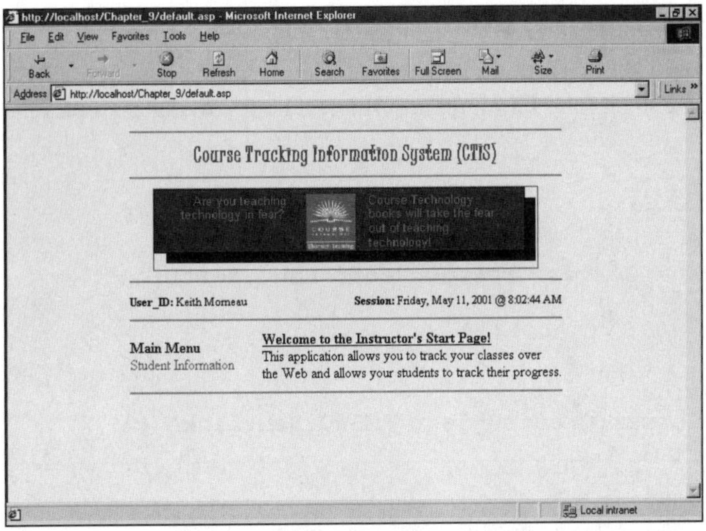

Figure 9-2   Course Tracking Information System start page

4. Look for the advertisement at the top of the page. The code that you wrote for the schedule file allows this advertisement to exist.

5. Click the ad. You will be taken to the new "site," just as if you were on the Internet.

6. Close your browser.

USING THE CONTENT LINKING COMPONENT

The sample application in this chapter contains a table of contents. At first glance, you might think the table of contents is nothing out of the ordinary. But in fact a special component is used to create a table of contents within a Web application. This component is called the Content Linking component.

The Content Linking component allows the programmer to create a table of contents with contents that are generated dynamically. Dynamic generation ensures that the table of contents will be updated every time the application's internal organization changes, without requiring the Web developer to recode everything by hand.

To use the Content Linking component, you have to do the following:

- Create the Content Linking Component Object.
- Create the Content Linking List File.

Once again, our bulleted list provides a convenient outline for further discussion, which begins next.

Create the Content Linking Component Object

To use the Content Linking component in your applications, you must first create an instance of the Content Linking Component Object. The following examples show how to create this object:

Code Example

```
Dim objContent
set objContent = Server.CreateObject("MSWC.NextLink")
```

or

```
var objContent;
objContent = Server.CreateObject("MSWC.NextLink");
```

Code Dissection

- The MSWC component contains the Next Link object.
- The first line of code declares the object variable.
- The second line of code creates an instance of the Content Linking Object.

Once the Web application creates an instance of the Content Linking Object, the Web application has access to the Content Linking Object's properties and methods. Table 9-2 shows important methods of the Content Linking Object.

Table 9-2 Useful Methods of the Content Linking Object

Name	Description
GetListCount(file)	Determines the number of items in the list
GetListIndex(file)	Determines the index of the current page in the list; starts at 1
GetNextURL(file)	Determines the next URL in the list
GetNextDescription(file)	Determines the description of the next page in the list
GetPreviousURL(file)	Determines the previous URL in the list
GetNthURL(file,n)	Determines the URL of the nth item in the list
GetNthDescription(file,n)	Determines the description of the nth item in the list

The following code shows how to use the properties and methods of the Content Linking Object:

Code Example

```
1 Dim objContent, i, intCount
2 set objContent = Server.CreateObject("MSWC.NextLink")
3 i = objContent.GetListCount("/Chapter_9/toc/toc.txt")
4 For intCount = 1 to i
5    Response.Write("<a href=" &_
6    objContent.GetNthURL("/Chapter_9/toc/toc.txt",intCount) &
">" &_
7    objContent.GetNthDescription("/Chapter_9/toc/toc.txt",
intCount) &_
8    "</a><BR>")
9 Next
```

Code Dissection

- Line 1 declares the object variable (objContent) and the index (i) of the list. The list is stored as toc.txt in the toc folder of the Chapter_9 folder of your Data Disk.

- Line 2 creates an instance of the Content Linking Object.

- Line 3 determines the number of items in the list.

- Lines 4–9 create a loop that will iterate through the list one item at a time and display the contents of the list.

Now that you have examined the Content Linking Object, you need to learn how to create a list file.

Creating the Content Linking List File

The Content Linking Component Object retrieves the table of contents from a list file called toc.txt. The general structure of this list file is as follows:

Syntax Example

URL1 DESCRIPTION1   COMMENT1
URL2 DESCRIPTION2   COMMENT2

. . .

Syntax Dissection

- The *URL* field includes the complete path to the next page as a link. The *DESCRIPTION* field includes a description of a table of contents entry. You can use the *COMMENT* field to record more information about a specific table of contents entry. Each list file can contain one or more items. A tab space separates each field in this file from the next.

Code Example

```
/Chapter_9/register/search.htm    Student Information
/Chapter_9/classes/search.htm     Class Information
```

Code Dissection

- This example file contains only two fields, the URL field and the Description field. The resulting table of contents will show two items: Student Information and Class Information.

It is now time to finish the functionality of the Content Linking component for this chapter.

To finish the functionality:

1. Open **Toc.txt** in the Toc folder of your Data Disk.

2. Add the following code:

   ```
   /Chapter_9/classes/search.htm <HIT TAB KEY> Class
   Information
   ```

3. Save your work.

4. Open your browser and navigate to **http://localhost/Chapter_9/default.asp**. Your screen should resemble Figure 9-3. The dynamically generated table of contents is the main menu on the left side of the screen. Figure 9-2 contained the same table of contents, but clicking the links will now provide additional information. Note that the font shown depends on your system configuration.

5. Close your browser.

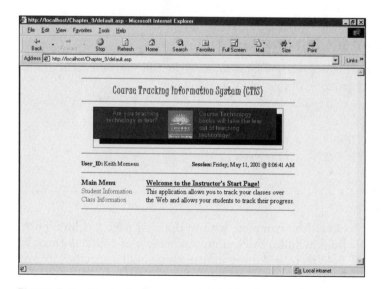

Figure 9-3   Dynamically generated table of contents

USING COUNTERS

In this section you will learn how to incorporate yet another feature into your applications—counters. You can employ two different counters in your applications:

- **PageCounter**: Counts the number of times a user has accessed a Web page

- **Counters**: Counts a variety of events, including the number of times a user has accessed a Web page, the number of times a particular person has sent e-mail, or the number of times a user requests help

The PageCounter Object is useful if you are only interested in the number of hits on a particular page. For this purpose, it is the most efficient alternative. However, the Counters Object gives you more flexibility because you can use it to count just about anything else you wish in your Web applications.

Many beginning ASP programmers wonder why the skill of working with counters is so important to acquire. After all, they argue, isn't this something that you can double-click within FrontPage just as easily as you can code it by hand? The answer to this argument, of course, is that you need to understand the logic and structure of these objects before you can use tools that automate the process. It's the same reason that you weren't allowed to use calculators in math class until you could do basic math in your head.

9

Using the PageCounter Object

The PageCounter Object provides a very simple interface. It works like this: Every time a user accesses the site, the Hit Count Data file stores and retrieves page hits. Even if the Web server goes down and then comes back up, the PageCounter Object will pick up again where it left off. The PageCounter Object is very simple and provides two methods, as shown in Table 9-3.

Table 9-3   Useful Methods of the PageCounter Object

Name	Description
Hits	Returns and increments the page counter
Reset	Resets the counter to zero

The following example shows how to create a PageCounter Object in VBScript and in JavaScript.

Code Example

```
Dim objPageCounter
set objPageCounter = Server.CreateObject("MSWC.PageCounter")
Response.Write("The number of hits: " & objPageCounter.Hits)
```

and

```javascript
var objPageCounter;
objPageCounter = Server.CreateObject("MSWC.PageCounter");
Response.Write("The number of hits: " + objPageCounter.Hits());
```

Code Dissection

- Lines 1 and 2 show you how to create an instance of the PageCounter Object.

- Line 3 shows you how to increment and display the number of visitors to a particular page. You can include this script in any Web page for which you need to count page hits.

Using the Counters Object

While the PageCounter Object is useful in limited circumstances, you will generally want to use the more powerful counter object, Counters. The Counters Object stores information about all counters in a file called counters.txt in the directory where counters.dll resides.

To use the Counters Object, you must first declare an instance of it. It's helpful to create an instance of the Counters Object in the global.asa file. After creating this one instance in the global.asa file, you can use multiple counters from the single instance. When the application starts, the global.asa loads into memory, and the Counters Object instance is created. Thus it is unnecessary for each page to create its own counters; this in turn saves crucial processing time.

You can use the global.asa file to create the instance of a counter, using the following OBJECT tag:

Code Example

```
<OBJECT
RUNAT=Server
SCOPE=Application
ID=Counter
PROGID="MSWC.Counters">
</OBJECT>
```

Code Dissection

- The RUNAT attribute tells ASP to run this on the server.

- The SCOPE attribute tells ASP to use the Application scope, which means that all sessions and all pages can see the object.

- The ID attribute tells ASP the name of the instance.

- The PROGID attribute tells ASP where the Counters component can be found.

- The OBJECT tag provides the programmer with a method of creating instances of objects that everyone needs to use in the application. This prevents the programmer from having to create instances on the fly in an ASP script if the counters are used over and over again in Web pages.

The Counters tag has four methods, as listed in Table 9-4.

Table 9-4 Useful Methods of the Counters Object

Name	Description
Set(counter,value)	Allows the counter to be initialized to some value
Increment(counter)	Increments a counter by one and returns the new value
Get(counter)	Gets the value of a counter
Remove(counter)	Removes a counter

Once you create the object, you initialize it in order to set the counter to zero, as shown below. Initialization is done to provide the application with a known starting point against which to make comparisons.

Code Example

```
Counter.Set("defaultInstructorPageHits",0)
```

or

```
Counter.Set("defaultInstructorPageHits",0);
```

It is now time to put code into your application that increments the counter by a particular unit every time a certain event happens. Then, your code needs to retrieve that incrementation information. We will put this functionality into our application next.

To add the counter functionality:

1. Open the **default.asp** file in your text editor.

2. Add the following code right before the </TABLE> tag. This new code will increment the counter and permit later retrieval of that information.

```
<TR>
  <TD COLSPAN=2>
  <FONT SIZE=-1>You are visitor number
<%=Counter.Increment("defaultInstructorPageHits")%>.</FONT>
  </TD>
</TR>
```

3. Save the file. Open your browser, and then navigate to **http://localhost/ Chapter_9/default.asp**. Note the counter information at the bottom of the screen.

9

4. Close your browser, open your browser, and then navigate to **http://localhost/ Chapter_9/default.asp**. Click the **Refresh** button. Note that the counter has incremented by one, as shown in Figure 9-4.

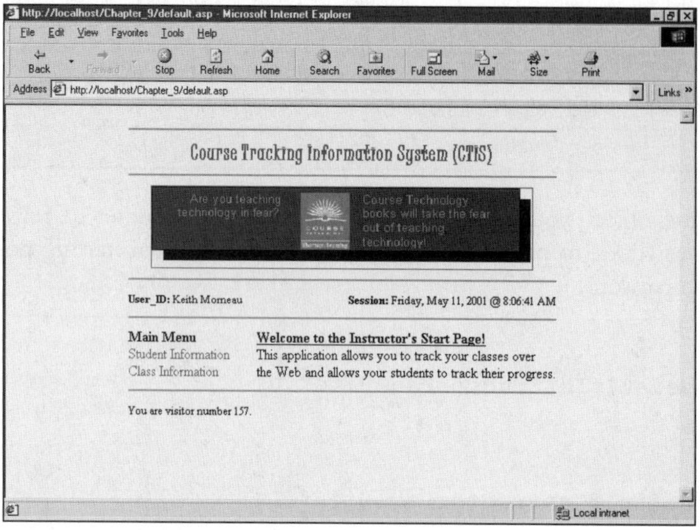

Figure 9-4   Successful incrementation

5. Close your browser.

REVIEWING THE COURSE TRACKING INFORMATION SYSTEM START PAGE

Each of the functionalities in this chapter has its core representation in the default.asp start page. Let's examine the code of default.asp:

Code Example

```
1 <%@ Language=VBScript%>
2 <%Option Explicit%>
3 <%Response.buffer=true%>
4 <!-- #include file="./login/login.asp" -->
5 <HTML>
6 <HEAD>
7 <%
8 Dim strHTML,objRotator
9 set objRotator = Server.CreateObject("MSWC.AdRotator")
10 objRotator.Border = 1
11 objRotator.Clickable = True
12 strHTML =
13 objRotator.GetAdvertisement("/Chapter_9/Advertisements/
ad.txt")
14 %>
```

```
15  </HEAD>
16  <BODY BGCOLOR=LIGHTYELLOW>
17  <CENTER>
18  <TABLE BORDER=0>
19    <TR>
20     <TD COLSPAN=4>
21        <HR COLOR=RED>
22     </TD>
23    </TR>
24    <TR>
25     <TD ALIGN=CENTER COLSPAN=2>
26        <B><FONT SIZE=+2 FACE="Juice ITC" COLOR=BLUE>Course
Tracking
27  Information System (CTIS)</FONT></B>
28     </TR>
29    <TR>
30     <TD COLSPAN=2>
31        <HR COLOR=RED>
32     </TD>
33    </TR>
34    <TR>
35     <TD COLSPAN=2>
36        <CENTER><%Response.Write(strHTML)%></CENTER>
37     </TD>
38    </TR>
39    <TR>
40     <TD COLSPAN=2>
41        <HR COLOR=RED>
42     </TD>
43    </TR>
44    <TR>
45     <TD ALIGN=LEFT>
46        <FONT SIZE=-1><B>User_ID:</B>
47  <%=Request.Cookies("LOGININFO")("FIRST_NAME") & " " &_
48  Request.Cookies("LOGININFO")("LAST_NAME")%></FONT>
49       </TD>
50      <TD ALIGN=RIGHT>
51       <FONT SIZE=-1><B>Session:</B> <%=FormatDateTime(Now,1)
& " @ " &_
52  FormatDateTime(Now,3)%></FONT>
53       </TD>
54     </TR>
55    <TR>
56     <TD COLSPAN=2>
57        <HR COLOR=RED>
58     </TD>
59    </TR>
60    <TR>
61     <TD WIDTH=30%>
```

9

```
62          <B>Main Menu</B><BR>
63          <% Dim objContent, i, intCount
64          set objContent = Server.CreateObject("MSWC.NextLink")
65          i = objContent.GetListCount("/Chapter_9/toc/toc.txt")
66          For intCount = 1 to i
67             Response.Write("<a href=" &_
68   objContent.GetNthURL("/Chapter_9/toc/toc.txt",
intCount) & ">" &_
69
70   objContent.GetNthDescription("/Chapter_9/toc/toc.txt",
intCount) &_
71             "</a><BR>")
72          Next
73       %>
74       </TD>
75       <TD WIDTH=70% VALIGN=top>
76        <B><U>Welcome to the Instructor's Start Page!</U></B><BR>
77        This application allows you to track your classes over<BR>
78        the Web and allows your students to track their
progress.<BR>
79       </TD>
80
81   </TR>
82   <TR>
83     <TD COLSPAN=4>
84       <HR COLOR=RED>
85     </TD>
86   </TR>
87   <TR>
88     <TD COLSPAN=2>
89     <FONT SIZE=-1>You are visitor number
90   <%=Counter.Increment("defaultInstructorPageHits")%>.</FONT>
91     </TD>
92   </TR>
93   </TABLE>
94   </CENTER>
95   </BODY>
96   </HTML>
```

Code Dissection

- Lines 8–14 show the use of the AdRotator Object.

- Lines 63–73 show the use of the Content Linking Object.

- Lines 89–90 show the use of the Counters Object.

CHAPTER SUMMARY

❏ Rotating ads—so called because they are swapped in and out of circulation on a prede-termined schedule—are made possible by the Ad Rotator component. When the Ad Rotator component receives the ad request from default.asp, it returns the ad that the schedule file, which is named ad.txt, dictates should be sent. The schedule file determines the number of ads and the configuration of each ad.

❏ To use the Ad Rotator component in your applications, you must first create an instance of the Ad Rotator Component Object. The Ad Rotator component uses a schedule file, called ad.txt, to determine which advertisements will be sent back to default.asp and ultimately displayed in the browser for the viewing pleasure of the end user. The redirec-tion file, which contains the ad.asp script, provides the necessary code to redirect the browser to the advertiser's site.

❏ The Content Linking component allows the programmer to generate a table of contents with contents that are generated dynamically. To use the Content Linking component in your applications, you must first create an instance of the Content Linking Component Object. The Content Linking Component Object retrieves the table of contents from a list file called toc.txt.

❏ You can employ two different counters in your applications: PageCounter and Counters. The PageCounter Object is useful if you are only interested in the number of hits on a particular page. For this purpose, it is the most efficient alternative. However, the Counters Object gives you more flexibility because you can use it to count just about anything else you wish in your Web applications.

REVIEW QUESTIONS

1. Which object displays advertisements on a Web page?

   a. Content Linking

   b. AdRotator

   c. Counters

   d. PageCounter

2. Which object is used to create a table of contents?

   a. Content Linking

   b. AdRotator

   c. Counters

   d. PageCounter

3. Which property of the AdRotator Object determines whether the advertisement is a hyperlink?

   a. TargetFrame

   b. GetAdvertisement

   c. Border

   d. Clickable

4. Which method of the Ad Rotator Object gets the details of the next advertisement and formats them as HTML?

   a. TargetFrame

   b. GetAdvertisement

   c. Border

   d. Clickable

5. Which method of the Content Linking Object determines the number of items in the list?

   a. GetListIndex

   b. GetListCount

   c. GetNextURL

   d. GetNextDescription

6. Which method of the Content Linking Object determines the next URL in the list?

   a. GetListIndex

   b. GetListCount

   c. GetNextURL

   d. GetNextDescription

7. Which method of the PageCounter Object returns and increments the page counter?

   a. Hits

   b. Reset

   c. Set

   d. Increment

8. Which method of the PageCounter Object resets the counter to zero?

   a. Hits

   b. Reset

   c. Set

   d. Increment

9. Which method of the Counters Object returns and increments the page counter?

   a. Hits

   b. Reset

   c. Set

   d. Increment

10. Which method of the Counter Object initializes a counter to a value?

   a. Hits

   b. Reset

   c. Set

   d. Increment

11. Which tag allows you to create an instance of an object in the global.asa file?

   a. HTML

   b. BODY

   c. OBJECT

   d. CreateObject

12. The PageCounter Object allows you to create one instance of the object, which can then create different counters to be used throughout your Web application. True or False?

13. The Content Linking Object allows you to display ads on a Web page. True or False?

14. Windows 98 requires you to create a Counters instance in the global.asa file. True or False?

15. An entry point into a Web application is called the _____ page.

   a. default

   b. next

   c. start

   d. none of the above

16. Which object requires a schedule file to be created?

   a. Content Linking

   b. PageCounter

   c. Counters

   d. AdRotator

17. Which object requires a list file to be created?

   a. Content Linking

   b. PageCounter

   c. Counters

   d. AdRotator

9

18. Which object requires a redirection file to be created?

   a. Content Linking

   b. PageCounter

   c. Counters

   d. AdRotator

19. With the Ad Rotator Object, the GetAdvertisement method gets the details of the next advertisement and formats them as _____.

20. A frame can be named any of the following: _top, _parent, or _self. True or False?

HANDS-ON PROJECTS

Project 9-1

Create an include file for the advertisements and replace the advertisements code with a server-side include in the default.asp script.

1. Create a file called ads.asp in the Chapter_9 folder of your Data Disk with the following code:

```
<%
Dim strHTML,objRotator
set objRotator = Server.CreateObject("MSWC.AdRotator")
objRotator.Border = 1
objRotator.Clickable = True
strHTML = objRotator.GetAdvertisement("/Chapter_9/" &_
"Advertisements/ad.txt")
%>
```

2. Save the file.

3. Open Default.asp, remove the script between the <HEAD> and </HEAD> tags, and replace that script with the following line of code:

```
<!-- #include file="ads.asp" -->
```

4. Save the file.

5. Test the new application in your browser by browsing to *http://localhost/Chapter_9/ default.asp*. You should see the start page appear with the ads at the top of the page.

6. Close your browser.

Project 9-2

Your instructor decides it would be nice to count the number of hits to the register part of the application. You decide to add a counter to the Form.asp page of the Register folder of the Chapter_9 folder of your Data Disk.

1. Open the form.asp page of the Register folder of the Chapter_9 folder of your Data Disk, and add the following bolded code:

```
<%@ Language=VBScript%>
...
<%Case "Delete" %>
<center><p><input id="cmdSubmit" type="submit" value="Delete
">
</center>
<%Case "Browse"%>
<center><p>Back to <a href=search.htm>Search</a>.</center>
</center>
<% End Select %>
</form>
<HR>
<FONT SIZE=-1>You are visitor number

<%=Counter.Increment("defaultRegisterPageHits")%>.</FONT>
<HR>

</body>
</html>
```

2. Save the file.

3. Test your changed application by browsing to *http://localhost/Chapter_9/default.asp*, leaving the site, and returning to the site in order to view the change in the counter.

Project 9-3

Your instructor decides it would be nice to count the number of hits to the classes part of the application. You decide to add a counter to the form.asp page of the Classes folder of the Chapter_9 folder of your Data Disk.

1. Open the Form.asp page of the Classes folder of the Chapter_9 folder of your Data Disk, and add the following bolded code:

```
<%@ Language=VBScript%>
...
<% End Select %>
</form>
<HR>
<FONT SIZE=-1>You are visitor number
<%=Counter.Increment("defaultClassPageHits")%>.</FONT>
<HR>
</body>
</html>
```

2. Save the file.

3. Test your changed application by browsing to *http://localhost/Chapter_9/default.asp* and viewing a valid class to see if the counter is working properly.

4. Close your browser.

Project 9-4

Now, your instructor really needs a counter reports page that displays the number of visitors to the Start, Register, and Classes pages.

1. Create a file called report.asp in the Chapter_9 folder of your Data Disk, containing the following code:

```
<%@ Language=VBScript%>
<%Option Explicit%>
<%Response.buffer=true%>
<html>

<head>
<title>Counters Report</title>
</head>
<body>
<center>
<H1>Counters Report</H1>
Start page count:
<%=Counter.Get("defaultInstructorPageHits") %><BR>
Register page count:
<%=Counter.Get("defaultRegisterPageHits") %><BR>
Classes page count:
<%=Counter.Get("defaultClassPageHits") %><BR>
</center>
</body>
</html>
```

2. Open your browser. Test your code by browsing to *http://localhost/Chapter_9/report.asp.*

3. Close your browser.

Project 9-5

As a student of ASP, you decide that you would like to keep a list of all of your favorite ASP sites on the Web. You decide that you need to use the Content Linking component to do this, so that you only have to update an ASCII text file instead of having to update a page every time.

1. Create a folder called favorites.

2. Create a folder called toc in the favorites folder.

3. Create a file called toc.txt in the toc folder, containing the following data:

```
http://www.activeserverpages.com    Learn ASP Tutorials
http://www.asptoday.com   ASP Today
```

4. Save the file.

5. Create a file called favorites.asp in the favorites folder with the following code:

```
<%@ Language=VBScript%>
<%Option Explicit%>
<%Response.buffer=true%>
<HTML>
<HEAD>
</HEAD>
<BODY>
<CENTER>
<B>My Favorite ASP Sites</B><BR>
<% Dim objContent, i, intCount
   set objContent = Server.CreateObject("MSWC.NextLink")
   i = objContent.GetListCount("/Chapter_9/favorites/" &_
"toc/toc.txt")
   For intCount = 1 to i
      Response.Write("<a href=" &_
objContent.GetNthURL("/Chapter_9/favorites/toc/toc.txt" &_
,intCount) &_
">" &_
objContent.GetNthDescription("/Chapter_9/favorites/toc/
toc.txt",intCount) & "</a><BR>")
   Next
%>
</CENTER>
</BODY>
</HTML>
```

6. Save the file.

7. Test your code by browsing to *http://localhost/Chapter_9/favorites/favorites.asp*.

9

CASE PROJECTS

1. John's Software has retained you to help them develop a start page for the gift management system you created in Chapters 5–7. Using the application in Chapter 7, create a start page and reorganize the application into folders similar to those in this chapter.

2. Interstate Bank has retained you to help them develop a start page for the budget management system you created in Chapters 5–7. Using the application in Chapter 7, create a start page and reorganize the application into folders similar to those in this chapter.

3. Interstate Bank has retained you to help them develop a start page for the checkbook management system you created in Chapters 5–7. Using the application in Chapter 7, create a start page and reorganize the application into folders similar to those in this chapter.

10

CREATING USER-DEFINED COMPONENTS IN VISUAL BASIC 6.0

In this chapter you will:

♦ Learn about components and their role in a Web application
♦ Explore components in the Visual Basic 6.0 environment
♦ Transform scripts into components
♦ Test the validity of transformed scripts
♦ Learn about and implement transaction processing
♦ Learn about high-level functions and strategies for software applications

To bring about a successful completion of a programming activity, you must complete front-line tasks and overseer tasks, and learn the management environment toward which the efficacy of your code is directed. In this chapter, you will do all three as you create user-defined components in Visual Basic 6.0.

Note that you should not attempt this chapter until you have a firm introductory knowledge of Visual Basic. Diane Zak's *Programming with Microsoft Visual Basic*, published by Course Technology, is an excellent introduction to the subject.

COMPONENTS IN WEB APPLICATIONS

Components are self-contained precompiled software units (code) that can be reused in one or more applications. (In this chapter, you will base your components on Active Server Pages that you have already created.) Components provide specific functionality to an application, contain one or more objects, and perform front-line tasks. In a way, they are like privates in the military; they have a particular job that requires them to complete certain tasks.

Components, like privates, belong to a certain unit but can also work with other units doing similar jobs. Thus, they can be moved from job to job. This "movability" makes them very valuable, as in this business scenario: You are working on a project and want to include a reporting component in the project, but you do not have the time or the money to create a complete reporting component yourself. Instead, you look around in magazines and on the Internet to find a vendor that sells a suitable reporting component for your applications. You select a component and then plug it into your program with very little effort, without necessarily understanding all the details of how the component works. With this scenario, both you and the original developer win; the original developer can sell his or her work many times over, and you can buy premade functionality. And so goes the software industry.

Some components fall into the category of middleware. **Middleware** allows clients and servers to communicate with each other over a network, as shown in Figure 10-1. Middleware hides the details and complexities of the operating system and the network software from the programmer.

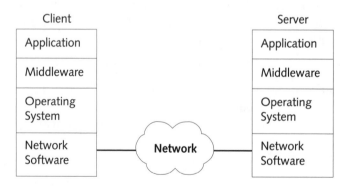

Figure 10-1   Role of middleware in a networked environment

Middleware can be built on various technologies. For instance, if you need to accomplish programming in a Windows environment, you will use object-specific middleware technology such as **Component Object Model (COM)**. COM is Microsoft's standard technology that allows an object to supply its services to another object, and vice versa, so that the objects can communicate with each other.

You can create COM objects in languages such as Visual Basic, Visual J++, and Visual C++. COM only handles interaction of objects on a single machine. **Distributed Component**

Object Model (DCOM) is Microsoft's technology that enhances COM and that allows interaction among objects located across machines on the network. Figure 10-2 illustrates the high-level tasks that programmers can accomplish with COM/DCOM.

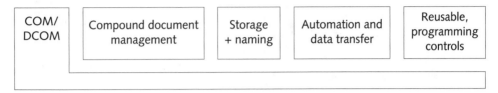

Figure 10-2 Tasks that programmers accomplish with COM/DCOM

COM/DCOM allows programmers to do the following:

- **Compound Document Management**: Microsoft Office supplies **object linking and embedding (OLE)** capability in each of its applications. With OLE, you can link or embed an Excel spreadsheet in a Word document. When you need to change the spreadsheet, you double-click on the Excel object. If the object is embedded (i.e., a copy of the Excel object is part of Word), then the Excel application opens in Word and allows you to change the object. In this case, Word is called a **container object** because Word contains the Excel object. If the object is linked (i.e., a copy of the Excel object is stored in its own file), Excel opens the spreadsheet in the Excel window. After you change the spreadsheet, the updated object appears in Word.

- **Storage and naming**: You can store COM/DCOM objects by using a dynamic-link library (dll), an executable (exe), or a control (ocx). Windows uses a class identifier (CLSID) to uniquely identify each component stored. The Windows Registry stores the CLSIDs and the name of the component (PROGID), which is the name of the project with a period and the name of the class. If you need to find your component in the Registry, you need to search for PROGID first, determine the CLSID, and use the CLSID to find all instances of the component in the Registry.

- **Automation and data transfer**: Windows supports two types of automation. The first is an in-process server (ActiveX DLL), which allows your component to run in the same address space as your application. The second is an out-of-process server (ActiveX EXE), which allows your component to run in its own address space separate from the application that called it.

- **Reusable, programmable controls**: ActiveX controls are special COM objects that are created as a mini-GUI application that runs in the context of an application; they are reusable. Examples of controls are text boxes, labels, and command buttons. You can reuse these controls in any application.

10

Figure 10–3 shows the interaction between COM/DCOM objects on a network.

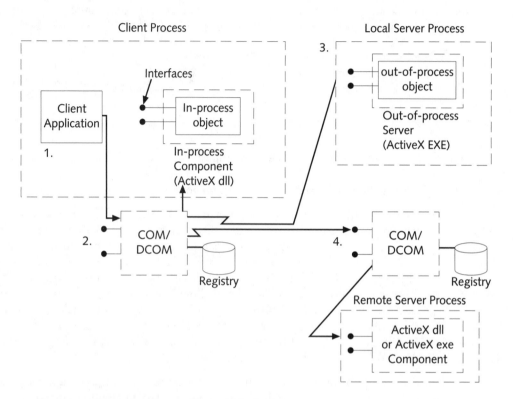

1. Client requests services from a dll. COM looks up component in Registry and tells application where it is. COM then loads the component.
2. Client requests services from a local ActiveX EXE.
3. COM loads and runs remote server process after the Registry lookup. Application calls services from local server.
4. Client requests services from remote server. DCOM looks up and locates remote server. Client application then communicates with it.

Figure 10-3 COM/DCOM object interaction

We've provided the definition of a component, explained its value, and described where the component lies within programming logic so that you can see where you will "plug" in your component. Now, you are ready to create your own component, or, to follow our military analogy, your own "private" who will carry out specific tasks. Because you will create this component in the Visual Basic 6.0 environment, we will review that environment next.

Components and the Visual Basic 6.0 Environment

You need to have Visual Basic 6.0 completely installed to use this chapter effectively.

Visual Basic Integrated Development Environment gives you a graphical way of designing Visual Basic Applications. From a single environment, you manage your files in a project, code your program, and run your program to see the results immediately. Figure 10-4 shows the Visual Basic 6.0 environment.

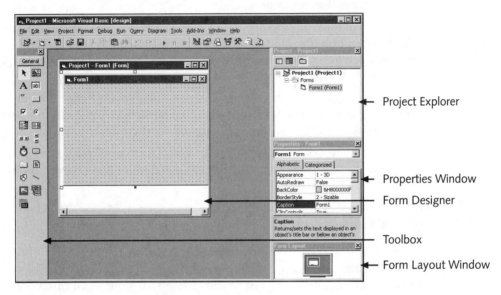

Figure 10-4 Visual Basic 6.0 environment

Visual Basic contains the following windows:

- **Toolbox**: By default, the toolbox stores all of the controls you can use. You can add controls to the toolbox, if necessary.

- **Form Designer**: The Form Designer is where you create Visual Basic forms in your projects.

- **Code Editor window**: The Code Editor window is an ASCII text editor that allows you to enter code.

- **Form Layout window**: The Form Layout window allows you to position the forms on your screen.

- **Properties window**: The Properties window allows you to view and update control and object properties used in Visual Basic.

- **Project Explorer**: The Project Explorer is a window that allows you to manage all the files you use in your Visual Basic application.

Coding the comDBUtility Component in Visual Basic

In previous chapters, you have used a utility class called clsForm in a script. In this section, you will transform this script into a comDBUtility component in Visual Basic. Once created, this component will interact with a database such as Microsoft Access. There are several benefits of creating an ActiveX component:

- In its present form, the clsForm script is interpreted each time it is run in an ASP. The ActiveX component, on the other hand, is a compiled (prerun) program that will run faster than its scripting counterpart.

- In its present form, the clsForm script is an ASCII text file and can be easily downloaded from the site and used by other programmers who are creating sites. ActiveX components are compiled programs and are harder to reuse; this protects your intellectual property.

- In its present form, the class script will work well in an ASP page but not in any other languages or environments. Once converted, however, it can also be used in Visual Basic, Visual C++, Visual J++, and other Microsoft applications.

- You can deploy ActiveX components in a traditional or Web application and anywhere on the network. A script cannot be deployed on the network; it can only work from a Web server.

Now that you have seen the benefits of ActiveX components, let's use Visual Basic to create the comDBUtility component.

To create the comDBUtility component in Visual Basic:

1. Click the **Start** button on your desktop. Point to **Programs**, and then point to **Microsoft Visual Studio 6.0** (if you installed VB alone, click **Microsoft Visual Basic 6.0**).

2. Click **Microsoft Visual Basic 6.0** to start Visual Basic.

3. In the New Project dialog box, click **ActiveX DLL**, and then click **Open**.

4. In the Properties window, change the Name of the class to **clsDBUtility**.

5. Click **Project1** in the Project Explorer.

6. In the Properties window, change the Name of the project to **comDBUtility**.

7. In the code window for clsDBUtility class, type the following code:

```
Option Explicit

Private strMode As String
Private objRS As Object
Private objConn As Object
Private strServerConnectionString As String

Public Sub Class_Initialize()

  strMode = "Browse"
  strServerConnectionString = "DRIVER=" &_
"{Microsoft Access Driver (*.mdb)};" &_
"DBQ=" & App.Path & "\..\db\course.mdb"

End Sub
```

```vb
Public Sub Open_Recordset(strSQL As String)

  Set objConn = CreateObject("ADODB.Connection")
  Set objRS = CreateObject("ADODB.Recordset")

  On Error GoTo TransactionError
  objConn.Open strServerConnectionString

  If Err.Number <> 0 Then
    Exit Sub
  End If

  objRS.CursorType = adOpenKeyset
  Set objRS = objConn.Execute(strSQL)

  If Err.Number <> 0 Then
    Exit Sub
  End If
  Exit Sub
TransactionError:

End Sub

Public Function Run_SQL(strSQL As String)

  Dim objConn As Object, objRS As Object

  Set objConn = CreateObject("ADODB.Connection")
  Set objRS = CreateObject("ADODB.Recordset")

  objConn.Open strServerConnectionString
  objConn.BeginTrans

  Set objRS = objConn.Execute(strSQL)

  If objConn.Errors.Count = 0 Then
    objConn.CommitTrans
    Run_SQL = ""
    Exit Function
  Else
    objConn.RollbackTrans
    Run_SQL = "Transaction Error!"
    Exit Function
  End If

  Run_SQL = ""
  Exit Function

End Function
```

10

```
'Create a property called Mode
Public Property Get Mode() As String

    Mode = strMode

End Property

Public Property Let Mode(newMode As String)

    strMode = newMode

End Property

'Create a property called ServerConnectionString
Public Property Get ServerConnectionString() As String

    ServerConnectionString = strServerConnectionString

End Property

Public Property Let ServerConnectionString(_
newServerConnectionString As String)

    strServerConnectionString = newServerConnectionString

End Property

Public Property Get RS() As ADODB.Recordset

    Set RS = objRS

End Property
```

You will notice that this code looks very similar to the clsForm script you have seen previously. You should review this code to see the differences between the script and the actual component.

8. Click **Project** on the menu bar, and then click **References**.

9. Select **Microsoft ActiveX Data Objects 2.1 Library**, and then click **OK**.

10. Click **File** on the menu bar, and then click **Save Project As** to begin the process of saving the project and the code.

11. Change the default folder to the **Chapter_10** folder of your Data Disk.

12. Create a new folder called **src**.

13. Double-click the **src** folder to open it in the Save File As dialog box.

14. Click the **Save** button in the Save File As dialog box.

15. Click the **Save** button in the Save Project As dialog box.

16. If you are prompted to save this project to SourceSafe, click **No**.

17. Now you are ready to compile this component into an ActiveX DLL. Click **File** on the menu bar, and then click **Make comDBUtility.dll**.

18. Click **OK** in the Make Project dialog box.

19. To verify that the component was created, click **Project** on the menu bar, and then click **References**. You should be able to find comDBUtility in the list, as shown in Figure 10-5. If you do not see the item, even after scrolling, repeat Step 17 and Step 18. Close the dialog box.

 If you do not see the comDBUtility in the dialog box, exit Visual Basic, reopen it and then reopen the project.

10

References - comDBUtility.vbp

Available References:

- [ ] Application Performance Explorer Worker Provider
- [ ] ATL 2.0 Type Library
- [ ] backstab 1.0 Type Library
- [ ] BldWizMg 1.0 Type Library
- [ ] CCrsWpp 1.0 Type Library
- [ ] CFtpWpp 1.0 Type Library
- [ ] cic 1.0 Type Library
- [ ] comBudDBUtility
- [ ] comChkDBUtility
- [ ] comClasses
- [x] comDBUtility
- [ ] comFormUtility
- [ ] comFormUtility
- [ ] comFormUtility

OK Cancel Browse... Priority Help

comDBUtility

Location: E:\Solutions\Chapter_10\INCLUDES\comDBUtility.dll
Language: Standard

Figure 10-5   comDBUtility

Testing the Component

You have successfully converted your script into a component. As with all programming, once you create, you must test. The easiest way to do this is to change the project from an ActiveX DLL to a Standard EXE and code a MAIN subroutine to test each function of the clsClassData class. Once the testing is complete, change the project back to an ActiveX DLL and compile.

 You may think it would be easier to simply compile the ActiveX DLL as is. However, if you do that, Visual Basic will create a comDBUtility.DLL file that is not easy to debug.

To code the MAIN subroutine:

1. Click **Project** on the menu bar, and then click **comDBUtility Properties**.

2. Change the Project Type to **Standard EXE** and Startup Object to **SubMain**.

3. Click **OK**, and then click **OK** again in the message box.
4. Click **Project** on the menu bar, click **Add Module**, and then click the **Open** button in the Add Module dialog box.
5. Type the following in the Module's code window:

```
Private Sub Main()
  Dim objDB As New clsDBUtility
  Dim strResult As String

  strResult = objDB.Run_SQL("INSERT INTO STUDENTS" & _
  "(FIRST_NAME,LAST_NAME,HOME_PHONE,WORK_PHONE,E_MAIL)" &_
  " VALUES(" & _
           "'" & "Jack" & "'," & _
           "'" & "Lee" & "'," & _
           "'" & "7033333333" & "'," & _
           "'" & "7033333333" & "'," & _
           "'" & "jlee@erols.com" & "')")
  If strResult <> "" Then
     MsgBox strResult
  End If
  Set objDB = Nothing
End Sub
```

6. Click the **Run** button on the Standard toolbar.
7. Verify that the record was entered in Microsoft Access by checking that a new row appears in the STUDENTS table, as shown in Figure 10-6.

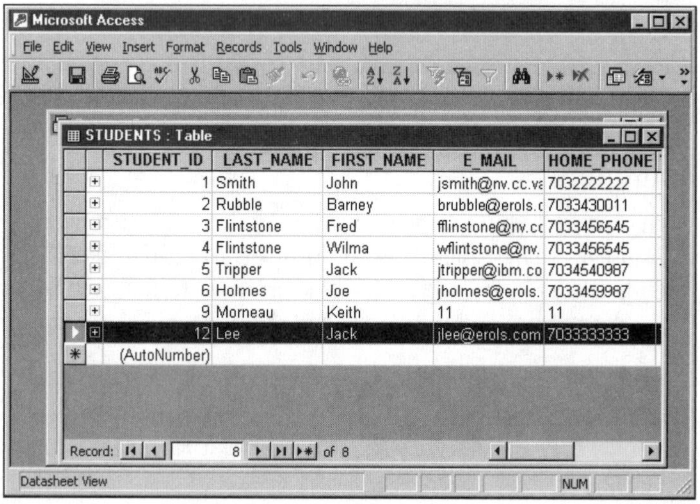
Microsoft Access
File Edit View Insert Format Records Tools Window Help
STUDENTS : Table
STUDENT_ID LAST_NAME FIRST_NAME E_MAIL HOME_PHONE
1 Smith John jsmith@nv.cc.va 7032222222
2 Rubble Barney brubble@erols.c 7033430011
3 Flintstone Fred fflinstone@nv.cc 7033456545
4 Flintstone Wilma wflintstone@nv. 7033456545
5 Tripper Jack jtripper@ibm.co 7034540987
6 Holmes Joe jholmes@erols. 7033459987
9 Morneau Keith 11 11
12 Lee Jack jlee@erols.com 7033333333
(AutoNumber)
Record: 8 of 8
Datasheet View
NUM

Figure 10-6 Successful compile

8. Right-click **Module1** in Project Explorer, and then click **Remove module1**.

9. Click **No**, click **File** on the menu bar, and then click **Exit**.

10. Click **No** to the final dialog box.

Coding the comClasses Component

Back when it was a script, comDBUtility interacted with comClasses. Since you have already converted the former, we will convert the latter so that they can be deployed together.

To create the comClasses component in Visual Basic:

1. Click the **Start** button on your desktop. Point to **Programs**, and then point to **Microsoft Visual Studio 6.0**.

2. Click **Microsoft Visual Basic 6.0** to start Visual Basic.

3. In the New Project dialog box, click **ActiveX DLL**, and then click **Open**.

4. In the Properties window, change the Name of the class to **clsClasses**.

5. Click **Project1** in Project Explorer.

6. In the Properties window, change the name of the project to **comClasses**.

7. In the code window for clsClasses class, type the following code:

```
Private intClass_ID As Integer
Private strClass_number As String
Private strClass_name As String

Private objFormUtility As New comDBUtility.clsDBUtility

Private strMode As String

Public Sub Class_Initialize()

    strMode = "Browse"
    intClass_ID = 0
    strClass_number = ""
    strClass_name = ""

End Sub

Public Function ExecuteMode() As String
    Dim strSQL, strErr As String
    Select Case strMode
    Case "New"
     strErr = objFormUtility.Run_SQL("" &_
"INSERT INTO CLASSES" & _
                    "(CLASS_NUMBER,CLASS_NAME)" & _
                    " VALUES(" & _
                    "'" & strClass_number & "'," & _
                    "'" & strClass_name & "')")
```

10

```vb
          Case "Update"

             strErr = objFormUtility.Run_SQL("UPDATE CLASSES" & _
                     " SET CLASS_NUMBER = " & _
                     "'" & strClass_number & "'," & _
                     "CLASS_NAME = " & _
                     "'" & strClass_name & "'" & _
                     " WHERE CLASS_ID = " & _
                        intClass_ID)


      Case "Delete"
          strErr = objFormUtility.Run_SQL"" &_
("DELETE FROM CLASSES" & _
                     " WHERE CLASS_ID = " & _
                     intClass_ID)

    End Select

ExecuteMode = strErr

End Function

Public Function Search() As Boolean

  Dim strSQL As String
  Dim strMessage As String
  Dim objRS As ADODB.Recordset

  strSQL = "select * from classes where " & _
           " class_number = '" & strClass_number & "'"

  objFormUtility.Open_Recordset (strSQL)

  Set objRS = objFormUtility.RS

  If Not objRS.BOF Then
    Search = True
    intClass_ID = objRS("CLASS_ID")
    strClass_number = objRS("CLASS_NUMBER")
    strClass_name = objRS("CLASS_NAME")
  Else
    Search = False
  End If

End Function
'Create a property called Mode
Public Property Get Mode() As String

  Mode = strMode
```

```
End Property

Public Property Let Mode(newMode As String)

  strMode = newMode

End Property

Public Property Get Class_ID() As Integer

  Class_ID = intClass_ID

End Property

Public Property Let Class_ID(newClass_ID As Integer)

  intClass_ID = newClass_ID

End Property

Public Property Get Class_number() As String

  Class_number = strClass_number

End Property

Public Property Let Class_number(newClass_number As String)

  strClass_number = newClass_number

End Property

Public Property Get Class_name() As String

  Class_name = strClass_name

End Property


Public Property Let Class_name(newClass_name As String)

  strClass_name = newClass_name

End Property
```

10

8. Click **Project** on the menu bar, and then click **References** to add references to ADO.

9. Select **Microsoft ActiveX Data Objects 2.1 Library**, and then click **comDBUtility**.

10. Click **OK**.

11. Click **File** on the menu bar, click **Save Project As**, and then change the default folder to the **Chapter_10** folder of your Data Disk.

12. Navigate to the **src** folder.

13. Click the **Save** button in the Save File As dialog box, and then click the **Save** button in the Save Project As dialog box.

14. If you are prompted to save this project to SourceSafe, click **No**. Now, you are ready to compile this component into an ActiveX DLL.

15. Click **File** on the menu bar, click **Make comClasses.dll**, and then click **OK** in the resulting dialog box.

16. To verify that the component is created, click **Project** on the menu bar, click **References**, and then verify that comClasses is in the list, as shown in Figure 10-7. If the item is not in the list, repeat Step 15. Close the dialog box and exit VB.

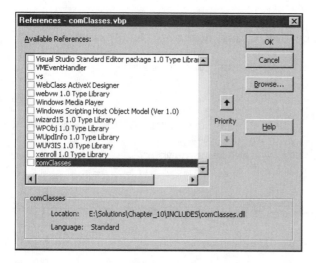

Figure 10-7   comClasses

THE ROLE OF TRANSACTION PROCESSING

In the last several sections, you created components (or "privates," if we continue our military analogy) that directly interacted with the database. Your code now needs to verify that changes made to the database are permanent and correct. One way to do this is to use transaction processing.

To build on our military analogy, transaction processing is the sergeant who controls one or more privates and tells them what to do. Specifically, transaction processing dictates a **transaction**, which is a unit of activity. This unit can be a series of insert, update, and delete statements or a grouping of components that do various jobs.

A transaction (which occurs during transaction processing) must adhere to the following properties or states:

- **Atomicity**: Atomicity characterizes a unit of work that you define. All of the actions in the transaction succeed or fail as a unit.

- **Consistency**: Consistency allows a system to be in a correct stable state at the end of the transaction or when the transaction aborts. It returns the system to the initial state before the transaction ran.

- **Isolation**: An isolated transaction cannot be affected by other transactions that execute concurrently. A transaction is isolated from other simultaneous transactions. This means that a transaction will not see partial results of another transaction while it is running.

- **Durability**: After the transaction has been successfully completed, a durable transaction is permanent and survives any type of failure, including power failures.

You may be tempted to view transaction processing as too much precaution that is too time-intensive. However, it is worth the effort. Consider the following scenario:

- You receive an order for a product. You have an order component that now needs to update the billing database and the inventory database.

- The order component adds information to the inventory database to show that an item has sold, and the order component adds information to the billing database so that you can bill your customer for the work.

- After the processing of the inventory information, the power fails.

- Without a transaction, the billing information never makes it to the billing database. This leaves your system in an incomplete state and may mean that your customer doesn't receive a bill. (If customers don't pay, you don't get paid!)

- With transaction processing, however, your application will remove the inventory information and leave your system in the state it was in before the customer order. When power is restored, your system can rerun your transaction from the beginning to make sure that the data updates properly in both databases.

Implementing Transaction Processing

ADO provides a mechanism for creating transactions in your code. Your application can start a transaction and either commit, if successful, or roll back, if not successful. Let's look at examples of each of these lines of code.

Code Example

```
objComm.BeginTrans
```

Code Dissection

- This line of code sets up a transaction in ADO.

After you set up a transaction for your code, you make sure to commit or roll back that transaction, depending on whether your component is successful or unsuccessful, as shown in the following code:

Code Example

```
objConn.CommitTrans
objConn.RollbackTrans
```

Code Dissection

- The first line commits an ADO transaction.

- The second line rolls back an ADO transaction.

The final files that will allow us to showcase this new functionality have not yet been created (you'll do that in the next section). However, we can still review the core transaction processing code. In this code, the bolded sections begin a new transaction, commit a transaction, and roll back a transaction, respectively.

Code Example

```
Public Function Run_SQL(strSQL As String)

  Dim objConn As Object, objRS As Object

  Set objConn = CreateObject("ADODB.Connection")
  Set objRS = CreateObject("ADODB.Recordset")

  objConn.Open strServerConnectionString
  objConn.BeginTrans

  Set objRS = objConn.Execute(strSQL)

  If objConn.Errors.Count = 0 Then
    objConn.CommitTrans
    Run_SQL = ""
    Exit Function
  Else
    objConn.RollbackTrans
    Run_SQL = "Transaction Error!"
    Exit Function
  End If

  Run_SQL = ""
  Exit Function

End Function
```

HIGH-LEVEL FUNCTIONS AND ORGANIZATION STRATEGIES FOR A SOFTWARE APPLICATION

Well, we've heard from the privates (components) and we've heard from the sergeants (transactions). Now it's time to have a chat with the general who dictated the overall strategy of the application in this chapter. As in real life, our general had to decide how to achieve mandated goals. These goals can be divided into four categories: presentation management, application logic, data access logic, and data storage.

Presentation management is the part of the program that displays information on the computer screen in the form of windows, dialog boxes, and graphs. Presentation management includes the graphical user interface (GUI) in a Windows application and managing user input.

Application logic, or **business rules**, is the part of the program that decides what the program should do in various situations. For example, suppose an application requires a clerk to enter customer information such as last name, first name, address, city, state, and zip code. The application logic of the program might only accept two-letter abbreviations for state entries; the program would display an error when this rule is broken.

Data storage is the part of the program that stores and retrieves data. The data can take the form of a **file**, which is an unstructured and unorganized collection of data, or a **database**, which is a structured and organized collection of data. Examples of databases are Microsoft Access, Microsoft SQL Server, and Oracle. The term **data access logic** refers to software that allows the presentation management and application logic to interact with data storage.

While the previous functions are logical divisions, **tiers**, which are one or more networked computers on which the application software is actually installed, are physical divisions. You can create single-tier, two-tier, three-tier, or *n*-tier applications, as described in the following sections.

10

Single Tier

Single-tier applications are applications that provide the presentation management, application logic, data access logic, and data storage services from a single machine. Examples of single-tier applications are word-processing applications such as Microsoft Word and spreadsheet applications such as Microsoft Excel.

Two Tiers

While a single-tier application consists of a single application on a single computer, two-tier applications are composed of two components on two separate computers. As an example of a two-tier application, consider an e-mail system. It has two components: the client component that allows a user to type a mail message and the server component that handles the delivery of the message to a recipient.

Three Tiers

Just as two-tier applications consist of two components residing on two computers, three-tier applications consist of three components residing on three separate computers. The three components consist of a client application (which contains the presentation management function), an application server application (which contains the application logic and data access logic), and a database server application, which contains the data access logic and data storage.

N-Tier Applications

While three-tier applications provide three services on three machines, *n*-tier applications are typically Internet/intranet applications that provide the application functions on three or more computers. For instance, the presentation management function might exist on the client computer, while an application server computer provides the application logic and data access logic. Meanwhile, the Web server would provide Web services, and the database server would handle data access logic and data storage.

Creating the New Classes ASP Scripts

Well, it's time to let you know that you have been promoted from "ASP" programmer to "general" programmer, and your first assignment is to execute Operation Component Software. Because you have already created the new comDBUtility component and the comClasses component, you now need to update the Form.asp and save_class.asp files to interact with the new component team.

To create the new Form.asp file:

1. Create a file named **Form.asp** in the Classes folder in the Chapter_10 folder of your Data Disk, and insert the following code:

```
<%@ Language=VBScript%>
<%Option Explicit%>
<%Response.buffer=true%>
<!-- #include file="../includes/adovbs.inc" -->
<html>

<head>
<title>Class Form</title>
<!--
    *************************************************
    *** Form Name:      frmClass              ***
    *** Author:         Keith Morneau         ***
    *** Date:           8/6/01               ***
    *** Description:                          ***
    ***    This form allows user to enter     ***
    ***    the class information.             ***
    ***                                       ***
    *** Revisions:                            ***
    *************************************************
-->
```

```
<%
  Dim objForm,strEval
  set objForm = Server.CreateObject
("comClasses.clsClasses")

  objForm.Mode = Request.QueryString("Mode")
  objForm.Class_number = Request.QueryString
("txtClassNumber")
  objForm.Class_name = ""

  If Request.QueryString("Mode") = "New" Then

        If (objForm.Search) Then
          objForm.Mode = "Update"
        End If
    Else

    If objForm.Mode = "Browse" or objForm.Mode = "Update" _
or objForm.Mode = "Delete" Then

        If Not (objForm.Search) Then
          Response.Write("<CENTER><H1>Error Information
</H1>")
          Response.Write("<H3>Class not found!</H3><BR>")
          Response.Write("Back to <a href=search.htm>Class
Form</a>.</center>")
          Response.End
        Else
         If Request.QueryString("Mode") = "Browse" Then
          objForm.Mode = "Browse"
        Else
          if Request.QueryString("Mode") = "Delete" Then
            objForm.Mode = "Delete"
          End If
        End If
      End If
    Else
          Response.Write("<CENTER><H1>Error Information
</H1>")
          Response.Write("<H3>You did not select a mode!
</H3><BR>")
          Response.Write("Click on the Back button of your
browser to fix!</center>")
          Response.End
    End If
End If

%>

</head>
```

10

```
<body BGCOLOR=LIGHTYELLOW>

<H1 align="center">Class Form</H1>

<form id="frmClass" name="frmClass" action="save_class.asp"
 method="post">

<center><p><b>Class Information</b></p></center>

<center>Form Mode: <% = objForm.Mode %><input id="Mode"
 type="hidden" name="Mode" size="35" value="<% =
objForm.Mode %>" >
<input id="CLASS_ID" type="hidden" name="CLASS_ID" size=
"35" value="<% = objForm.Class_ID %>" >


<p>Class number: <input id="CLASS_NUMBER" type="text"
name="CLASS_NUMBER" size="35" value="<% =
objForm.Class_number %>" >*<br>
  Class name: 

<input id="CLASS_NAME" type = "text" name="CLASS_NAME" size
="35" value="<% = objForm.Class_name %>"><strong>*</strong>
</label></p>
</center>

<%Select Case objForm.Mode %>
<% Case "New"%>
<center><p><input id="cmdSubmit" type="submit" value=
"Create">
<input id="cmdReset" type="reset" value="Reset">
</p></center>
<%Case "Update" %>
<center><p><input id="cmdSubmit" type="submit" value=
"Update">
</center>
<%Case "Delete" %>
<center><p><input id="cmdSubmit" type="submit" value=
"Delete">
</center>
<%Case "Browse"%>
<center><p>Back to <a href=search.htm>Class Form
</a>.</center>
</center>
<% End Select %>
</form>

</body>
</html>
```

2. Save the file.

3. Create a file named **save_class.asp** in the Classes folder in the Chapter_10 folder of your Data Disk with the following code:

```
<%@ Language=VBScript %>
<% Response.Buffer = True %>

<html>

<head>

<title>Class Response</title>
<%
Sub FormValidation

Dim blnOK

    blnOK = (Trim(Request.Form("CLASS_NUMBER")) = "") OR
(Trim(Request.Form("CLASS_NAME")) = "")
    If blnOK Then
        Response.Write("<CENTER><H1>Error Information</H1>")
        Response.Write("<H3>You must enter all the
information.</H3><BR>")
        Response.Write("Click the Back button on your
browser to fix your errors!</CENTER>")
        Response.End
    End If

End Sub

  Dim objForm,strEval,strErr
  Call FormValidation
  set objForm = Server.CreateObject
("comClasses.clsClasses")
  objForm.Mode = Request.Form("Mode")
  objForm.Class_ID = cint(Request.Form("CLASS_ID"))
  objForm.Class_number = Request.Form("CLASS_NUMBER")
  objForm.Class_name = Request.Form("CLASS_NAME")
  strErr = objForm.ExecuteMode

  If strErr <> "" Then
      Response.Write("<CENTER><H1>Error Information</H1>")
      Response.Write(strErr & "</CENTER>")
      Response.End
  End If


%>
</head>
<body BGCOLOR=LIGHTYELLOW>
```

10

```
<center><h1>Class Response</h1></center>
<center>
<p>Thank you for using the Class form!<p>

<% If Request.Form("Mode") <> "Delete" Then %>
<p>The information you entered: <br>
<ul>
<li>Class number: <%=Request.Form("CLASS_NUMBER")%></li>
<li>Class name: <%=Request.Form("CLASS_NAME")%></li>
</ul>
<% End If %>
</center>
<center>Back to <a href="search.htm">Class Form</a>.
</center>
</body>
</html>
```

4. Save the file.

5. Exit your text editor.

6. Create a virtual directory to your Chapter_10 folder and name that virtual directory **Chapter_10**.

7. Start your browser.

8. Type **http://localhost/Chapter_10/default.asp** in the Address field, and then press **Enter**.

9. If the Login page appears, then enter your first name and last name, and then click **Submit**. The Course Tracking Information System start page loads.

10. Open the Class Information page.

11. Add a new class.

12. Delete the new class.

Your transactions were successfully executed. If, for example, a power outage had happened during the addition or deletion of the file, the entire transaction would have been rolled back in preparation for a "retry." If you hadn't had the transaction functionality in place, you could have ended up with a partial record entered in the database.

CHAPTER SUMMARY

❑ Components are self-contained precompiled software units (code) that can be reused in one or more applications. Components provide specific functionality to an application, contain one or more objects, and perform front-line tasks.

❑ Visual Basic Integrated Development Environment gives you a graphical way of designing Visual Basic applications. From a single environment, you manage your files in a project, code your program, and run your program to see the results immediately.

❏ The easiest way to test a component is to change the project from an ActiveX DLL to a Standard EXE and code a MAIN subroutine to test each function of the clsClassData class. Once the testing is complete, change the project back to an ActiveX DLL and compile.

❏ Transaction processing dictates a transaction, which is a unit of activity. This unit can be a series of insert, update, and delete statements or a grouping of components that do various jobs. A transaction (which occurs during transaction processing) must adhere to the following properties or states: atomicity, consistency, isolation, and durability. ADO provides a mechanism for creating transactions in your code. Your application can start a transaction and either commit, if successful, or roll back, if not successful.

❏ Programs are written to achieve mandated goals. These goals can be divided into four categories: presentation management, application logic, data access logic, and data storage. Tiers, which are one or more networked computers on which the application software is actually installed, are physical divisions. You can create single-tier, two-tier, three-tier, or *n*-tier applications.

REVIEW QUESTIONS

10

1. _____ are self-contained precompiled software units (code) that can be reused in one or more applications.

    a. Objects

    b. Classes

    c. Components

    d. none of the above

2. _____ is a broad category of software needed to allow clients and server to communicate with each other over a network.

    a. MTS

    b. MSMQ

    c. Middleware

    d. none of the above

3. _____ is Microsoft's standard for object interaction and supplies the "plumbing" needed for objects to communicate with each other.

    a. Middleware

    b. MTS

    c. COM

    d. none of the above

4. You can create components in which of the following languages? [Choose all that apply.]

   a. Visual Basic

   b. Visual C++

   c. Visual J++

   d. Visual InterDev

5. Windows uses a(n) _____ to uniquely identify each component stored in the Registry.

   a. CLSID

   b. ID

   c. CLS

   d. none of the above

6. An in-process server is also known as a(n) _____.

   a. ActiveX EXE

   b. ActiveX DLL

   c. Standard EXE

   d. Add-In

7. An out-of-process server is also known as a(n) _____.

   a. ActiveX EXE

   b. ActiveX DLL

   c. Standard EXE

   d. Add-In

8. A(n) _____ is a mini-application that enhances the functionality of the Visual Basic environment.

   a. ActiveX EXE

   b. ActiveX DLL

   c. Standard EXE

   d. Add-In

9. A(n) _____ is a unit of work that you define.

   a. object

   b. class

   c. transaction

   d. none of the above

10. Because of _____, all the actions in a transaction succeed or fail as a unit.

    a. atomicity

    b. consistency

    c. isolation

    d. durability

11. A transaction that cannot be affected by other transactions that execute concurrently has the state of _____.

    a. atomicity

    b. consistency

    c. isolation

    d. durability

12. _____ allows a system to be in a correct state at the end of a transaction.

    a. Atomicity

    b. Consistency

    c. Isolation

    d. Durability

13. A transaction that is permanent and that survives any type of failure, including power failures, has the state of _____.

    a. atomicity

    b. consistency

    c. isolation

    d. durability

14. _____ is Microsoft's transaction processing system for databases.

    a. ADO

    b. MTS

    c. MSMQ

    d. none of the above

15. Components can be reused. True or False?

16. All components are middleware. True or False?

17. Within Microsoft technology, COM enhances DCOM, allowing interaction among objects located across machines on the network. True or False?

18. With _____, you can link or embed files from one application into another.

19. Windows supports only one type of automation: Active X DLL. True or False?

20. With Active XEXE, a component can have its own _____ space.

10

HANDS-ON PROJECTS

Project 10-1

You created the comDBUtility component in this chapter. Write a test client to test the Update functionality in the clsDBUtility object.

To test the comDBUtility component Update functionality:

1. Click the Start menu.
2. Point to Programs, point to Microsoft Visual Studio 6.0, and then click Microsoft Visual Basic 6.0.
3. In the New Project window, select Standard EXE, and then click Open.
4. Click Project1 Properties in the Project menu.
5. In Startup Object, select Sub Main.
6. Click OK.
7. Click Add Module in the Project menu.
8. Click Module in the New Tab, and then click Open.
9. Type the following code in the Module's code window:

```
Private Sub Main()
Dim objForm As Object
Dim strResult As String
Set objForm = CreateObject("comDBUtility.clsDBUtility")
    strResult = objForm.Run_SQL("UPDATE STUDENTS " & _
        "SET HOME_PHONE = '7031111111'" & _
        " WHERE STUDENT_ID = 1")
    If strResult <> "" Then
        MsgBox strResult
    End If
```

10. Click Run on the toolbar.
11. Verify the results of the code.
12. Quit Visual Basic and discard any changes to the src folder.

Project 10-2

Create a component called comStudent and a class called clsStudent for the student contact application.

To create the comStudent component in Visual Basic:

1. Click Start. Point to Programs and Microsoft Visual Studio 6.0. Click on Microsoft Visual Basic 6.0 to start Visual Basic.
2. In the New Project dialog box, click on ActiveX DLL and click Open.
3. In the Properties window, change the Name of the class to clsStudent.

4. Click on Project1 in the Project Explorer.

5. In the Properties window, change the Name of the project to comStudent.

6. In the code window for clsStudent class, type the following code:

```
Private intStudent_ID As Integer
Private strLast_name As String
Private strFirst_name As String
Private strEmail As String
Private strHome_phone As String
Private strWork_phone As String

Private objFormUtility As New comDBUtility.clsDBUtility

Private strMode As String

Public Sub Class_Initialize()

   strMode = "Browse"
   intStudent_ID = 0
   strLast_name = ""
   strFirst_name = ""
   strEmail = ""
   strHome_phone = ""
   strWork_phone = ""

End Sub

Public Function ExecuteMode() As String
   Dim strSQL, strErr As String
   Select Case strMode
   Case "New"
     strErr = objFormUtility.Run_SQL("" &_
"INSERT INTO STUDENTS" &_
     "(LAST_NAME,FIRST_NAME,E_MAIL,HOME_PHONE,WORK_PHONE)" &_
     " VALUES(" & _
     "'" & strLast_name & "'," & _
     "'" & strFirst_name & "'," & _
     "'" & strEMail & "'," & _
     "'" & strHome_phone & "'," & _
     "'" & strWork_phone & "')")


   Case "Update"

       strErr = objFormUtility.Run_SQL("UPDATE CLASSES" & _
              " SET LAST_NAME = " & _
              "'" & strLast_name & "'," & _
              " SET FIRST_NAME = " & _
              "'" & strFirst_name & "'," & _
```

10

```
                    " SET E_MAIL = " & _
                    "'" & strEmail & "'," & _
                    " SET HOME_PHONE = " & _
                    "'" & strHome_phone & "'," & _
                    " SET WORK_PHONE = " & _
                    "'" & strWork_phone & "'" & _
                    " WHERE STUDENT_ID = " & _
                       intStudent_ID)


        Case "Delete"
            strErr = objFormUtility.Run_SQL("" &_
  DELETE FROM STUDENTS" &_
                    " WHERE STUDENT_ID = " & _
                       intStudent_ID)

      End Select

  ExecuteMode = strErr

  End Function

  Public Function Search() As Boolean

    Dim strSQL As String
    Dim strMessage As String
    Dim objRS As ADODB.Recordset

    strSQL = "select * from students where " & _
             " LAST_NAME = '" & strLast_name & "'" & _
             " AND " & _
             "FIRST_NAME = '" & strFirst_name & "'"

    objFormUtility.Open_Recordset (strSQL)

    Set objRS = objFormUtility.RS

    If Not objRS.BOF Then
      Search = True
      intStudent_ID = objRS("STUDENT_ID")
      strLast_name = objRS("LAST_NAME")
      strFirst_name = objRS("FIRST_NAME")
      strEmail = objRS("E_MAIL")
      If (IsNull(objRS("HOME_PHONE"))) Then
        strHome_phone = ""
      Else
        strHome_phone = objRS("HOME_PHONE")
      End If

      If (IsNull(objRS("WORK_PHONE"))) Then
        strWork_phone = ""
```

```
      Else
        strWork_phone = objRS("WORK_PHONE")
      End If
    Else
      Search = False
    End If

End Function
'Create a property called Mode
Public Property Get Mode() As String

  Mode = strMode

End Property

Public Property Let Mode(newMode As String)

  strMode = newMode

End Property

Public Property Get Student_ID() As Integer

  Student_ID = intStudent_ID

End Property

Public Property Let Student_ID(newID As Integer)

  intStudent_ID = newID

End Property

Public Property Get Last_name() As String

  Last_name = strLast_name

End Property

Public Property Let Last_name(newLast_name As String)

  strLast_name = newLast_name

End Property


Public Property Get First_name() As String

  First_name = strFirst_name
```

```vb
    End Property

    Public Property Let First_name(newFirst_name As String)

      strFirst_name = newFirst_name

    End Property

    Public Property Get Email() As String

      Email = strEmail

    End Property

    Public Property Let Email(newEmail As String)

      strEmail = newEmail

    End Property

    Public Property Get Home_phone() As String

      Home_phone = strHome_phone

    End Property

    Public Property Let Home_phone(newHome_phone As String)

      strHome_phone = newHome_phone

    End Property

    Public Property Get Work_phone() As String

      Work_phone = strWork_phone

    End Property

    Public Property Let Work_phone(newWork_phone As String)

      strWork_phone = newWork_phone

    End Property
```

7. Click on References in the Project menu to add a reference to ADO.
8. Select Microsoft ActiveX Data Objects 2.1 Library.
9. Select comDBUtility.
10. Click OK.
11. Click on Save Project As in the File menu to save the project and the code.

12. Change the default folder to the Chapter_10 folder of your Data Disk.

13. Navigate to the src folder.

14. Click the Save button in the Save File As dialog box.

15. Click the Save button in the Save Project As dialog box.

16. If you are prompted to save this project to SourceSafe, click No.

17. Now you are ready to compile this component into an ActiveX DLL. Click Make comStudent.dll in the File menu.

18. Click OK in the Make Project dialog box.

19. To verify that the component has been created, click on References in the Project menu and search for comStudent in the list. If the item is not in the list, repeat Step 17 and Step 18.

20. Exit Visual Basic. If you are asked to save changes, do so.

Project 10-3

You created the comStudent component in Hands-on Project 10-2. Write a test client to test the ExecuteMode functionality in the clsStudent object.

To test the comStudent component ExecuteMode functionality:

1. Click the Start menu.

2. Point to Programs, point to Microsoft Visual Studio 6.0, and then click Microsoft Visual Basic 6.0.

3. In the New Project window, select Standard EXE, and then click Open.

4. Click Project1 Properties in the Project menu.

5. In Startup Object, select Sub Main.

6. Click OK.

7. Click Add Module in the Project menu.

8. Click Module in the New Tab, and then click Open.

9. Type the following code in the Module's code window:

```
Private Sub Main()
Dim objForm As Object
Dim strResult As String
Set objForm = CreateObject("comStudent.clsStudent")
objForm.Mode = "New"
objForm.Last_name = "Brown"
objForm.First_name = "Joe"
objForm.Email = "jbrown@happy.com"
objForm.Home_phone = "7033333333"
objForm.Work_phone = "7033333333"
  strResult = objForm.ExecuteMode
  If strResult <> "" Then
    MsgBox strResult
  End If
```

10

10. Click Run on the toolbar.

11. Verify the results of the code using Access.

12. Quit Visual Basic and discard any changes to the src folder.

Project 10-4

Update the student contacts application in the register folder to use the newly created comStudent component.

To create the new Form.asp file:

1. Replace a file Form.asp in the register folder of the Chapter_10 folder of your Data Disk with the following code:

```
<%@ Language=VBScript%>
<%Option Explicit%>
<%Response.buffer=true%>
<!-- #include file="../includes/adovbs.inc" -->
<html>

<head>
<title>Class Registration Form</title>
<!--
    ************************************************
    *** Form Name:      frmRegister         ***
    *** Author:         Keith Morneau       ***
    *** Date:           8/6/01              ***
    *** Description:                        ***
    ***    This form allows user to enter   ***
    ***    the student information.          ***
    ***                                     ***
    *** Revisions:                          ***
    ************************************************
-->
<%
  Dim objForm,strEval
  set objForm = Server.CreateObject("comStudent.clsStudent")

  objForm.Mode = Request.QueryString("Mode")
  objForm.Last_name = Request.QueryString("txtLastName")
  objForm.First_name = Request.QueryString("txtFirstName")

  If Request.QueryString("Mode") = "New" Then

        If objForm.Search Then
          objForm.Mode = "Update"
        End If
    Else

    If objForm.Mode = "Browse" or objForm.Mode = "Update" _
  or objForm.Mode = "Delete" Then
```

```
        If Not objForm.Search Then
           Response.Write("<CENTER><H1>Error Information
</H1>")
           Response.Write("<H3>Student not found!</H3><BR>")
           Response.Write("Back to <a href=search.htm>Student
 Form</a>.</center>")
           Response.End
        Else
          If Request.QueryString("Mode") = "Browse" Then
          objForm.Mode = "Browse"
          Else
          if Request.QueryString("Mode") = "Delete" Then
          objForm.Mode = "Delete"
          End If
        End If
    End If
  Else
           Response.Write("<CENTER><H1>Error Information
</H1>")
           Response.Write("<H3>You did not select a mode!
</H3><BR>")
           Response.Write("Click on the Back button of your
browser to fix!</center>")
           Response.End
  End If
End If

%>

</head>

<body BGCOLOR=LIGHTYELLOW>

<H1 align="center">Class Registration Form</H1>

<p align="center"><strong>Instructions:</strong>  You
need to fill in this information <br> so that I can
contact you in an emergency.<br>  All mandatory
fields have an &quot;*&quot; next to them. <br> Please
fill in all mandatory fields before hitting SUBMIT.</p>

<form id="frmRegister" name="frmRegister" action=
"register_me.asp" method="post">

<center><p><b>Personal Information</b></p></center>

<center>Form Mode: <% = objForm.Mode %><input id="Mode"
type="hidden" name="Mode" size="35" value="<% = objForm.Mode
%>" >
<input id="STUDENT_ID" type="hidden" name="STUDENT_ID" size=
"35" value="<% = objForm.Student_ID%>" >
```

10

```
<p>First name: <input id="First_Name" type="text"
name="First_Name" size="35" value="<% = objForm.First_name%>
" >*<br>
  Last name: 

<input id="txtLastName" type = "text" name="Last_Name" size=
"35" value="<% = objForm.Last_name%>"><strong>*</strong>
</label></p>
</center>

<center><p><b>Contact Information</b></p>
</center>

<center><p>Home phone:<input type="text" name="Home_Phone"
size="12" value="<% = objForm.Home_phone%>"><br>

Work phone:<input type="text" name="Work_Phone" size="12"
value="<% = objForm.Work_phone%>"><br>

E-mail: <input type="text" name="E_mail" size="30"
value="<% = objForm.Email%>"><strong>*</strong></p>
</center>

<%Select Case objForm.Mode %>
<% Case "New"%>
<center><p><input id="cmdSubmit" type="submit" value="Create
">
<input id="cmdReset" type="reset" value="Reset"> </p>
</center>
<%Case "Update" %>
<center><p><input id="cmdSubmit" type="submit" value=
"Update">
</center>
<%Case "Delete" %>
<center><p><input id="cmdSubmit" type="submit" value=
"Delete">
</center>
<%Case "Browse"%>
<center><p>Back to <a href=search.htm>Search</a>.</center>
</center>
<% End Select %>
</form>

</body>
</html>
```

2. Save the file.

3. Replace register_me.asp in the register folder in the Chapter_10 folder of your Data Disk with the following code:

```
<%@ Language=VBScript %>
<% Response.Buffer = True %>

<html>

<head>

<title>Class Registration Response</title>
<%
Sub FormValidation

Dim blnOK

    blnOK = (Trim(Request.Form("First_Name")) = "") OR (Trim
(Request.Form("Last_Name")) = "") OR (Trim(Request.Form
("e_mail")) = "")
    If blnOK Then
      Response.Write("<CENTER><H1>Error Information</H1>")
      Response.Write("<H3>You must enter all the
information that has *'s!</H3><BR>")
      Response.Write("You click the back button on your
browser to fix your errors!</CENTER>")
      Response.End
    End If

End Sub

  Dim objForm,strEval,strErr
  Call FormValidation
  set objForm = Server.CreateObject("comStudent.clsStudent")

  objForm.Mode = Request.Form("Mode")
  objForm.Student_ID = Request.Form("STUDENT_ID")
  objForm.Last_name = Request.Form("LAST_NAME")
  objForm.First_name = Request.Form("FIRST_NAME")
  objForm.Email = Request.Form("E_MAIL")
  objForm.Home_phone = Request.Form("HOME_PHONE")
  objForm.Work_phone = Request.Form("WORK_PHONE")

  strErr = objForm.ExecuteMode

  If strErr <> "" Then
    Response.Write("<CENTER><H1>Error Information</H1>")
    Response.Write(strErr & "</CENTER>")
    Response.End
  End If


%>
</head>
<body BGCOLOR=LIGHTYELLOW>
```

10

```
<center><h1>Class Registration Response</h1></center>
<center>
<p>Thank you for using the Class Registration form!<p>

<% If Request.Form("Mode") <> "Delete" Then %>
<p>The information you entered: <br>
<ul>
<li>First name: <%=Request.Form("First_Name")%>*</li>
<li>Last name: <%=Request.Form("Last_Name")%>*</li>
<li>Home phone: <%=Request.Form("Home_Phone")%>*</li>
<li>Work phone: <%=Request.Form("Work_Phone")%>*</li>
<li>E-Mail: <%=Request.Form("e_mail")%>*</li>
</ul>
<% End If %>
</center>
<center>Back to <a href="search.htm">Search</a>.</center>
</body>
</html>
```

4. Save the file.

5. Exit your text editor.

6. Open your Web browser and navigate to *http://localhost/Chapter_10/default.asp*. Test the changes using the Student Information link.

CASE PROJECTS

1. John's Software has retained you to help them develop components for the gift management system you created in Chapters 5–7. Using the application in Chapter 9, create components and change the ASP scripts as needed. You must create and compile the Utility component before you create and compile the main component. If you do not, the ASP scripts will not work.

2. Interstate Bank has retained you to help them develop components for the budget management system you created in Chapters 5–7. Using the application in Chapter 9, create components and change the ASP scripts as needed. You must create and compile the Utility component before you create and compile the main component. If you do not, the ASP scripts will not work.

3. Interstate Bank has retained you to help them develop components for the checkbook management system you created in Chapters 5–7. Using the application in Chapter 9, create components and change the ASP scripts as needed. You must create and compile the Utility component before you create and compile the main component. If you do not, the ASP scripts will not work.

Index

A

Access. *see also* database
data types, 131
as file-based DBMS, 206
typical scenario, 206–207
accessor methods, JavaScript, 40
Active Server Pages (ASP)
functionality, scripts, 3–4
process description, 3
ActiveX controls, 3
Extensible Markup Language, 3
Java Applets, 3
thread, 3
run-time errors, 173–174
ActiveX controls, 3
ActiveX Data Objects (ADO)
Field object, 168
Fields collection, 168
column and field referencing,
172–173
implementing
changing data source
configuration, 169–170
in general, 168–169
Recordset object, 166–168
data insertion, 172
database query, 170–172
role, 165
understanding, 165
Ad Rotator component
in action, 276–277

creating, 272–274
redirection file, 275–276
schedule file, 274–275
using, 272
ADO. *see* ActiveX Data Objects
ADO command object, calling
stored procedures, 218–220
aggregate functions, SELECT
statement, 144–145
alias, query, 145
application logic, software, 311
application object
ASP object model, 43–44
variable scope, 22
argument, functions, 33
arrays. *see also* collections
collections and, 54, 56
in general, 54
subscript, 54
in JavaScript, 54–55
two-dimensional, 55–56
in VBScript, 54–55
ASCII file, 89
ASP. *see* Active Server Pages
ASP object model. *see also* objects
application object, 43–44
request object, 44–45
response object, 45–46
session object, 44
assignment statement, variables, 24
atomicity, transactions, 309
automation, data transfer and, 297

B

binary file, 89
Browscap.ini file, 244
Browser Capabilities component.
see also Web application
browscap.ini file, 244
maintaining, 248–249
in general, 244
understanding, 244–246
using, 246–248
business rules, software, 311

C

case sensitivity, IFTHENELSE
statement, 68
CASE statement, IFTHENELSE
statement, 68–70
CGI. *see* Common Gateway
Interface
class
instance, 40
object creation
in general, 36–37
JavaScript, 38–40
VBScript, 37–38
object declaration, 40
using
JavaScript, 42–43
Server-Side Include file, 40–41
VBScript, 40–42
clsForm.cls
in general, 177, 179–183

student contacts application,
103–107
colFormElements, 104
logical path, 104
physical path, 104
strMode, 104
strServerFilePath, 104
Code Editor window, 299
col-list argument, SELECT statement, 141
colFormElements, 104
collections. *see also* arrays
arrays and, 54, 56
creating, 57–58
dictionary object
modifying, 58–59
reviewing, 59–62
keys, 56–57
columns. *see also* database
management
in general, 127–128
referencing, 172–173
COM. *see* Component
Object Model
comDBUtility component coding
coding, 305–308
testing, 303–305
Visual Basic 6.0, 299–303
Command object, 165
Common Gateway Interface
(CGI), 2
Component Object Model
(COM), 296
components. *see* Web application
components
compound condition,
IFTHENELSE statement, 65–66
Compound Document
Management, 297
connect, SELECT statement,
145–146

Connection object, 165
consistency, transactions, 309
constants. *see also* variables
declaring, 24
in general, 20
using in application, 25–29
constraint, database, 133
container object, 297
Content Linking component
Content Linking Component
Object creation, 278–279
Content Linking list file, 279–280
in general, 277
control structures
in general, 62
IFTHENELSE statement
case sensitivity, 68
CASE statement, 68–70
in general, 63
logical operators, 65–66
nested, 66–67
relational operators, 64–65
loop, 72
repetition control structure
FOR loop, 73–76
in general, 72–73
WHILE loop, 76–77
selection control structure, in
general, 62
server-side validation, 70
cookies. *see also* Web application
in general, 250
history, 250–251
incorporating into applications,
252–258
login.asp, 258–259
request object, 252
response object, 251–252
counters, 73
using, 281

Counters Object, 282–284
PageCounter object, 281–282
Counters Object, using, 282–284

D
data access logic, 311
data insertion, Recordset
object, 172
data source, 174
data source configuration, changing, 169–170
data storage. *see also* storage
software, 311
data transfer, automation and, 297
data types
in database, 131
in SQL server, 213
variant, 21–22
database, 127. *see also* Access
data storage, 311
designing, 131–134
constraint, 133
denormalizing data, 133
entity relationship diagram, 132
normalizing data, 132
querying with SQL
DELETE statement, 148
INSERT statement, 146–147
SELECT statement, 139–146
UPDATE statement, 148
Web application creation for,
134–139
database management system
(DBMS)
database concepts
data types, 131
keys, 128–129
relational database, 128–129
relationships, 129–130
tables, rows, columns, 127–128

in general, 126–127
    extensibility concerns, 127
database overview, DBMS
    overview, 126–127
DBMS. *see* database management
    system
DCOM. *see* Distributed
    Component Object Model
default.asp, 284–286
default.htm, 102–103, 177
    discussed, 178–179
    mode, 178
    option button, 178
DELETE statement, 148
denormalizing data, database, 133
dictionary object
    modification, 58–59
    reviewing, 59–62
Distributed Component Object
    Model (DCOM), 296–297
documents, Compound
    Document Management, 297
drive object, 90–91
drives, review, 88–89
durability, transactions, 309

E

end user, 88–89. *see also* software
    application
    program interface interactions,
        162–164, 175–177
entity relationship diagram
    (ERD), 132
ERD. *see* entity relationship
    diagram
error handling. *see also* run-time
    errors
    variables, 215
expressionlist, 69
Extensible Markup Language
    (XML), 3

F

field. *see* columns
Field object, 168
Fields collection
    ADO, 168
    column and field referencing,
        172–173
file object, 92
filefield, 111
files
    ASCII, 89
    attributes
        alias, 88
        archive, 88
        compressed, 88
        directory, 88
        hidden, 88
        normal, 88
        read only, 88
        system, 88
    binary, 89
    data storage, 311
    opening, 99–100
    review, 88–89
    Unicode, 89
    uploading to server
        in general, 111
        SiteGalaxy upload component,
            111–116
FileSystemObject Object
    overview
        displaying file and folder infor-
            mation, 92–99
        drive object, 90–91
        file object, 92
        folder object, 91–92
        in general, 89–90
        opening new and existing files,
            99–100
        student contacts application

clsForm.cls, 103–107
default.htm, 102–103
form.asp, 107–110, 178,
    183–187
QueryString property of
    request object, 101–102
registerme.asp, 110–111, 178,
    187–190
TextStream object, 100–101
uploading files to server
    in general, 111
    SiteGalaxy upload component,
        111–116
flow control, variables, 214–215
folder, review, 88–89
folder object, 91–92
FOR loop. *see also* control
    structures
    repetition control structure,
        73–76
        counter, 73
form, 111
Form Designer, 299
Form Layout window, 299
form.asp, 107–110, 178
    discussed, 183–187
functions
    adding VBScript function, 34–35
    calling, 34
    in general, 33–34
        argument, 33
    reviewing JavaScript function,
        35–36

G

global variable, 22
Global.asa file, 8
graphics, defined, 2

H

HTML. *see* Hypertext Markup
    Language

Hypertext Markup Language (HTML), documents in, 2

I

IFTHENELSE statement, 63
case sensitivity, 68
CASE statement, 68–70
logical operators, 65–66
nested, 66–67
relational operators, 64–65
server-side validation, 70
reviewing, 70–72
INSERT statement, database, 146–147
instance, class, 40
isolation, transactions, 309

J

Java Applets, described, 3
JavaScript
arrays, 54–55
classes, 38–40
accessor methods, 40
using, 42–43
client-side script, 5
function, 35–36
server-side scripting, 6–7
subroutine, 32–33
join, SELECT statement, 145–146

K

keys
collections and, 56–57
match, 129–130
relational databases and, 128–129
foreign key, 128
primary key, 128

L

logical operators
IFTHENELSE statement, 65–66
compound condition, 65–66

logical path, 104
login.asp
cookies, 258–259
save login.asp, 259–260
loop, control structures, 72

M

match, keys in tables, 129–130
Microsoft Access. *see* Access
Microsoft Data Link, setting up, 175
Microsoft Management Console (MMC), 209
middleware, 296
MMC. *see* Microsoft Management Console
mode, default.htm, 178
modularization, 29
modules, subroutines/procedures, 29–33

N

n-tier applications, 312
naming, COM/DCOM objects, 297
normalizing data, database, 132
Notepad, ASP creation with, 3

O

object linking and embedding (OLE), 297
objects, 43. *see also* ASP object model
creating from class
in general, 36–37
JavaScript, 38–40
VBScript, 37–38
declaring from class, 40–42
in Web application, 8
ODBC, considerations for using, 174–175
OLE. *see* object linking and embedding

OLE DB providers, 175
option button, 178
ORDER BY clause, SELECT statement, 143–144

P

PageCounter object, using, 281–282
path
logical path, 104
physical path, 104
virtual path, 41
performance degradation, causes, 206–207
presentation management, 311
procedural language, stored procedures, 212
procedural language variables. *see also* variables
assigning values to variables, 214
error handling, 215
flow control, 214–215
Project Explorer, 299
Properties window, 299

Q

QueryString property, request object, 101–102

R

record. *see* rows
Recordset object, 165, 166–168
cursor, 166
data insertion, 172
database query, 170–172
redirection file, creating, 275–276
registerme.asp, 110–111, 178
discussed, 187–190
relational database. *see also* database management system
keys and, 128–129
relational operators, IFTHENELSE statement, 64–65

relationships
  database, 129–130
    many-to-many, 130
    one-to-many, 130
    one-to-one, 129–130
request object
  ASP object model, 44–45
  cookies, 252
  QueryString property, 101–102
response object
  ASP object model, 45–46
  cookies, 251–252
result set, 170
rows. *see also* database management
  in general, 127–128
run-time errors. *see also* error
  handling
  in ASP, 173–174

S

save login.asp, 259–260
schedule file, creating, 274–275
script, 3–4
  subscript, 54
  variable declaration, 22
scripting languages
  client-side scripting
    JavaScript, 5
    VBScript, 4–5
  in general, 4
  server-side scripting
    JavaScript, 6–7
    VBScript, 6
SELECT statement
  aggregate functions use, 144–145
  col-list argument, 141
  in general, 139–140
  joining with, 145–146
  ORDER BY clause, 143–144
  WHERE clause, 141–143

SERVER name, updating, 220
Server-Side Include (SSI)
  file, 40–41
server-side validation
  in general, 70
  reviewing, 70–72
session object, 22
  ASP object model, 44
session variable, 21
sessions, 8
share, 88
single-tier application, 311
SiteGalaxy upload component,
  111–116
  filefield, 111
  form, 111
  using, 112–116
software application. *see also* end
  user; Visual Basic 6.0; Web
  application
  ASP scripts creation, 312–316
  in general, 311
  n-tier, 312
  single-tier, 311
  three-tier, 312
  two-tier, 311
SQL Server 7.0
  converting Access database to,
    207–208
    database restoration, 210–211
    Microsoft Management
      Console, 209
    SQL Server Enterprise
      Manager, 208–209
    SQL shell preparation, 209–210
  final product examination,
    221–222
  key code points, 222–230
  logic flow and characteristics,
    206–207
  stored procedures

calling with ADO Command
  object, 218–220
creating, 216–218
in general, 212
procedural language, 212
procedural language variables,
  212–215
syntax, 216
Transact-SQL, 212
SSI. *see* Server-Side Include file
storage. *see also* data storage
  COM/DCOM objects, 297
  terabytes, 126
stored procedures
  ADO role, 165
  calling with ADO Command
    object, 218–220
    updating SERVER name, 220
  creating, 216–218
  procedural language, 212
  syntax, 216
strMode, 104
strServerFilePath, 104
student contacts application
  clsForm.cls, 103–107, 179–183
  default.htm, 102–103
  form.asp, 107–110, 178, 183–187
  QueryString property of request
    object, 101–102
  registerme.asp, 110–111, 178,
    187–190
subroutine
  modules, 29–33
    JavaScript subroutine, 32–33
    VBScript subroutine, 30–32
subscript, arrays, 54

T

tables. *see also* database
  management
  in general, 127–128

terabytes, storage, 126

testexpression, 69

TextStream object, 100–101

thread, 3

three-tier application, 312

tiers

data, 311

n-tier applications, 312

single-tier application, 311

three-tier application, 312

two-tier application, 311

Toolbox, 299

transaction, 308

transaction processing

in general, 308–309

implementing, 309–310

two-tier application, 311

U

UCASE function, case sensitivity, 68

Unicode file, 89

UPDATE statement, 148

V

values, assigning to variables, 214

variables. *see also* constants; procedural language variables

application and session, 21

declaring, 24

assigning value to, 214

counter, 73

data types, 21–22

declaring, 23–24, 213

assignment statement, 24

in general, 20, 212

global, 22

local, 213

scope

application object, 22

procedure, 22

script, 22

session object, 22

using in application, 25–29

VBScript

arrays, 54–55

classes, 37–38

using, 40–42

client-side scripting, 4–5

function, 34–35

server-side scripting, 6

subroutine, 30–32

virtual path, 41

Visual Basic 6.0. *see also* software application

comClasses component, coding, 305–308

comDBUtility component

coding, 299–303

testing, 303–305

component testing, 303–305

in general, 298–299

Code Editor window, 299

Form Designer, 299

Form Layout window, 299

Project Explorer, 299

Properties window, 299

Toolbox, 299

transaction processing

in general, 308–309

implementing, 309–310

Visual InterDev, ASP creation with, 3

W

Web application. *see also* Browser Capabilities component; cookies; software application

creating, 10–13

to interact with database, 134–139

process description, 7–9

testing, 13–14

Web application components

in general, 296–298

Component Object Model, 296

container object, 297

Distributed Component Object Model, 296–297

middleware, 296

object linking and embedding, 297

Visual Basic 6.0 environment, in general, 298–299

Web server, role, 9–10

WHERE clause, SELECT statement, 141–143

WHILE loop, repetition control structure, 76–77

X

XML. *see* Extensible Markup Language